HEMINGWAY'S AFRICAN STORIES:

The Stories, Their Sources, Their Critics

SCRIBNER
RESEARCH
ANTHOLOGIES

Martin Steinmann, Jr., GENERAL EDITOR

the lovers bored her. She had been married to a man who had never
bored her and these people bored her very much.

Then one of her two children was killed in a plane crash and
after that was over she did not want the lovers and drink being no
anaesthetic she had to make another life. Suddenly she had been
acutely frightened of being alone. But she wanted someone that
she respected with her. He, Henry Walden, had become ~~that life.~~

It had begun very simply. She liked what he wrote and she had
always envied the life he led. She thought he did exactly what he
wanted to. The steps by which she had acquired him and the way in
which she had finally fallen in love with him were all part of a
regular progression in which she had built herself a new life and he
had traded away what remained of his old life. He had traded it
for security, for comfort too, there was no denying that, and for
what else? He did not know. She would have bought him anything he
wanted. He knew that. She was a damned nice woman too. He would
as soon be in bed with her as anyone; rather with her, because she was
richer, because she was very pleasant and appreciative and because
she never made scenes. And now this life that she had built again was
coming to a term because he had not used iodine two weeks ago when a
thorn had scratched his knee as they moved forward trying to photograph
a herd of waterbuck standing, their heads up, peering while their
nostrils searched the air, and their ears spread wide to hear the
first noise that would send them rushing into the bush. They had
bolted, too, before he got the picture.

Here she came now. He turned his head on the cot to
look toward her. "Hello," he said.

"I shot a Tommy ram," she told him. "He'll make you good
broth and I'll have them mash some potatoes with the Klim. How do

From the typescript of "The Snows of Kilimanjaro."

JOHN M. HOWELL
Southern Illinois University, Carbondale

HEMINGWAY'S AFRICAN STORIES:
The Stories, Their Sources, Their Critics

SCRIBNER
RESEARCH
ANTHOLOGIES

CHARLES SCRIBNER'S SONS   New York

Printed in the United States of America
Library of Congress Catalog Card Number 69-14263

For SUE

I wish to express my gratitude to the many authors who appear in this anthology; to my colleagues at Southern Illinois University, Carbondale, Alan M. Cohn of the Morris Library and Thomas M. Davis of the Department of English; to my colleagues at Charles Scribner's Sons; and to the general editor of this series, Martin Steinmann, Jr.

Preface

Each Scribner Research Anthology is a collection of written sources upon a single historical, political, literary, or scientific topic or problem—the Hungarian Revolt, Shakespeare's *Julius Cæsar*, or extrasensory perception, for example. In addition to these sources, it contains (1) "Guide to Research," an account of the rationale and the methods of research and of research-paper writing, (2) an introduction to the topic of the anthology, (3) suggested topics for controlled research, and (4) suggested sources and topics for library research.

Each anthology is designed to serve two purposes. First, each gives the student access to important sources—texts, documents, letters, diaries, essays, articles, reports, transcripts of hearings, for instance—on a given topic. Some of these sources are otherwise available in only a few libraries, some (manuscripts and historical and government documents) in only one. In any case, the collection as a whole is not otherwise available in one volume. Second, each anthology gives the student either all his sources for a controlled-research paper or some of them for a library-research paper. Each anthology can be valuable either for readings in courses in history, literature, science, or humanities or as the basis for a research paper in these or in other courses.

A controlled-research paper—a paper in which the student's search for sources is limited to, and in certain ways controlled by, those sources contained in one anthology—is not so noble an undertaking as a library-research paper. But it is often more successful—more rewarding for the student and easier for his instructor to teach effectively and judge fairly. Its advantages for both student and instructor are often considerable.

For the student, it sometimes provides sources unavailable in his school library. And it enables him to learn a good deal about research (selection, interpretation, and evaluation of sources; quotation and paraphrase; and documentation) without prior instruction in use of the library (and, incidentally, without overtaxing the facilities and the resources of his library and without loss of, or damage to, sources either irreplaceable or difficult and expensive to replace).

For the instructor, it permits focus of class discussion upon a limited set of topics. It enables him to track down the student's sources conveniently. And—perhaps the greatest advantage of all—it enables him to judge both conveniently and exactly how well the student has selected, interpreted, and evaluated his sources and how well he has quoted and paraphrased them.

In many schools, a controlled-research paper is either a preliminary to or a part of a library-research paper. A library-research paper is probably the most difficult paper that the student can be assigned to write. The problems that confront him are not simply those common to any paper —organization, paragraphing, and transitions, for instance—and those (already mentioned) common to all research papers. He has, in addition, the problem of using the library well—of, for example, using the card catalogue, periodical indexes, and other reference works. But, if the instructor assigns a controlled-research paper as a preliminary to or, as it were, an early part of a library-research paper, the student need not come to grips with all these problems at once.

Each Scribner Research Anthology is compiled according to the following editorial principles. Each source that is not anonymous is prefaced by a biographical note on its author. At the foot of the same page is a bibliographical note. Each source is reprinted exactly as it appears in the original except for (1) some typographical peculiarities, (2) explanatory notes, given in brackets, and (3) omissions, indicated by ellipses (". . ."). And, finally, for each source that has pagination in the original, page numbers are given in brackets within the source itself—thus: "[**320/321**]," where everything before the slash (and after the preceding slash, if any) is from page 320, and everything after the slash (and before the next slash, if any) is from page 321. For a source hitherto unpublished, no page numbers are given; and the student who uses it should cite the page numbers of the Scribner Research Anthology. Footnotes to a source are given as in the original. Where the original pagination of a footnote is not evident, its page number precedes it in brackets.

MARTIN STEINMANN, JR.

Bingham Bay
Lake Gogebic
August, 1960

Contents

ix

Introduction

Ernest Hemingway committed himself and his art to portraying the "truth" of his experience—"the way it was." No writer, consequently, is better approached through the study of his experience and its creative growth into art. And no two stories in the Hemingway canon depend more intensely on "the way it was" than "The Short Happy Life of Francis Macomber" and "The Snows of Kilimanjaro."

The stories, sources, and criticism in this volume are collected in five parts: "Stories," "Theory," "Experience," "Context," and "Criticism." Each part is intended as a critical tool for achieving a more profound appreciation of Hemingway's art.

Part II, through a collection of his most significant comments on writing, reflects Hemingway's opinion of American writers and literature; his problems as an apprentice writer in Paris; his creative search for the "action that produced the emotion"; his esthetic concept of omission—and its metaphor the "iceberg"; and, throughout, his continued emphasis on finding the "truth" of his experience in life and objectifying it in fiction.

Part III collects all known accounts of the life experiences which Hemingway later objectified in the African stories. Introducing this section is a brief but comprehensive study by Carlos Baker of the autobiographical details in "The Snows of Kilimanjaro." This is followed by Charles A. Fenton's discussion of Hemingway's dispatches on the Greco-Turkish war; relevant excerpts from Hemingway's memories of Paris from *A Moveable Feast;* "letters" from Tanganyika published in *Esquire;* excerpts from *Green Hills of Africa* (a book-length account of his African experience); an excerpt from *Death in the Afternoon* on the significance of the

kill in the bullring; and an excerpt from his introduction to *Men at War* on the courage to face death in battle.

Part IV collects evidence bearing on questions of historical and literary context. Was there actually a leopard on Kilimanjaro? Or was it really an antelope? Historical accounts by Hans Meyer, H. W. Tilman, and Richard Reusch conflict. Robert O. Stephens finds a literary solution. Further complication is added by Robert W. Lewis, Jr.'s noting that there was a second epigraph, taken from Vivienne de Watteville's *Speak to the Earth,* in the original typescript. But there was also, as the facsimile of the typescript in the frontispiece indicates, a tentative gesture toward giving Harry the surname "Walden"—even the Christian name "Henry."

Finally, Part V collects criticism selected for both its quality and its ability to represent varying critical approaches and interpretations. In treating "The Short Happy Life of Francis Macomber," for example, Carlos Baker focuses on tone and structure; Philip Young on the psychological implications of Macomber's initiation into the "code"; Warren Beck on a defense of Margot Macomber; R. S. Crane, in response to three student essays, on a comprehensive application of Aristotelian theory; and Robert Holland on the ambiguity which the critics have imposed on the story. Complementing these essays in emphasis and approach are essays on "The Snows of Kilimanjaro" by Caroline Gordon and Allen Tate, by Marion Montgomery, by Oliver Evans, and by Gloria Dussinger, which comment, for example, on Hemingway's failure to develop the mountain as a controlling metaphor, on his failure to develop the leopard as a symbol, on his success in unifying the story through the thematic polarities of death-in-life on the plain versus life-in-death on the mountain, and on the failure of the critics to see that the dying Harry is given a "second chance" as a writer.

The question of Harry's "second chance" is, like all the questions raised by the sources and the criticism reprinted in this anthology, a matter for research, analysis, and discussion. There is no question, however, that for Hemingway himself Africa was indeed a source of psychic and artistic renewal. Always dependent on experience for inspiration, he was, like the contemporary America of the thirties, temporarily overdrawn. He had used the Michigan experiences of his boyhood in the stories *In Our Time* (1925); and, along with the experiences of his twenties, in *Men Without Women* (1927). His Paris experiences, of course, had been the inspiration for *The Sun Also Rises* (1926). And then, breaking chronology, he had turned back to his World War I experiences—always in or behind his early stories—and brought them to a focus in *A Farewell to Arms* (1929). Though he had taken up big-game fishing after moving to Key West, in 1927, it would be twenty-five years before the perceptions of age and accumulated experience would produce *The Old Man and the Sea* (1952). And though his long interest in bullfighting produced one of the best treatises of its kind, *Death in the Afternoon* (1932), he had already used the bullfight to inform *The Sun Also Rises*. Apart from publishing a number of magazine stories, collected, along with six originals, under the symptomatic title *Winner Take Nothing* (1933), he had, in his own mind at least, created little since 1929 to justify the enormous popularity and critical acclaim that, by 1933, had finally become his. When he sailed for Africa in November of that year, he went, like Harry of "The Snows of Kilimanjaro," to "work the fat off his soul." Like Joseph Conrad before him, he went deeper into the truth of his experience than ever before.

JOHN M. HOWELL

PART ONE

STORIES

The Short Happy Life of Francis Macomber *

ERNEST HEMINGWAY (1899–1961) wrote "The Short Happy Life of Francis Macomber" early in 1936. Though he had originally intended it for *Esquire,* he met an earlier deadline with *Cosmopolitan* by sending them the story and promising *Esquire* his next, which, as it happened, was "The Snows of Kilimanjaro." *Cosmopolitan* published "The Short Happy Life of Francis Macomber" in September, 1936. It was reprinted, with minor revisions, in *The Fifth Column and the First Forty-nine Stories.* It is the text of this final version that is reprinted here.

It was now lunch time and they were all sitting under the double green fly of the dining tent pretending that nothing had happened.

"Will you have lime juice or lemon squash?" Macomber asked.

"I'll have a gimlet," Robert Wilson told him.

"I'll have a gimlet too. I need something," Macomber's wife said.

"I suppose it's the thing to do," Macomber agreed. "Tell him to make three gimlets."

The mess boy had started them already, lifting the bottles out of the canvas cooling bags that sweated wet in the wind that blew through the trees that shaded the tents.

"What had I ought to give them?" Macomber asked.

"A quid would be plenty," Wilson told him. "You don't want to spoil them."

"Will the headman distribute it?"

"Absolutely."

Francis Macomber had, half an hour before, been carried to his tent from the edge of the camp in triumph on the arms and shoulders of the cook, the personal boys, the skinner and the porters. The gun-bearers had taken no part in the demonstration. When the native boys put him down at the door of his tent, he had shaken all their hands, received their congratulations, and then gone into the tent and sat on the bed until his wife came in. She did not speak to him when she came in and he left the tent at once to wash his face and hands in the port- [102/103] able wash basin outside and go over to the dining tent to sit in a comfortable canvas chair in the breeze and the shade.

"You've got your lion," Robert Wilson said to him, "and a damned fine one too."

Mrs. Macomber looked at Wilson quickly. She was an extremely handsome and well-kept woman of the beauty and social position which had, five years before, commanded five thousand dollars as the price of endorsing, with photographs, a beauty product which she had never used. She had been married to Francis Macomber for eleven years.

"He is a good lion, isn't he?" Macomber said. His wife looked at him now. She looked at both these men as though she had never seen them before.

One, Wilson, the white hunter, she knew she had never truly seen before. He was about middle height with sandy hair, a stubby mustache, a very red face and extremely cold blue eyes with faint white wrinkles at the corners that grooved merrily when he smiled. He smiled at her now and she looked away from his face at the way his shoulders sloped in the loose tunic he wore with the four big cartridges held in loops where the left breast pocket should have been, at his big brown hands, his old slacks, his very dirty boots and back to his red face again. She noticed where the baked red of his face stopped in a white line that marked the circle left by his Stetson hat that hung now from one of the pegs of the tent pole.

"Well, here's to the lion," Robert Wilson said. He smiled at her again and, not smiling, she looked curiously at her husband.

Francis Macomber was very tall, very well built if you did not mind that length of bone, dark, his hair cropped like an oarsman, rather thin-lipped, and was considered handsome. He was dressed in the same sort of safari clothes that Wilson wore except that his were new, he was thirty-five years old, kept himself very fit, was good at court games, had a number of big-game fishing records, and had just shown himself, very publicly, to be a coward. [103/104]

"Here's to the lion," he said. "I can't ever thank you for what you did."

Margaret, his wife, looked away from him and back to Wilson.

"Let's not talk about the lion," she said.

Wilson looked over at her without smiling and now she smiled at him.

"It's been a very strange day," she said. "Hadn't you ought to put your hat on even under the canvas at noon? You told me that, you know."

"Might put it on," said Wilson.

"You know you have a very red face, Mr. Wilson," she told him and smiled again.

"Drink," said Wilson.

"I don't think so," she said. "Francis drinks a great deal, but his face is never red."

"It's red today," Macomber tried a joke.

"No," said Margaret. "It's mine that's red today. But Mr. Wilson's is always red."

"Must be racial," said Wilson. "I say, you wouldn't like to drop my beauty as a topic, would you?"

"I've just started on it."

"Let's chuck it," said Wilson.

"Conversation is going to be so difficult," Margaret said.

"Don't be silly, Margot," her husband said.

"No difficulty," Wilson said. "Got a damn fine lion."

Margot looked at them both and they both saw that she was going to cry. Wilson had seen it coming for a long time and he dreaded it. Macomber was past dreading it.

"I wish it hadn't happened. Oh, I wish it hadn't happened," she said and started for her tent. She made no noise of crying but they could see that her shoulders were shaking under the rose-colored, sun-proofed shirt she wore.

"Women upset," said Wilson to the tall man. "Amounts to nothing. Strain on the nerves and one thing'n another." [104/105]

"No," said Macomber. "I suppose that I rate that for the rest of my life now."

"Nonsense. Let's have a spot of the giant killer," said Wilson. "Forget the whole thing. Nothing to it anyway."

"We might try," said Macomber. "I won't forget what you did for me though."

"Nothing," said Wilson. "All nonsense."

So they sat there in the shade where the camp was pitched under some wide-topped acacia trees with a boulder-strewn cliff behind them, and a stretch of grass that ran to the bank of a boulder-filled stream in front with forest beyond it, and drank their just-cool lime drinks and avoided one another's eyes while the boys set the table for lunch. Wilson could tell that the boys all knew about it now and when he saw Macomber's personal boy looking curiously at his master while he was putting dishes on the table he snapped at him in Swahili. The boy turned away with his face blank.

"What were you telling him?" Macomber asked.

"Nothing. Told him to look alive or I'd see he got about fifteen of the best."

"What's that? Lashes?"

"It's quite illegal," Wilson said. "You're supposed to fine them."

"Do you still have them whipped?"

"Oh, yes. They could raise a row if they chose to complain. But they don't. They prefer it to the fines."

"How strange!" said Macomber.

"Not strange, really," Wilson said. "Which would you rather do? Take a good birching or lose your pay?"

Then he felt embarrassed at asking it and before Macomber could answer he went on, "We all take a beating every day, you know, one way or another."

This was no better. "Good God," he thought. "I am a diplomat, aren't I?"

"Yes, we take a beating," said Macomber, still not looking at [**105/106**] him. "I'm awfully sorry about that lion business. It doesn't have to go any further, does it? I mean no one will hear about it, will they?"

"You mean will I tell it at the Mathaiga Club?" Wilson looked at him now coldly. He had not expected this. So he's a bloody four-letter man as well as a bloody coward, he thought. I rather liked him too until today. But how is one to know about an American?

"No," said Wilson. "I'm a professional hunter. We never talk about our clients. You can be quite easy on that. It's supposed to be bad form to ask us not to talk though."

He had decided now that to break would be much easier. He would eat, then, by himself and could read a book with his meals. They would eat by themselves. He would see them through the safari on a very formal basis—what was it the French called it? Distinguished consideration—and it would be a damn sight easier than having to go through this emotional trash. He'd insult him and make a good clean break. Then he could read a book with his meals and he'd still be drinking their whisky. That was the phrase for it when a safari went bad. You ran into

another white hunter and you asked, "How is everything going?" and he answered, "Oh, I'm still drinking their whisky," and you knew everything had gone to pot.

"I'm sorry," Macomber said and looked at him with his American face that would stay adolescent until it became middle-aged, and Wilson noted his crew-cropped hair, fine eyes only faintly shifty, good nose, thin lips and handsome jaw. "I'm sorry I didn't realize that. There are lots of things I don't know."

So what could he do, Wilson thought. He was all ready to break it off quickly and neatly and here the beggar was apologizing after he had just insulted him. He made one more attempt. "Don't worry about me talking," he said. "I have a living to make. You know in Africa no woman ever misses her lion and no white man ever bolts."

"I bolted like a rabbit," Macomber said. [**106/107**]

Now what in hell were you going to do about a man who talked like that, Wilson wondered.

Wilson looked at Macomber with his flat, blue, machine-gunner's eyes and the other smiled back at him. He had a pleasant smile if you did not notice how his eyes showed when he was hurt.

"Maybe I can fix it up on buffalo," he said. "We're after them next, aren't we?"

"In the morning if you like," Wilson told him. Perhaps he had been wrong. This was certainly the way to take it. You most certainly could not tell a damned thing about an American. He was all for Macomber again. If you could forget the morning. But, of course, you couldn't. The morning had been about as bad as they come.

"Here comes the Memsahib," he said. She was walking over from her tent looking refreshed and cheerful and quite lovely. She had a very perfect oval face, so perfect that you expected her to be stupid. But she wasn't stupid, Wilson thought, no, not stupid.

"How is the beautiful red-faced Mr.

Wilson? Are you feeling better, Francis, my pearl?"

"Oh, much," said Macomber.

"I've dropped the whole thing," she said, sitting down at the table. "What importance is there to whether Francis is any good at killing lions? That's not his trade. That's Mr. Wilson's trade. Mr. Wilson is really very impressive killing anything. You do kill anything, don't you?"

"Oh, anything," said Wilson. "Simply anything." They are, he thought, the hardest in the world; the hardest, the cruelest, the most predatory and the most attractive and their men have softened or gone to pieces nervously as they have hardened. Or is it that they pick men they can handle? They can't know that much at the age they marry, he thought. He was grateful that he had gone through his education on American women before now because this was a very attractive one.

"We're going after buff in the morning," he told her. [**107/108**]

"I'm coming," she said.

"No, you're not."

"Oh, yes, I am. Mayn't I, Francis?"

"Why not stay in camp?"

"Not for anything," she said. "I wouldn't miss something like today for anything."

When she left, Wilson was thinking, when she went off to cry, she seemed a hell of a fine woman. She seemed to understand, to realize, to be hurt for him and for herself and to know how things really stood. She is away for twenty minutes and now she is back, simply enamelled in that American female cruelty. They are the damnedest women. Really the damnedest.

"We'll put on another show for you tomorrow," Francis Macomber said.

"You're not coming," Wilson said.

"You're very mistaken," she told him. "And I want *so* to see you perform again. You were lovely this morning. That is if blowing things' heads off is lovely."

"Here's the lunch," said Wilson. "You're very merry, aren't you?"

"Why not? I didn't come out here to be dull."

"Well, it hasn't been dull," Wilson said. He could see the boulders in the river and the high bank beyond with the trees and he remembered the morning.

"Oh, no," she said. "It's been charming. And tomorrow. You don't know how I look forward to tomorrow."

"That's eland he's offering you," Wilson said.

"They're the big cowy things that jump like hares, aren't they?"

"I suppose that describes them," Wilson said.

"It's very good meat," Macomber said.

"Did you shoot it, Francis?" she asked.

"Yes."

"They're not dangerous, are they?"

"Only if they fall on you," Wilson told her.

"I'm so glad." [**108/109**]

"Why not let up on the bitchery just a little, Margot," Macomber said, cutting the eland steak and putting some mashed potato, gravy and carrot on the down-turned fork that tined through the piece of meat.

"I suppose I could," she said, "since you put it so prettily."

"Tonight we'll have champagne for the lion," Wilson said. "It's a bit too hot at noon."

"Oh, the lion," Margot said. "I'd forgotten the lion!"

So, Robert Wilson thought to himself, she *is* giving him a ride, isn't she? Or do you suppose that's her idea of putting up a good show? How should a woman act when she discovers her husband is a bloody coward? She's damn cruel but they're all cruel. They govern, of course, and to govern one has to be cruel sometimes. Still, I've seen enough of their damn terrorism.

"Have some more eland," he said to her politely.

That afternoon, late, Wilson and Macomber went out in the motor car with the native driver and the two gun-bearers. Mrs. Macomber stayed in the camp. It was too hot to go out, she said, and she was going with them in the early morning. As they drove off Wilson saw her standing under the big tree, looking pretty rather than beautiful in her faintly rosy khaki, her dark hair drawn back off her forehead and gathered in a knot low on her neck, her face as fresh, he thought, as though she were in England. She waved to them as the car went off through the swale of high grass and curved around through the trees into the small hills of orchard bush.

In the orchard bush they found a herd of impala, and leaving the car they stalked one old ram with long, wide-spread horns and Macomber killed it with a very creditable shot that knocked the buck down at a good two hundred yards and sent the herd off bounding wildly and leaping over one another's backs in long, leg-drawn-up leaps as unbelievable and as floating as those one makes sometimes in dreams.

"That was a good shot," Wilson said. "They're a small target."

"Is it a worth-while head?" Macomber asked. [**109/110**]

"It's excellent," Wilson told him. "You shoot like that and you'll have no trouble."

"Do you think we'll find buffalo tomorrow?"

"There's a good chance of it. They feed out early in the morning and with luck we may catch them in the open."

"I'd like to clear away that lion business," Macomber said. "It's not very pleasant to have your wife see you do something like that."

I should think it would be even more unpleasant to do it, Wilson thought, wife or no wife, or to talk about it having done it. But he said, "I wouldn't think about that any more. Any one could be upset by his first lion. That's all over."

But that night after dinner and a whisky and soda by the fire before going to bed, as Francis Macomber lay on his cot with the mosquito bar over him and listened to the night noises it was not all over. It was neither all over nor was it beginning. It was there exactly as it happened with some parts of it indelibly emphasized and he was miserably ashamed at it. But more than shame he felt cold,

hollow fear in him. The fear was still there like a cold slimy hollow in all the emptiness where once his confidence had been and it made him feel sick. It was still there with him now.

It had started the night before when he had wakened and heard the lion roaring somewhere up along the river. It was a deep sound and at the end there were sort of coughing grunts that made him seem just outside the tent, and when Francis Macomber woke in the night to hear it he was afraid. He could hear his wife breathing quietly, asleep. There was no one to tell he was afraid, nor to be afraid with him, and, lying alone, he did not know the Somali proverb that says a brave man is always frightened three times by a lion; when he first sees his track, when he first hears him roar and when he first confronts him. Then while they were eating breakfast by lantern light out in the dining tent, before the sun was up, the lion roared again and Francis thought he was just at the edge of camp. [**110/111**]

"Sounds like an old-timer," Robert Wilson said, looking up from his kippers and coffee. "Listen to him cough."

"Is he very close?"

"A mile or so up the stream."

"Will we see him?"

"We'll have a look."

"Does his roaring carry that far? It sounds as though he were right in camp."

"Carries a hell of a long way," said Robert Wilson. "It's strange the way it carries. Hope he's a shootable cat. The boys said there was a very big one about here."

"If I get a shot, where should I hit him," Macomber asked, "to stop him?"

"In the shoulders," Wilson said. "In the neck if you can make it. Shoot for bone. Break him down."

"I hope I can place it properly," Macomber said.

"You shoot very well," Wilson told him. "Take your time. Make sure of him. The first one in is the one that counts."

"What range will it be?"

"Can't tell. Lion has something to say

about that. Don't shoot unless it's close enough so you can make sure."

"At under a hundred yards?" Macomber asked.

Wilson looked at him quickly.

"Hundred's about right. Might have to take him a bit under. Shouldn't chance a shot at much over that. A hundred's a decent range. You can hit him wherever you want at that. Here comes the Memsahib."

"Good morning," she said. "Are we going after that lion?"

"As soon as you deal with your breakfast," Wilson said. "How are you feeling?"

"Marvellous," she said. "I'm very excited."

"I'll just go and see that everything is ready," Wilson went off. As he left the lion roared again.

"Noisy beggar," Wilson said. "We'll put a stop to that."

"What's the matter, Francis?" his wife asked him.

"Nothing," Macomber said. [**111/112**]

"Yes, there is," she said. "What are you upset about?"

"Nothing," he said.

"Tell me," she looked at him. "Don't you feel well?"

"It's that damned roaring," he said. "It's been going on all night, you know."

"Why didn't you wake me," she said. "I'd love to have heard it."

"I've got to kill the damned thing," Macomber said, miserably.

"Well, that's what you're out here for, isn't it?"

"Yes. But I'm nervous. Hearing the thing roar gets on my nerves."

"Well then, as Wilson said, kill him and stop his roaring."

"Yes, darling," said Francis Macomber. "It sounds easy, doesn't it?"

"You're not afraid, are you?"

"Of course not. But I'm nervous from hearing him roar all night."

"You'll kill him marvellously," she said. "I know you will. I'm awfully anxious to see it."

"Finish your breakfast and we'll be starting."

"It's not light yet," she said. "This is a ridiculous hour."

Just then the lion roared in a deep-chested moaning, suddenly guttural, ascending vibration that seemed to shake the air and ended in a sigh and a heavy, deep-chested grunt.

"He sounds almost here," Macomber's wife said.

"My God," said Macomber. "I hate that damned noise."

"It's very impressive."

"Impressive. It's frightful."

Robert Wilson came up then carrying his short, ugly, shockingly big-bored .505 Gibbs and grinning.

"Come on," he said. "Your gun-bearer has your Springfield and the big gun. Everything's in the car. Have you solids?"

"Yes."

"I'm ready," Mrs. Macomber said. [**112/ 113**]

"Must make him stop that racket," Wilson said. "You get in front. The Memsahib can sit back here with me."

They climbed into the motor car and, in the gray first daylight, moved off up the river through the trees. Macomber opened the breech of his rifle and saw he had metal-cased bullets, shut the bolt and put the rifle on safety. He saw his hand was trembling. He felt in his pocket for more cartridges and moved his fingers over the cartridges in the loops of his tunic front. He turned back to where Wilson sat in the rear seat of the doorless, box-bodied motor car beside his wife, them both grinning with excitement, and Wilson leaned forward and whispered,

"See the birds dropping. Means the old boy has left his kill."

On the far bank of the stream Macomber could see, above the trees, vultures circling and plummeting down.

"Chances are he'll come to drink along here," Wilson whispered. "Before he goes to lay up. Keep an eye out."

They were driving slowly along the high bank of the stream which here cut deeply to its boulder-filled bed, and they wound in and out through big trees as they drove. Macomber was watching the opposite bank when he felt Wilson take hold of his arm. The car stopped.

"There he is," he heard the whisper. "Ahead and to the right. Get out and take him. He's a marvellous lion."

Macomber saw the lion now. He was standing almost broadside, his great head up and turned toward them. The early morning breeze that blew toward them was just stirring his dark mane, and the lion looked huge, silhouetted on the rise of bank in the gray morning light, his shoulders heavy, his barrel of a body bulking smoothly.

"How far is he?" asked Macomber, raising his rifle.

"About seventy-five. Get out and take him."

"Why not shoot from where I am?"

"You don't shoot them from cars," he heard Wilson saying in his ear. "Get out. He's not going to stay there all day."

Macomber stepped out of the curved opening at the side of [**113/114**] the front seat, onto the step and down onto the ground. The lion still stood looking majestically and coolly toward this object that his eyes only showed in silhouette, bulking like some super-rhino. There was no man smell carried toward him and he watched the object, moving his great head a little from side to side. Then watching the object, not afraid, but hesitating before going down the bank to drink with such a thing opposite him, he saw a man figure detach itself from it and he turned his heavy head and swung away toward the cover of the trees as he heard a cracking crash and felt the slam of a .30–06 220-grain solid bullet that bit his flank and ripped in sudden hot scalding nausea through his stomach. He trotted, heavy, big-footed, swinging wounded full-bellied, through the trees toward the tall grass and cover, and the crash came again to go past him ripping the air apart. Then it crashed again and he felt the blow as it hit his lower ribs and ripped on through, blood sudden hot and frothy in his mouth, and he galloped toward the high grass where he could crouch and not be seen and make them bring the crashing thing close

enough so he could make a rush and get the man that held it.

Macomber had not thought how the lion felt as he got out of the car. He only knew his hands were shaking and as he walked away from the car it was almost impossible for him to make his legs move. They were stiff in the thighs, but he could feel the muscles fluttering. He raised the rifle, sighted on the junction of the lion's head and shoulders and pulled the trigger. Nothing happened though he pulled until he thought his finger would break. Then he knew he had the safety on and as he lowered the rifle to move the safety over he moved another frozen pace forward, and the lion seeing his silhouette now clear of the silhouette of the car, turned and started off at a trot, and, as Macomber fired, he heard a whunk that meant that the bullet was home; but the lion kept on going. Macomber shot again and every one saw the bullet throw a spout of dirt beyond the trotting lion. He shot again, remembering to lower his aim, and they all heard the bullet hit, and the lion [**114/115**] went into a gallop and was in the tall grass before he had the bolt pushed forward.

Macomber stood there feeling sick at his stomach, his hands that held the Springfield still cocked, shaking, and his wife and Robert Wilson were standing by him. Beside him too were the two gun-bearers chattering in Wakamba.

"I hit him," Macomber said. "I hit him twice."

"You gut-shot him and you hit him somewhere forward," Wilson said without enthusiasm. The gun-bearers looked very grave. They were silent now.

"You may have killed him," Wilson went on. "We'll have to wait a while before we go in to find out."

"What do you mean?"

"Let him get sick before we follow him up."

"Oh," said Macomber.

"He's a hell of a fine lion," Wilson said cheerfully. "He's gotten into a bad place though."

"Why is it bad?"

"Can't see him until you're on him."

"Oh," said Macomber.

"Come on," said Wilson. "The Memsahib can stay here in the car. We'll go to have a look at the blood spoor."

"Stay here, Margot," Macomber said to his wife. His mouth was very dry and it was hard for him to talk.

"Why?" she asked.

"Wilson says to."

"We're going to have a look," Wilson said. "You stay here. You can see even better from here."

"All right."

Wilson spoke in Swahili to the driver. He nodded and said, "Yes, Bwana."

Then they went down the steep bank and across the stream, climbing over and around the boulders and up the other bank, pulling up by some projecting roots, and along it until they found where the lion had been trotting when Macomber first shot. There was dark blood on the short grass that the gun- [115/116] bearers pointed out with grass stems, and that ran away behind the river bank trees.

"What do we do?" asked Macomber.

"Not much choice," said Wilson. "We can't bring the car over. Bank's too steep. We'll let him stiffen up a bit and then you and I'll go in and have a look for him."

"Can't we set the grass on fire?" Macomber asked.

"Too green."

"Can't we send beaters?"

Wilson looked at him appraisingly. "Of course we can," he said. "But it's just a touch murderous. You see we know the lion's wounded. You can drive an unwounded lion—he'll move on ahead of a noise—but a wounded lion's going to charge. You can't see him until you're right on him. He'll make himself perfectly flat in cover you wouldn't think would hide a hare. You can't very well send boys in there to that sort of a show. Somebody bound to get mauled."

"What about the gun-bearers?"

"Oh, they'll go with us. It's their *shauri*. You see, they signed on for it. They don't look too happy though, do they?"

"I don't want to go in there," said Macomber. It was out before he knew he'd said it.

"Neither do I," said Wilson very cheerily. "Really no choice though." Then, as an afterthought, he glanced at Macomber and saw suddenly how he was trembling and the pitiful look on his face.

"You don't have to go in, of course," he said. "That's what I'm hired for, you know. That's why I'm so expensive."

"You mean you'd go in by yourself? Why not leave him there?"

Robert Wilson, whose entire occupation had been with the lion and the problem he presented, and who had not been thinking about Macomber except to note that he was rather windy, suddenly felt as though he had opened the wrong door in a hotel and seen something shameful.

"What do you mean?" [116/117]

"Why not just leave him?"

"You mean pretend to ourselves he hasn't been hit?"

"No. Just drop it."

"It isn't done."

"Why not?"

"For one thing, he's certain to be suffering. For another, some one else might run onto him."

"I see."

"But you don't have to have anything to do with it."

"I'd like to," Macomber said. "I'm just scared, you know."

"I'll go ahead when we go in," Wilson said, "with Kongoni tracking. You keep behind me and a little to one side. Chances are we'll hear him growl. If we see him we'll both shoot. Don't worry about anything. I'll keep you backed up. As a matter of fact, you know, perhaps you'd better not go. It might be much better. Why don't you go over and join the Memsahib while I just get it over with?"

"No, I want to go."

"All right," said Wilson. "But don't go in if you don't want to. This is my *shauri* now, you know."

"I want to go," said Macomber.

They sat under a tree and smoked.

"Want to go back and speak to the Memsahib while we're waiting?" Wilson asked.

"No."

"I'll just step back and tell her to be patient."

"Good," said Macomber. He sat there, sweating under his arms, his mouth dry, his stomach hollow feeling, wanting to find courage to tell Wilson to go on and finish off the lion without him. He could not know that Wilson was furious because he had not noticed the state he was in earlier and sent him back to his wife. While he sat there Wilson came up. "I have your big gun," he said. "Take it. We've given him time, I think. Come on."

Macomber took the big gun and Wilson said: [117/118]

"Keep behind me and about five yards to the right and do exactly as I tell you." Then he spoke in Swahili to the two gun-bearers who looked the picture of gloom.

"Let's go," he said.

"Could I have a drink of water?" Macomber asked. Wilson spoke to the older gun-bearer, who wore a canteen on his belt, and the man unbuckled it, unscrewed the top and handed it to Macomber, who took it noticing how heavy it seemed and how hairy and shoddy the felt covering was in his hand. He raised it to drink and looked ahead at the high grass with the flat-topped trees behind it. A breeze was blowing toward them and the grass rippled gently in the wind. He looked at the gun-bearer and he could see the gun-bearer was suffering too with fear.

Thirty-five yards into the grass the big lion lay flattened out along the ground. His ears were back and his only movement was a slight twitching up and down of his long, black-tufted tail. He had turned at bay as soon as he had reached this cover and he was sick with the wound through his full belly, and weakening with the wound through his lungs that brought a thin foamy red to his mouth each time he breathed. His flanks were wet and hot and flies were on the little openings the solid bullets had made in his tawny hide, and

his big yellow eyes, narrowed with hate, looked straight ahead, only blinking when the pain came as he breathed, and his claws dug in the soft baked earth. All of him, pain, sickness, hatred and all of his remaining strength, was tightening into an absolute concentration for a rush. He could hear the men talking and he waited, gathering all of himself into this preparation for a charge as soon as the men would come into the grass. As he heard their voices his tail stiffened to twitch up and down, and, as they came into the edge of the grass, he made a coughing grunt and charged.

Kongoni, the old gun-bearer, in the lead watching the blood spoor, Wilson watching the grass for any movement, his big gun ready, the second gun-bearer looking ahead and listening, [118/119] Macomber close to Wilson, his rifle cocked, they had just moved into the grass when Macomber heard the blood-choked coughing grunt, and saw the swishing rush in the grass. The next thing he knew he was running; running wildly, in panic in the open, running toward the stream.

He heard the *ca-ra-wong!* of Wilson's big rifle, and again in a second crashing *carawong!* and turning saw the lion, horrible-looking now, with half his head seeming to be gone, crawling toward Wilson in the edge of the tall grass while the red-faced man worked the bolt on the short ugly rifle and aimed carefully as another blasting *carawong!* came from the muzzle, and the crawling, heavy, yellow bulk of the lion stiffened and the huge, mutilated head slid forward and Macomber, standing by himself in the clearing where he had run, holding a loaded rifle, while two black men and a white man looked back at him in contempt, knew the lion was dead. He came toward Wilson, his tallness all seeming a naked reproach, and Wilson looked at him and said:

"Want to take pictures?"

"No," he said.

That was all any one had said until they reached the motor car. Then Wilson had said:

"Hell of a fine lion. Boys will skin him

out. We might as well stay here in the shade."

Macomber's wife had not looked at him nor he at her and he had sat by her in the back seat with Wilson sitting in the front seat. Once he had reached over and taken his wife's hand without looking at her and she had removed her hand from his. Looking across the stream to where the gunbearers were skinning out the lion he could see that she had been able to see the whole thing. While they sat there his wife had reached forward and put her hand on Wilson's shoulder. He turned and she had leaned forward over the low seat and kissed him on the mouth.

"Oh, I say," said Wilson, going redder than his natural baked color. [**119/120**]

"Mr. Robert Wilson," she said. "The beautiful red-faced Mr. Robert Wilson."

Then she sat down beside Macomber again and looked away across the stream to where the lion lay, with uplifted, white-muscled, tendon-marked naked forearms, and white bloating belly, as the black men fleshed away the skin. Finally the gunbearers brought the skin over, wet and heavy, and climbed in behind with it, rolling it up before they got in, and the motor car started. No one had said anything more until they were back in camp.

That was the story of the lion. Macomber did not know how the lion had felt before he started his rush, nor during it when the unbelievable smash of the .505 with a muzzle velocity of two tons had hit him in the mouth, nor what kept him coming after that, when the second ripping crash had smashed his hind quarters and he had come crawling on toward the crashing, blasting thing that had destroyed him. Wilson knew something about it and only expressed it by saying, "Damned fine lion," but Macomber did not know how Wilson felt about things either. He did not know how his wife felt except that she was through with him.

His wife had been through with him before but it never lasted. He was very wealthy, and would be much wealthier,

and he knew she would not leave him ever now. That was one of the few things that he really knew. He knew about that, about motor cycles—that was earliest—about motor cars, about duck-shooting, about fishing, trout, salmon and big-sea, about sex in books, many books, too many books, about all court games, about dogs, not much about horses, about hanging on to his money, about most of the other things his world dealt in, and about his wife not leaving him. His wife had been a great beauty and she was still a great beauty in Africa, but she was not a great enough beauty any more at home to be able to leave him and better herself and she knew it and he knew it. She had missed the chance to leave him and he knew it. If he had been better with women she would probably have started to worry [**120/121**] about him getting another new, beautiful wife; but she knew too much about him to worry about him either. Also, he had always had a great tolerance which seemed the nicest thing about him if it were not the most sinister.

All in all they were known as a comparatively happily married couple, one of those whose disruption is often rumored but never occurs, and as the society columnist put it, they were adding more than a spice of *adventure* to their much envied and ever-enduring *Romance* by a *Safari* in what was known as *Darkest Africa* until the Martin Johnsons lighted it on so many silver screens where they were pursuing *Old Simba* the lion, the buffalo, *Tembo* the elephant and as well collecting specimens for the Museum of Natural History. This same columnist had reported them *on the verge* at least three times in the past and they had been. But they always made it up. They had a sound basis of union. Margot was too beautiful for Macomber to divorce her and Macomber had too much money for Margot ever to leave him.

It was now about three o'clock in the morning and Francis Macomber, who had been asleep a little while after he had stopped thinking about the lion, wakened and then slept again, woke suddenly, frightened in a dream of the bloody-headed lion standing over him, and listening while his heart pounded, he realized that his wife was not in the other cot in the tent. He lay awake with that knowledge for two hours.

At the end of that time his wife came into the tent, lifted her mosquito bar and crawled cozily into bed.

"Where have you been?" Macomber asked in the darkness.

"Hello," she said. "Are you awake?"

"Where have you been?"

"I just went out to get a breath of air."

"You did, like hell."

"What do you want me to say, darling?"

"Where have you been?"

"Out to get a breath of air."

"That's a new name for it. You *are* a bitch." [**121/122**]

"Well, you're a coward."

"All right," he said. "What of it?"

"Nothing as far as I'm concerned. But please let's not talk, darling, because I'm very sleepy."

"You think that I'll take anything."

"I know you will, sweet."

"Well, I won't."

"Please, darling, let's not talk. I'm so very sleepy."

"There wasn't going to be any of that. You promised there wouldn't be."

"Well, there is now," she said sweetly.

"You said if we made this trip that there would be none of that. You promised."

"Yes, darling. That's the way I meant it to be. But the trip was spoiled yesterday. We don't have to talk about it, do we?"

"You don't wait long when you have an advantage, do you?"

"Please let's not talk. I'm so sleepy, darling."

"I'm going to talk."

"Don't mind me then, because I'm going to sleep." And she did.

At breakfast they were all three at the table before daylight and Francis Macomber found that, of all the many men that he had hated, he hated Robert Wilson the most.

"Sleep well?" Wilson asked in his throaty voice, filling a pipe.

"Did you?"

"Topping," the white hunter told him.

You bastard, thought Macomber, you insolent bastard.

So she woke him when she came in, Wilson thought, looking at them both with his flat, cold eyes. Well, why doesn't he keep his wife where she belongs? What does he think I am, a bloody plaster saint? Let him keep her where she belongs. It's his own fault.

"Do you think we'll find buffalo?" Margot asked, pushing away a dish of apricots. [**122/123**]

"Chance of it," Wilson said and smiled at her. "Why don't you stay in camp?"

"Not for anything," she told him.

"Why not order her to stay in camp?" Wilson said to Macomber.

"You order her," said Macomber coldly.

"Let's not have any ordering, nor," turning to Macomber, "any silliness, Francis," Margot said quite pleasantly.

"Are you ready to start?" Macomber asked.

"Any time," Wilson told him. "Do you want the Memsahib to go?"

"Does it make any difference whether I do or not?"

The hell with it, thought Robert Wilson. The utter complete hell with it. So this is what it's going to be like. Well, this is what it's going to be like, then.

"Makes no difference," he said.

"You're sure you wouldn't like to stay in camp with her yourself and let me go out and hunt the buffalo?" Macomber asked.

"Can't do that," said Wilson. "Wouldn't talk rot if I were you."

"I'm not talking rot. I'm disgusted."

"Bad word, disgusted."

"Francis, will you please try to speak sensibly?" his wife said.

"I speak too damned sensibly," Macomber said. "Did you ever eat such filthy food?"

"Something wrong with the food?" asked Wilson quietly.

"No more than with everything else."

"I'd pull yourself together, laddybuck," Wilson said very quietly. "There's a boy waits at table that understands a little English."

"The hell with him."

Wilson stood up and puffing on his pipe strolled away, speaking a few words in Swahili to one of the gun-bearers who was standing waiting for him. Macomber and his wife sat on at the table. He was staring at his coffee cup. [123/124]

"If you make a scene I'll leave you, darling," Margot said quietly.

"No, you won't."

"You can try it and see."

"You won't leave me."

"No," she said. "I won't leave you and you'll behave yourself."

"Behave myself? That's a way to talk. Behave myself."

"Yes. Behave yourself."

"Why don't *you* try behaving?"

"I've tried it so long. So very long."

"I hate that red-faced swine," Macomber said. "I loathe the sight of him."

"He's really *very* nice."

"Oh, *shut up*," Macomber almost shouted. Just then the car came up and stopped in front of the dining tent and the driver and the two gun-bearers got out. Wilson walked over and looked at the husband and wife sitting there at the table.

"Going shooting?" he asked.

"Yes," said Macomber, standing up. "Yes."

"Better bring a woolly. It will be cool in the car," Wilson said.

"I'll get my leather jacket," Margot said.

"The boy has it," Wilson told her. He climbed into the front with the driver and Francis Macomber and his wife sat, not speaking, in the back seat.

Hope the silly beggar doesn't take a notion to blow the back of my head off, Wilson thought to himself. Women *are* a nuisance on safari.

The car was grinding down to cross the river at a pebbly ford in the gray daylight and then climbed, angling up the steep bank, where Wilson had ordered a way shovelled out the day before so they could reach the parklike wooded rolling country on the far side.

It was a good morning, Wilson thought. There was a heavy dew and as the wheels went through the grass and low bushes [124/125] he could smell the odor of the crushed fronds. It was an odor like verbena and he liked this early morning smell of the dew, the crushed bracken and the look of the tree trunks showing black through the early morning mist, as the car made its way through the untracked, parklike country. He had put the two in the back seat out of his mind now and was thinking about buffalo. The buffalo that he was after stayed in the daytime in a thick swamp where it was impossible to get a shot, but in the night they fed out into an open stretch of country and if he could come between them and their swamp with the car, Macomber would have a good chance at them in the open. He did not want to hunt buff with Macomber in thick cover. He did not want to hunt buff or anything else with Macomber at all, but he was a professional hunter and he had hunted with some rare ones in his time. If they got buff today there would only be rhino to come and the poor man would have gone through his dangerous game and things might pick up. He'd have nothing more to do with the woman and Macomber would get over that too. He must have gone through plenty of that before by the look of things. Poor beggar. He must have a way of getting over it. Well, it was the poor sod's own bloody fault.

He, Robert Wilson, carried a double size cot on safari to accommodate any windfalls he might receive. He had hunted for a certain clientele, the international, fast, sporting set, where the women did not feel they were getting their money's worth unless they had shared that cot with the white hunter. He despised them when he was away from them although he liked some of them well enough at the time, but he made his living by them; and their standards were his standards as long as they were hiring him.

They were his standards in all except the shooting. He had his own standards about the killing and they could live up to them or get some one else to hunt them. He knew, too, that they all respected him for this. This Macomber was an odd one though. Damned if he wasn't. Now the wife. Well, the wife. [125/126] Yes, the wife. Hm, the wife. Well he'd dropped all that. He looked around at them. Macomber sat grim and furious. Margot smiled at him. She looked younger today, more innocent and fresher and not so professionally beautiful. What's in her heart God knows, Wilson thought. She hadn't talked much last night. At that it was a pleasure to see her.

The motor car climbed up a slight rise and went on through the trees and then out into a grassy prairie-like opening and kept in the shelter of the trees along the edge, the driver going slowly and Wilson looking carefully out across the prairie and all along its far side. He stopped the car and studied the opening with his field glasses. Then he motioned to the driver to go on and the car moved slowly along, the driver avoiding wart-hog holes and driving around the mud castles ants had built. Then, looking across the opening, Wilson suddenly turned and said,

"By God, there they are!"

And looking where he pointed, while the car jumped forward and Wilson spoke in rapid Swahili to the driver, Macomber saw three huge, black animals looking almost cylindrical in their long heaviness, like big black tank cars, moving at a gallop across the far edge of the open prairie. They moved at a stiff-necked, stiff bodied gallop and he could see the upswept wide black horns on their heads as they galloped heads out; the heads not moving.

"They're three old bulls," Wilson said. "We'll cut them off before they get to the swamp."

The car was going a wild forty-five miles an hour across the open and as Macomber watched, the buffalo got bigger and bigger until he could see the gray, hairless, scabby look of one huge bull and how his neck was a part of his shoulders and the shiny black of his horns as he galloped a little behind the others that were strung out in that steady plunging gait; and then, the car swaying as though it had just jumped a road, they drew up close and he could see the plunging hugeness of the bull, and the dust in his sparsely haired hide, the wide boss of [126/127] horn and his outstretched, wide-nostrilled muzzle, and he was raising his rifle when Wilson shouted, "Not from the car, you fool!" and he had no fear, only hatred of Wilson, while the brakes clamped on and the car skidded, plowing sideways to an almost stop and Wilson was out on one side and he on the other, stumbling as his feet hit the still speeding-by of the earth, and then he was shooting at the bull as he moved away, hearing the bullets whunk into him, emptying his rifle at him as he moved steadily away, finally remembering to get his shots forward into the shoulder, and as he fumbled to re-load, he saw the bull was down. Down on his knees, his big head tossing, and seeing the other two still galloping he shot at the leader and hit him. He shot again and missed and he heard the *carawonging* roar as Wilson shot and saw the leading bull slide forward onto his nose.

"Get that other," Wilson said. "Now you're shooting!"

But the other bull was moving steadily at the same gallop and he missed, throwing a spout of dirt, and Wilson missed and the dust rose in a cloud and Wilson shouted, "Come on. He's too far!" and grabbed his arm and they were in the car again, Macomber and Wilson hanging on the sides and rocketing swayingly over the uneven ground, drawing up on the steady, plunging, heavy-necked, straight-moving gallop of the bull.

They were behind him and Macomber was filling his rifle, dropping shells onto the ground, jamming it, clearing the jam, then they were almost up with the bull when Wilson yelled "Stop," and the car skidded so that it almost swung over and Macomber fell forward onto his feet, slammed his bolt forward and fired as far forward as he could aim into the galloping, rounded black back, aimed and shot again, then again, then again, and the bullets, all of them hitting, had no effect on the buffalo that he could see. Then Wilson shot, the roar deafening him, and he could see the bull stagger. Macomber shot again, aiming carefully, and down he came, onto his knees. [**127/128**]

"All right," Wilson said. "Nice work. That's the three."

Macomber felt a drunken elation.

"How many times did you shoot?" he asked.

"Just three," Wilson said. "You killed the first bull. The biggest one. I helped you finish the other two. Afraid they might have got into cover. You had them killed. I was just mopping up a little. You shot damn well."

"Let's go to the car," said Macomber. "I want a drink."

"Got to finish off that buff first," Wilson told him. The buffalo was on his knees and he jerked his head furiously and bellowed in pig-eyed, roaring rage as they came toward him.

"Watch he doesn't get up," Wilson said. Then, "Get a little broadside and take him in the neck just behind the ear."

Macomber aimed carefully at the center of the huge, jerking, rage-driven neck and shot. At the shot the head dropped forward.

"That does it," said Wilson. "Got the spine. They're a hell of a looking thing, aren't they?"

"Let's get the drink," said Macomber. In his life he had never felt so good.

In the car Macomber's wife sat very white faced. "You were marvellous, darling," she said to Macomber. "What a ride."

"Was it rough?" Wilson asked.

"It was frightful. I've never been more frightened in my life."

"Let's all have a drink," Macomber said.

"By all means," said Wilson. "Give it to the Memsahib." She drank the neat whisky from the flask and shuddered a little when she swallowed. She handed the flask to Macomber who handed it to Wilson.

"It was frightfully exciting," she said. "It's given me a dreadful headache. I didn't know you were allowed to shoot them from cars though.

"No one shot from cars," said Wilson coldly.

"I mean chase them from cars."

"Wouldn't ordinarily," Wilson said. "Seemed sporting [**128/129**] enough to me though while we were doing it. Taking more chance driving that way across the plain full of holes and one thing and another than hunting on foot. Buffalo could have charged us each time we shot if he liked. Gave him every chance. Wouldn't mention it to any one though. It's illegal if that's what you mean."

"It seemed very unfair to me," Margot said, "chasing those big helpless things in a motor car."

"Did it?" said Wilson.

"What would happen if they heard about it in Nairobi?"

"I'd lose my licence for one thing. Other unpleasantnesses," Wilson said, taking a drink from the flask. "I'd be out of business."

"Really?"

"Yes, really."

"Well," said Macomber, and he smiled for the first time all day. "Now she has something on you."

"You have such a pretty way of putting things, Francis," Margot Macomber said. Wilson looked at them both. If a four-letter man marries a five-letter woman, he was thinking, what number of letters would their children be? What he said was, "We lost a gun-bearer. Did you notice it?"

"My God, no," Macomber said.

"Here he comes," Wilson said. "He's all right. He must have fallen off when we left the first bull."

Approaching them was the middle-aged gun-bearer, limping along in his knitted cap, khaki tunic, shorts and rubber sandals, gloomy-faced and disgusted looking.

As he came up he called out to Wilson in Swahili and they all saw the change in the white hunter's face.

"What does he say?" asked Margot.

"He says the first bull got up and went into the bush," Wilson said with no expression in his voice.

"Oh," said Macomber blankly.

"Then it's going to be just like the lion," said Margot, full of anticipation. [129/130]

"It's not going to be a damned bit like the lion," Wilson told her. "Did you want another drink, Macomber?"

"Thanks, yes," Macomber said. He expected the feeling he had had about the lion to come back but it did not. For the first time in his life he really felt wholly without fear. Instead of fear he had a feeling of definite elation.

"We'll go and have a look at the second bull," Wilson said. "I'll tell the driver to put the car in the shade."

"What are you going to do?" asked Margaret Macomber.

"Take a look at the buff," Wilson said.

"I'll come."

"Come along."

The three of them walked over to where the second buffalo bulked blackly in the open, head forward on the grass, the massive horns swung wide.

"He's a very good head," Wilson said. "That's close to a fifty-inch spread."

Macomber was looking at him with delight.

"He's hateful looking," said Margot. "Can't we go into the shade?"

"Of course," Wilson said. "Look," he said to Macomber, and pointed. "See that patch of bush?"

"Yes."

"That's where the first bull went in. The gun-bearer said when he fell off the bull was down. He was watching us helling along and the other two buff galloping. When he looked up there was the bull up and looking at him. Gun-bearer ran like hell and the bull went off slowly into that bush."

"Can we go in after him now?" asked Macomber eagerly.

Wilson looked at him appraisingly. Damned if this isn't a strange one, he thought. Yesterday he's scared sick and today he's a ruddy fire eater.

"No, we'll give him a while."

"Let's please go into the shade," Margot said. Her face was white and she looked ill. [130/131]

They made their way to the car where it stood under a single, wide-spreading tree and all climbed in.

"Chances are he's dead in there," Wilson remarked. "After a little we'll have a look."

Macomber felt a wild unreasonable happiness that he had never known before.

"By God, that was a chase," he said. "I've never felt any such feeling. Wasn't it marvellous, Margot?"

"I hated it."

"Why?"

"I hated it," she said bitterly. "I loathed it."

"You know I don't think I'd ever be afraid of anything again," Macomber said to Wilson. "Something happened in me after we first saw the buff and started after him. Like a dam bursting. It was pure excitement."

"Cleans out your liver," said Wilson. "Damn funny things happen to people."

Macomber's face was shining. "You know something did happen to me," he said. "I feel absolutely different."

His wife said nothing and eyed him strangely. She was sitting far back in the seat and Macomber was sitting forward talking to Wilson who turned sideways talking over the back of the front seat.

"You know, I'd like to try another lion," Macomber said. "I'm really not afraid of them now. After all, what can they do to you?"

"That's it," said Wilson. "Worst one can do is kill you. How does it go? Shakespeare. Damned good. See if I can remember. Oh, damned good. Used to quote it to myself at one time. Let's see. 'By my troth, I care not; a man can die but once; we owe God a death and let it go which way it will he that dies this year is quit for the next.' Damned fine, eh?"

He was very embarrassed, having

brought out this thing he had lived by, but he had seen men come of age before and it always moved him. It was not a matter of their twenty-first birthday. [131/132]

It had taken a strange chance of hunting, a sudden precipitation into action without opportunity for worrying beforehand, to bring this about with Macomber, but regardless of how it had happened it had most certainly happened. Look at the beggar now, Wilson thought. It's that some of them stay little boys so long, Wilson thought. Sometimes all their lives. Their figures stay boyish when they're fifty. The great American boy-men. Damned strange people. But he liked this Macomber now. Damned strange fellow. Probably meant the end of cuckoldry too. Well, that would be a damned good thing. Damned good thing. Beggar had probably been afraid all his life. Don't know what started it. But over now. Hadn't had time to be afraid with the buff. That and being angry too. Motor car too. Motor cars made it familiar. Be a damn fire eater now. He'd seen it in the war work the same way. More of a change than any loss of virginity. Fear gone like an operation. Something else grew in its place. Main thing a man had. Made him into a man. Women knew it too. No bloody fear.

From the far corner of the seat Margaret Macomber looked at the two of them. There was no change in Wilson. She saw Wilson as she had seen him the day before when she had first realized what his great talent was. But she saw the change in Francis Macomber now.

"Do you have that feeling of happiness about what's going to happen?" Macomber asked, still exploring his new wealth.

"You're not supposed to mention it," Wilson said, looking in the other's face. "Much more fashionable to say you're scared. Mind you, you'll be scared too, plenty of times."

"But you *have* a feeling of happiness about action to come?"

"Yes," said Wilson. "There's that. Doesn't do to talk too much about all this.

Talk the whole thing away. No pleasure in anything if you mouth it up too much."

"You're both talking rot," said Margot. "Just because you've chased some helpless animals in a motor car you talk like heroes." [132/133]

"Sorry," said Wilson. "I have been gassing too much." She's worried about it already, he thought.

"If you don't know what we're talking about why not keep out of it?" Macomber asked his wife.

"You've gotten awfully brave, awfully suddenly," his wife said contemptuously, but her contempt was not secure. She was very afraid of something.

Macomber laughed, a very natural hearty laugh. "You know I *have*," he said. "I really have."

Isn't it sort of late?" Margot said bitterly. Because she had done the best she could for many years back and the way they were together now was no one person's fault.

"Not for me," said Macomber.

Margot said nothing but sat back in the corner of the seat.

"Do you think we've given him time enough?" Macomber asked Wilson cheerfully.

"We might have a look," Wilson said. "Have you any solids left?"

"The gun-bearer has some."

Wilson called in Swahili and the older gun-bearer, who was skinning out one of the heads, straightened up, pulled a box of solids out of his pocket and brought them over to Macomber, who filled his magazine and put the remaining shells in his pocket.

"You might as well shoot the Springfield," Wilson said. "You're used to it. We'll leave the Mannlicher in the car with the Memsahib. Your gun-bearer can carry your heavy gun. I've this damned cannon. Now let me tell you about them." He had saved this until the last because he did not want to worry Macomber. "When a buff comes he comes with his head high and thrust straight out. The boss of the horns covers any sort of a brain shot. The only shot is straight into the nose. The only other shot is into his chest or, if you're to one side, into the neck or the shoulders. After they've been hit once they take a hell of a lot of killing. Don't try anything fancy. [133/134] Take the easiest shot there is. They've finished skinning out that head now. Should we get started?"

He called to the gun-bearers, who came up wiping their hands, and the older one got into the back.

"I'll only take Kongoni," Wilson said. "The other can watch to keep the birds away."

As the car moved slowly across the open space toward the island of brushy trees that ran in a tongue of foliage along a dry water course that cut the open swale, Macomber felt his heart pounding and his mouth was dry again, but it was excitement, not fear.

"Here's where he went in," Wilson said. Then to the gun-bearer in Swahili, "Take the blood spoor."

The car was parallel to the patch of bush. Macomber, Wilson and the gun-bearer got down. Macomber, looking back, saw his wife, with the rifle by her side, looking at him. He waved to her and she did not wave back.

The brush was very thick ahead and the ground was dry. The middle-aged gun-bearer was sweating heavily and Wilson had his hat down over his eyes and his red neck showed just ahead of Macomber. Suddenly the gun-bearer said something in Swahili to Wilson and ran forward.

"He's dead in there," Wilson said. "Good work," and he turned to grip Macomber's hand and as they shook hands, grinning at each other, the gun-bearer shouted wildly and they saw him coming out of the bush sideways, fast as a crab, and the bull coming, nose out, mouth tight closed, blood dripping, massive head straight out, coming in a charge, his little pig eyes bloodshot as he looked at them. Wilson, who was ahead was kneeling shooting, and Macomber, as he fired, unhearing his shot in the roaring of Wilson's gun,

saw fragments like slate burst from the huge boss of the horns, and the head jerked, he shot again at the wide nostrils and saw the horns jolt again and fragments fly, and he did not see Wilson now and, aiming carefully, shot again with the buffalo's huge bulk almost on him and his rifle almost level with the on-coming head, nose out, [134/135] and he could see the little wicked eyes and the head started to lower and he felt a sudden white-hot, blinding flash explode inside his head and that was all he ever felt.

Wilson had ducked to one side to get in a shoulder shot. Macomber had stood solid and shot for the nose, shooting a touch high each time and hitting the heavy horns, splintering and chipping them like hitting a slate roof, and Mrs. Macomber, in the car, had shot at the buffalo with the 6.5 Mannlicher as it seemed about to gore Macomber and had hit her husband about two inches up and a little to one side of the base of his skull.

Francis Macomber lay now, face down, not two yards from where the buffalo lay on his side and his wife knelt over him with Wilson beside her.

"I wouldn't turn him over," Wilson said.

The woman was crying hysterically.

"I'd get back in the car," Wilson said. "Where's the rifle?"

She shook her head, her face contorted. The gun-bearer picked up the rifle.

"Leave it as it is," said Wilson. Then, "Go get Abdulla so that he may witness the manner of the accident."

He knelt down, took a handkerchief from his pocket, and spread it over Francis Macomber's crew-cropped head where it lay. The blood sank into the dry, loose earth.

Wilson stood up and saw the buffalo on his side, his legs out, his thinly-haired belly crawling with ticks. "Hell of a good bull," his brain registered automatically. "A good fifty inches, or better. Better." He called to the driver and told him to spread a blanket over the body and stay by it. Then he walked over to the motor car where the woman sat crying in the corner.

"That was a pretty thing to do," he said in a toneless voice. "He *would* have left you too."

"Stop it," she said.

"Of course it's an accident," he said. "I know that."

"Stop it," she said.

"Don't worry," he said. "There will be a certain amount of unpleasantness but I will have some photographs taken that [135/136] will be very useful at the inquest. There's the testimony of the gunbearers and the driver too. You're perfectly all right."

"Stop it," she said.

"There's a hell of a lot to be done," he said. "And I'll have to send a truck off to the lake to wireless for a plane to take the three of us into Nairobi. Why didn't you poison him? That's what they do in England."

"Stop it. Stop it. Stop it," the woman cried.

Wilson looked at her with his flat blue eyes.

"I'm through now," he said. "I was a little angry. I'd begun to like your husband."

"Oh, please stop it," she said. "Please, please stop it."

"That's better," Wilson said. "Please is much better. Now I'll stop."

The Snows of Kilimanjaro *

ERNEST HEMINGWAY wrote "The Snows of Kilimanjaro" in April, 1936. The typescript was submitted with many additions and revisions (see frontispiece) to *Esquire* for publication in the August issue of 1936. Like "The Short Happy Life of Francis Macomber," it was reprinted, with minor revisions, in *The Fifth Column and the First Forty-nine Stories*. It is the text of this final version that is reprinted here.

Kilimanjaro is a snow covered mountain 19,710 feet high, and is said to be the highest mountain in Africa. Its western summit is called the Masai "Ngàje Ngài," the House of God. Close to the western summit there is the dried and frozen carcass of a leopard. No one has explained what the leopard was seeking at that altitude.

"The marvellous thing is that it's painless," he said. "That's how you know when it starts."

"Is it really?"

"Absolutely. I'm awfully sorry about the odor though. That must bother you."

"Don't! Please don't."

"Look at them," he said. "Now is it sight or is it scent that brings them like that?"

The cot the man lay on was in the wide shade of a mimosa tree and as he looked out past the shade onto the glare of the plain there were three of the big birds squatted obscenely, while in the sky a dozen more sailed, making quick-moving shadows as they passed.

"They've been there since the day the truck broke down," he said. "Today's the first time any have lit on the ground. I watched the way they sailed very carefully at first in case I ever wanted to use them in a story. That's funny now."

"I wish you wouldn't," she said.

"I'm only talking," he said. "It's much easier if I talk. But I don't want to bother you."

"You know it doesn't bother me," she said. "It's that I've gotten so very nervous not being able to do anything. I think we might make it as easy as we can until the plane comes."

"Or until the plane doesn't come."

"Please tell me what I can do. There must be something I can do."

"You can take the leg off and that might stop it, though I [150/151] doubt it. Or you can shoot me. You're a good shot now. I taught you to shoot didn't I?"

"Please don't talk that way. Couldn't I read to you?"

"Read what?"

"Anything in the book bag that we haven't read."

"I can't listen to it," he said. "Talking is the easiest. We quarrel and that makes the time pass."

"I don't quarrel. I never want to quarrel. Let's not quarrel any more. No matter how nervous we get. Maybe they will be back with another truck today. Maybe the plane will come."

"I don't want to move," the man said. "There is no sense in moving now except to make it easier for you."

"That's cowardly."

"Can't you let a man die as comfortably

as he can without calling him names? What's the use of slanging me?"

"You're not going to die."

"Don't be silly. I'm dying now. Ask those bastards." He looked over to where the huge, filthy birds sat, their naked heads sunk in the hunched feathers. A fourth planed down, to run quick-legged and then waddle slowly toward the others.

"They are around every camp. You never notice them. You can't die if you don't give up."

"Where did you read that? You're such a bloody fool."

"You might think about some one else."

"For Christ's sake," he said, "That's been my trade."

He lay then and was quiet for a while and looked across the heat shimmer of the plain to the edge of the bush. There were a few Tommies that showed minute and white against the yellow and, far off, he saw a herd of zebra, white against the green of the bush. This was a pleasant camp under big trees against a hill, with good water, and close by, a nearly dry water hole where sand grouse flighted in the mornings.

"Wouldn't you like me to read?" she asked. She was sitting on a canvas chair beside his cot. "There's a breeze coming up."

"No thanks."

"Maybe the truck will come." [151/152]

"I don't give a damn about the truck."

"I do."

"You give a damn about so many things that I don't."

"Not so many, Harry."

"What about a drink?"

"It's supposed to be bad for you. It said in Black's to avoid all alcohol. You shouldn't drink."

"Molo!" he shouted.

"Yes Bwana."

"Bring whiskey-soda."

"Yes Bwana."

"You shouldn't," she said. "That's what I mean by giving up. It says it's bad for you. I know it's bad for you."

"No," he said. "It's good for me."

So now it was all over, he thought. So now he would never have a chance to finish it. So this was the way it ended in a bickering over a drink. Since the gangrene started in his right leg he had no pain and with the pain the horror had gone and all he felt now was a great tiredness and anger that this was the end of it. For this, that now was coming, he had very little curiosity. For years it had obsessed him; but now it meant nothing in itself. It was strange how easy being tired enough made it.

Now he would never write the things that he had saved to write until he knew enough to write them well. Well, he would not have to fail at trying to write them either. Maybe you could never write them, and that was why you put them off and delayed the starting. Well he would never know, now.

"I wish we'd never come," the woman said. She was looking at him holding the glass and biting her lip. "You never would have gotten anything like this in Paris. You always said you loved Paris. We could have stayed in Paris or gone anywhere. I'd have gone anywhere. I said I'd go anywhere you wanted. If you wanted to shoot we could have gone shooting in Hungary and been comfortable."

"Your bloody money," he said. [152/153]

"That's not fair," she said. "It was always yours as much as mine. I left everything and I went wherever you wanted to go and I've done what you wanted to do. But I wish we'd never come here."

"You said you loved it."

"I did when you were all right. But now I hate it. I don't see why that had to happen to your leg. What have we done to have that happen to us?"

"I suppose what I did was to forget to put iodine on it when I first scratched it. Then I didn't pay any attention to it because I never infect. Then, later, when it got bad, it was probably using that weak carbolic solution when the other antiseptics ran out that paralyzed the minute blood vessels and started the gangrene." He looked at her, "What else?"

"I don't mean that."

"If we would have hired a good mechanic instead of a half baked kikuyu driver, he would have checked the oil and never burned out that bearing in the truck."

"I don't mean that."

"If you hadn't left your own people, your goddamned Old Westbury, Saratoga, Palm Beach people to take me on——"

"Why, I loved you. That's not fair. I love you now. I'll always love you. Don't you love me?"

"No," said the man. "I don't think so. I never have."

"Harry, what are you saying? You're out of your head."

"No. I haven't any head to go out of."

"Don't drink that," she said. "Darling, please don't drink that. We have to do everything we can."

"You do it," he said. "I'm tired."

Now in his mind he saw a railway station at Karagatch and he was standing with his pack and that was the headlight of the Simplon-Orient cutting the dark now and he was leaving Thrace then after the retreat. That was one of the things he had saved to write, with, in the morning at breakfast, looking out the window and seeing snow on the mountains in Bulgaria [153/154] and Nansen's Secretary asking the old man if it were snow and the old man looking at it and saying, No, that's not snow. It's too early for snow. And the Secretary repeating to the other girls, No, you see. It's not snow and them all saying, It's not snow we were mistaken. But it was the snow all right and he sent them on into it when he evolved exchange of populations. And it was snow they tramped along in until they died that winter.

It was snow too that fell all Christmas week that year up in the Gauertal, that year they lived in the woodcutter's house with the big square porcelain stove that filled half the room, and they slept on mattresses filled with beech leaves, the time the deserter came with his feet bloody in the snow. He said the police were right behind him and they gave him woolen socks and held the gendarmes talking until the tracks had drifted over.

In Schrunz, on Christmas day, the snow was so bright it hurt your eyes when you looked out from the weinstube and saw every one coming home from church. That was where they walked up the sleigh-smoothed urine-yellowed road along the river with the steep pine hills, skis heavy on the shoulder, and where they ran that great run down the glacier above the Madlener-haus, the snow as smooth to see as cake frosting and as light as powder and he remembered the noiseless rush the speed made as you dropped down like a bird.

They were snow-bound a week in the Madlener-haus that time in the blizzard playing cards in the smoke by the lantern light and the stakes were higher all the time as Herr Lent lost more. Finally he lost it all. Everything, the skischule money and all the season's profit and then his capital. He could see him with his long nose, picking up the cards and then opening, "Sans Voir." There was always gambling then. When there was no snow you gambled and when there was too much you gambled. He thought of all the time in his life he had spent gambling.

But he had never written a line of that, nor of that cold, bright Christmas day with the mountains showing across the plain that [154/155] Barker had flown across the lines to bomb the Austrian officers' leave train, machine-gunning them as they scattered and ran. He remembered Barker afterwards coming into the mess and starting to tell about it. And how quiet it got and then somebody saying, "You bloody murderous bastard."

Those were the same Austrians they killed then that he skied with later. No not the same. Hans, that he skied with all that year, had been in the Kaiser-Jägers and when they went hunting hares together up the little valley above the saw-mill they had talked of the fighting on Pasubio and of the attack on Pertica and Asalone and he had never written a word of that. Nor of Monte Corno, nor the Siete Commum, nor of Arsiedo.

*How many winters had he lived in the
Voralberg and the Arlberg? It was four
and then he remembered the man who
had the fox to sell when they had walked
into Bludenz, that time to buy presents,
and the cherry-pit taste of good kirsch, the
fast-slipping rush of running powder-
snow on crust, singing "Hi! Ho! said
Rolly!" as you ran down the last stretch to
the steep drop, taking it straight, then
running the orchard in three turns and
out across the ditch and onto the icy road
behind the inn. Knocking your bindings
loose, kicking the skis free and leaning
them up against the wooden wall of the
inn, the lamplight coming from the window, where inside, in the smoky, new-wine
smelling warmth, they were playing the
accordion.*

"Where did we stay in Paris?" he asked
the woman who was sitting by him in a
canvas chair, now, in Africa.

"At the Crillon. You know that."

"Why do I know that?"

"That's where we always stayed."

"No. Not always."

"There and at the Pavillion Henri-
Quatre in St. Germain. You said you
loved it there."

"Love is a dunghill," said Harry. "And
I'm the cock that gets on it to crow."

"If you have to go away," she said, "is it
absolutely necessary [155/156] to kill off
everything you leave behind? I mean do
you have to take away everything? Do you
have to kill your horse, and your wife and
burn your saddle and your armour?"

"Yes," he said. "Your damned money
was my armour. My Swift and my
Armour."

"Don't."

"All right. I'll stop that. I don't want to
hurt you."

"It's a little bit late now."

"All right then. I'll go on hurting you.
It's more amusing. The only thing I ever
really liked to do with you I can't do now."

"No, that's not true. You liked to do
many things and everything you wanted
to do I did."

"Oh, for Christ sake stop bragging, will
you?"

He looked at her and saw her crying.

"Listen," he said. "Do you think that it
is fun to do this? I don't know why I'm
doing it. It's trying to kill to keep yourself
alive, I imagine. I was all right when we
started talking. I didn't mean to start this,
and now I'm crazy as a coot and being as
cruel to you as I can be. Don't pay any
attention, darling, to what I say. I love
you, really. You know I love you. I've
never loved any one else the way I love
you."

He slipped into the familiar lie he made
his bread and butter by.

"You're sweet to me."

"You bitch," he said. "You rich bitch.
That's poetry. I'm full of poetry now.
Rot and poetry. Rotten poetry."

"Stop it. Harry, why do you have to
turn into a devil now?"

"I don't like to leave anything," the
man said. "I don't like to leave things
behind."

* * *

It was evening now and he had been
asleep. The sun was gone behind the hill
and there was a shadow all across the
plain and the small animals were feeding
close to camp; quick dropping heads and
switching tails, he watched them keeping
[156/157] well out away from the bush
now. The birds no longer waited on the
ground. They were all perched heavily in a
tree. There were many more of them. His
personal boy was sitting by the bed.

"Memsahib's gone to shoot," the boy
said. "Does Bwana want?"

"Nothing."

She had gone to kill a piece of meat and,
knowing how he liked to watch the game,
she had gone well away so she would not
disturb this little pocket of the plain that
he could see. She was always thoughtful,
he thought. On anything she knew about,
or had read, or that she had ever heard.

It was not her fault that when he went
to her he was already over. How could a
woman know that you meant nothing that

you said; that you spoke only from habit and to be comfortable? After he no longer meant what he said, his lies were more successful with women than when he had told them the truth.

It was not so much that he lied as that there was no truth to tell. He had had his life and it was over and then he went on living it again with different people and more money, with the best of the same places, and some new ones.

You kept from thinking and it was all marvellous. You were equipped with good insides so that you did not go to pieces that way, the way most of them had, and you made an attitude that you cared nothing for the work you used to do, now that you could no longer do it. But, in yourself, you said that you would write about these people; about the very rich; that you were really not of them but a spy in their country; that you would leave it and write of it and for once it would be written by some one who knew what he was writing of. But he would never do it, because each day of not writing, of comfort, of being that which he despised, dulled his ability and softened his will to work so that, finally, he did no work at all. The people he knew now were all much more comfortable when he did not work. Africa was where he had been happiest in the good time of his life, so he had come out here to start again. They [**157/158**] had made this safari with the minimum of comfort. There was no hardship; but there was no luxury and he had thought that he could get back into training that way. That in some way he could work the fat off his soul the way a fighter went into the mountains to work and train in order to burn it out of his body.

She had liked it. She said she loved it. She loved anything that was exciting, that involved a change of scene, where there were new people and where things were pleasant. And he had felt the illusion of returning strength of will to work. Now if this was how it ended, and he knew it was, he must not turn like some snake biting itself because its back was broken. It

wasn't this woman's fault. If it had not been she it would have been another. If he lived by a lie he should try to die by it. He heard a shot beyond the hill.

She shot very well this good, this rich bitch, this kindly caretaker and destroyer of his talent. Nonsense. He had destroyed his talent himself. Why should he blame this woman because she kept him well? He had destroyed his talent by not using it, by betrayals of himself and what he believed in, by drinking so much that he blunted the edge of his perceptions, by laziness, by sloth, and by snobbery, by pride and by prejudice, by hook and by crook. What was this? A catalogue of old books? What was his talent anyway? It was a talent all right but instead of using it, he had traded on it. It was never what he had done, but always what he could do. And he had chosen to make his living with something else instead of a pen or a pencil. It was strange, too, wasn't it, that when he fell in love with another woman, that woman should always have more money than the last one? But when he no longer was in love, when he was only lying, as to this woman, now, who had the most money of all, who had all the money there was, who had had a husband and children, who had taken lovers and been dissatisfied with them, and who loved him dearly as a writer, as a man, as a companion and as a proud possession; it was strange that when he did not love her at all and was lying, that [**158/159**] he should be able to give her more for her money than when he had really loved.

We must all be cut out for what we do, he thought. However you make your living is where your talent lies. He had sold vitality, in one form or another, all his life and when your affections are not too involved you give much better value for the money. He had found that out but he would never write that, now, either. No, he would not write that, although it was well worth writing.

Now she came in sight, walking across the open toward the camp. She was wearing jodphurs and carrying her rifle. The two boys had a Tommie slung and they were coming along behind her. She was still a good-looking woman, he thought, and she had a pleasant body. She had a great talent and appreciation for the bed, she was not pretty, but he liked her face, she read enormously, liked to ride and shoot and, certainly, she drank too much. Her husband had died when she was still a comparatively young woman and for a while she had devoted herself to her two just-grown children, who did not need her and were embarrassed at having her about, to her stable of horses, to books, and to bottles. She liked to read in the evening before dinner and she drank Scotch and soda while she read. By dinner she was fairly drunk and after a bottle of wine at dinner she was usually drunk enough to sleep.

That was before the lovers. After she had the lovers she did not drink so much because she did not have to be drunk to sleep. But the lovers bored her. She had been married to a man who had never bored her and these people bored her very much.

Then one of her two children was killed in a plane crash and after that was over she did not want the lovers, and drink being no anaesthetic she had to make another life. Suddenly, she had been acutely frightened of being alone. But she wanted some one that she respected with her.

It had begun very simply. She liked what he wrote and she had always envied the life he led. She thought he did exactly [**159/160**] what he wanted to. The steps by which she had acquired him and the way in which she had finally fallen in love with him were all part of a regular progression in which she had built herself a new life and he had traded away what remained of his old life.

He had traded it for security, for comfort too, there was no denying that, and for what else? He did not know. She would have bought him anything he wanted. He knew that. She was a damned nice woman too. He would as soon be in bed with her as any one; rather with her, because she was richer, because she was very pleasant and appreciative and because she never made scenes. And now this life that she had built again was coming to a term because he had not used iodine two weeks ago when a thorn had scratched his knee as they moved forward trying to photograph a herd of waterbuck standing, their heads up, peering while their nostrils searched the air, their ears spread wide to hear the first noise that would send them rushing into the bush. They had bolted, too, before he got the picture.

Here she came now.

He turned his head on the cot to look toward her. "Hello," he said.

"I shot a Tommy ram," she told him. "He'll make you good broth and I'll have them mash some potatoes with the Klim. How do you feel?"

"Much better."

"Isn't that lovely? You know I thought perhaps you would. You were sleeping when I left."

"I had a good sleep. Did you walk far?"

"No. Just around behind the hill. I made quite a good shot on the Tommy."

"You shoot marvellously, you know."

"I love it. I've loved Africa. Really. If *you're* all right it's the most fun that I've ever had. You don't know the fun it's been to shoot with you. I've loved the country."

"I love it too." [**160/161**]

"Darling, you don't know how marvellous it is to see you feeling better. I couldn't stand it when you felt that way. You won't talk to me like that again, will you? Promise me?"

"No," he said. "I don't remember what I said."

"You don't have to destroy me. Do you? I'm only a middle-aged woman who loves you and wants to do what you want to do. I've been destroyed two or three times already. You wouldn't want to destroy me again, would you?"

"I'd like to destroy you a few times in bed," he said.

"Yes. That's the good destruction. That's the way we're made to be destroyed. The plane will be here tomorrow."

"How do you know?"

"I'm sure. It's bound to come. The boys have the wood all ready and the grass to make the smudge. I went down and looked at it again today. There's plenty of room to land and we have the smudges ready at both ends."

"What makes you think it will come tomorrow?"

"I'm sure it will. It's overdue now. Then, in town, they will fix up your leg and then we will have some good destruction. Not that dreadful talking kind."

"Should we have a drink? The sun is down."

"Do you think you should?"

"I'm having one."

"We'll have one together. *Molo, letti dui whiskey-soda!*" she called.

"You'd better put on your mosquito boots," he told her.

"I'll wait till I bathe . . ."

While it grew dark they drank and just before it was dark and there was no longer enough light to shoot, a hyena crossed the open on his way around the hill.

"That bastard crosses there every night," the man said. "Every night for two weeks."

"He's the one makes the noise at night. I don't mind it. They're a filthy animal though."

Drinking together, with no pain now except the discomfort of lying in the one position, the boys lighting a fire, its shadow [161/162] jumping on the tents, he could feel the return of acquiescence in this life of pleasant surrender. She *was* very good to him. He had been cruel and unjust in the afternoon. She was a fine woman, marvellous really. And just then it occurred to him that he was going to die.

It came with a rush; not as a rush of water nor of wind; but of a sudden evil-smelling emptiness and the odd thing was that the hyena slipped lightly along the edge of it.

"What is it, Harry?" she asked him.

"Nothing," he said. "You had better move over to the other side. To windward."

"Did Molo change the dressing?"

"Yes. I'm just using the boric now."

"How do you feel?"

"A little wobbly."

"I'm going in to bathe," she said. "I'll be right out. I'll eat with you and then we'll put the cot in."

So, he said to himself, we did well to stop the quarrelling. He had never quarrelled much with this woman, while with the women that he loved he had quarrelled so much they had finally, always, with the corrosion of the quarrelling, killed what they had together. He had loved too much, demanded too much, and he wore it all out.

He thought about alone in Constantinople that time, having quarrelled in Paris before he had gone out. He had whored the whole time and then, when that was over, and he had failed to kill his loneliness, but only made it worse, he had written her, the first one, the one who left him, a letter telling her how he had never been able to kill it. . . . How when he thought he saw her outside the Regence one time it made him go all faint and sick inside, and that he would follow a woman who looked like her in some way, along the Boulevard, afraid to see it was not she, afraid to lose the feeling it gave him. How every one he had slept with had only made him miss her more. How what she had done could never matter since he knew he could [162/163] not cure himself of loving her. He wrote this letter at the Club, cold sober, and mailed it to New York asking her to write him at the office in Paris. That seemed safe. And that night missing her so much it made him feel hollow sick inside, he wandered up past Taxim's, picked a girl up and took her out to supper. He had gone to a place to dance with her afterward, she danced badly, and left her for a hot Armenian slut, that swung her belly against him so it almost scalded. He took her away from a British gunner subaltern after a row. The gunner asked him outside and they fought in the street on the cobbles in the dark. He'd hit him twice, hard, on the side of the jaw and when he didn't go down he knew he was in for a fight. The gunner hit him in the body, then beside his eye.

He swung with his left again and landed and the gunner fell on him and grabbed his coat and tore the sleeve off and he clubbed him twice behind the ear and then smashed him with his right as he pushed him away. When the gunner went down his head hit first and he ran with the girl because they heard the M. P.'s coming. They got into a taxi and drove out to Rimmily Hissa along the Bosphorus, and around, and back in the cool night and went to bed and she felt as over-ripe as she looked but smooth, rose-petal, syrupy, smooth-bellied, big-breasted and needed no pillow under her buttocks, and he left her before she was awake looking blousy enough in the first daylight and turned up at the Pera Palace with a black eye, carrying his coat because one sleeve was missing.

That same night he left for Anatolia and he remembered, later on that trip, riding all day through fields of the poppies that they raised for opium and how strange it made you feel, finally, and all the distances seemed wrong, to where they had made the attack with the newly arrived Constantine officers, that did not know a god-damned thing, and the artillery had fired into the troops and the British observer had cried like a child.

That was the day he'd first seen dead men wearing white ballet skirts and upturned shoes with pompons on them. The [163/164] *Turks had come steadily and lumpily and he had seen the skirted men running and the officers shooting into them and running then themselves and he and the British observer had run too until his lungs ached and his mouth was full of the taste of pennies and they stopped behind some rocks and there were the Turks coming as lumpily as ever. Later he had seen the things that he could never think of and later still he had seen much worse. So when he got back to Paris that time he could not talk about it or stand to have it mentioned. And there in the café as he passed was that American poet with a pile of saucers in front of him and a stupid look on his potato face talk-*

ing about the Dada movement with a Roumanian who said his name was Tristan Tzara, who always wore a monocle and had a headache, and, back at the apartment with his wife that now he loved again, the quarrel all over, the madness all over, glad to be home, the office sent his mail up to the flat. So then the letter in answer to the one he'd written came in on a platter one morning and when he saw the handwriting he went cold all over and tried to slip the letter underneath another. But his wife said, "Who is that letter from, dear?" and that was the end of the beginning of that.

He remembered the good times with them all, and the quarrels. They always picked the finest places to have the quarrels. And why had they always quarrelled when he was feeling best? He had never written any of that because, at first, he never wanted to hurt any one and then it seemed as though there was enough to write without it. But he had always thought that he would write it finally. There was so much to write. He had seen the world change; not just the events; although he had seen many of them and had watched the people, but he had seen the subtler change and he could remember how the people were at different times. He had been in it and he had watched it and it was his duty to write of it; but now he never would.

"How do you feel?" she said. She had come out from the tent now after her bath. [164/165]

"All right."

"Could you eat now?" He saw Molo behind her with the folding table and the other boy with the dishes.

"I want to write," he said.

"You ought to take some broth to keep your strength up."

"I'm going to die tonight," he said. "I don't need my strength up."

"Don't be melodramatic, Harry, please," she said.

"Why don't you use your nose? I'm rotted half way up my thigh now. What the hell should I fool with broth for? Molo bring whiskey-soda."

"Please take the broth," she said gently.

"All right."

The broth was too hot. He had to hold it in the cup until it cooled enough to take it and then he just got it down without gagging.

"You're a fine woman," he said. "Don't pay any attention to me."

She looked at him with her well-known, well-loved face from *Spur* and *Town and Country*, only a little the worse for drink, only a little the worse for bed, but *Town and Country* never showed those good breasts and those useful thighs and those lightly small-of-back-caressing hands, and as he looked and saw her well known pleasant smile, he felt death come again. This time there was no rush. It was a puff, as of a wind that makes a candle flicker and the flame go tall.

"They can bring my net out later and hang it from the tree and build the fire up. I'm not going in the tent tonight. It's not worth moving. It's a clear night. There won't be any rain."

So this was how you died, in whispers that you did not hear. Well, there would be no more quarrelling. He could promise that. The one experience that he had never had he was not going to spoil now. He probably would. You spoiled everything. But perhaps he wouldn't.

"You can't take dictation, can you?"

"I never learned," she told him. [**165/166**]

"That's all right."

There wasn't time, of course, although it seemed as though it telescoped so that you might put it all into one paragraph if you could get it right.

There was a log house, chinked white with mortar, on a hill above the lake. There was a bell on a pole by the door to call the people in to meals. Behind the house were fields and behind the fields was the timber. A line of lombardy poplars ran from the house to the dock. Other poplars ran along the point. A road went *up to the hills along the edge of the timber and along that road he picked blackberries. Then that log house was burned down and all the guns that had been on deer foot racks above the open fire place were* burned and afterwards their barrels, with the lead melted in the magazines, and the stocks burned away, lay out on the heap of ashes that were used to make lye for the big iron soap kettles, and you asked Grandfather if you could have them to play with, and he said, no. You see they were his guns still and he never bought any others. Nor did he hunt any more. The house was rebuilt in the same place out of lumber now and painted white and from its porch you saw the poplars and the lake beyond; but there were never any more guns. The barrels of the guns that had hung on the deer feet on the wall of the log house lay out there on the heap of ashes and no one ever touched them.*

In the Black Forest, after the war, we rented a trout stream and there were two ways to walk to it. One was down the valley from Triberg and around the valley road in the shade of the trees that bordered the white road, and then up a side road that went up through the hills past many small farms, with the big Schwarzwald houses, until that road crossed the stream. That was where our fishing began.

*The other way was to climb steeply up to the edge of the woods and then go across the top of the hills through the pine woods, and then out to the edge of a meadow and down across this meadow to the bridge. There were birches along the stream [**166/167**] and it was not big, but narrow, clear and fast, with pools where it had cut under the roots of the birches. At the Hotel in Triberg the proprietor had a fine season. It was very pleasant and we were all great friends. The next year came the inflation and the money he had made the year before was not enough to buy supplies to open the hotel and he hanged himself.*

You could dictate that, but you could not dictate the Place Contrescarpe where the flower sellers dyed their flowers in the

street and the dye ran over the paving
where the autobus started and the old
men and the women, always drunk on
wine and bad marc; and the children
with their noses running in the cold; the
smell of dirty sweat and poverty and
drunkenness at the Café des Amateurs
and the whores at the Bal Musette they
lived above. The Concierge who enter-
tained the trooper of the Garde Republi-
caine in her loge, his horse-hair-plumed
helmet on a chair. The locataire across the
hall whose husband was a bicycle racer and
her joy that morning at the Cremerie when
she had opened L'Auto and seen where he
placed third in Paris-Tours, his first big
race. She had blushed and laughed and
then gone upstairs crying with the yellow
sporting paper in her hand. The husband
of the woman who ran the Bal Musette
drove a taxi and when he, Harry, had to
take an early plane the husband knocked
upon the door to wake him and they each
drank a glass of white wine at the zinc of
the bar before they started. He knew his
neighbors in that quarter then because
they all were poor.

Around that Place there were two kinds;
the drunkards and the sportifs. The drunkards killed their poverty that way; the
sportifs took it out in exercise. They were
the descendants of the Communards and
it was no struggle for them to know their
politics. They knew who had shot their
fathers, their relatives, their brothers, and
their friends when the Versailles troops
came in and took the town after the Commune and executed any one they could
catch with calloused hands, or who wore a
cap, or carried any other sign he was a
working man. And in that poverty, and
in that quarter across the street from a
Boucherie [167/168] Chevaline and a
wine co-operative he had written the start
of all he was to do. There never was another part of Paris that he loved like that,
the sprawling trees, the old white plastered
houses painted brown below, the long
green of the autobus in that round square,
the purple flower dye upon the paving,
the sudden drop down the hill of the rue

Cardinal Lemoine to the River, and the
other way the narrow crowded world of
the rue Mouffetard. The street that ran up
toward the Pantheon and the other that he
always took with the bicycle, the only
asphalted street in all that quarter, smooth
under the tires, with the high narrow
houses and the cheap tall hotel where Paul
Verlaine had died. There were only two
rooms in the apartments where they lived
and he had a room on the top floor of that
hotel that cost him sixty francs a month
where he did his writing, and from it he
could see the roofs and chimney pots and
all the hills of Paris.

From the apartment you could only see
the wood and coal man's place. He sold
wine too, bad wine. The golden horse's
head outside the Boucherie Chevaline
where the carcasses hung yellow gold and
red in the open window, and the green
painted co-operative where they bought
their wine; good wine and cheap. The rest
was plaster walls and the windows of the
neighbors. The neighbors who, at night,
when some one lay drunk in the street,
moaning and groaning in that typical
French ivresse that you were propaganded
to believe did not exist, would open their
windows and then the murmur of talk.

"Where is the policeman? When you
don't want him the bugger is always there.
He's sleeping with some concierge. Get
the Agent." Till some one threw a bucket
of water from a window and the moaning
stopped. "What's that? Water. Ah, that's
intelligent." And the windows shutting.
Marie, his femme de menage, protesting
against the eight-hour day saying, "If a
husband works until six he gets only a
little drunk on the way home and does not
waste too much. If he works only until five
he is drunk every night and one has no
money. It is the wife of the working man
who suffers from this shortening of hours."
[168/169]

"Wouldn't you like some more broth?"
the woman asked him now.

"No, thank you very much. It is awfully
good."

"Try just a little."

"I would like a whiskey-soda."

"It's not good for you."

"No. It's bad for me. Cole Porter wrote the words and the music. This knowledge that you're going mad for me."

"You know I like you to drink."

"Oh yes. Only it's bad for me."

When she goes, he thought. I'll have all I want. Not all I want but all there is. Ayee he was tired. Too tired. He was going to sleep a little while. He lay still and death was not there. It must have gone around another street. It went in pairs, on bicycles, and moved absolutely silently on the pavements.

No, he had never written about Paris. Not the Paris that he cared about. But what about the rest that he had never written?

What about the ranch and the silvered gray of the sage brush, the quick, clear water in the irrigation ditches, and the heavy green of the alfalfa. The trail went up into the hills and the cattle in the summer were shy as deer. The bawling and the steady noise and slow moving mass raising a dust as you brought them down in the fall. And behind the mountains, the clear sharpness of the peak in the evening light and, riding down along the trail in the moonlight, bright across the valley. Now he remembered coming down through the timber in the dark holding the horse's tail when you could not see and all the stories that he meant to write.

About the half-wit chore boy who was left at the ranch that time and told not to let any one get any hay, and that old bastard from the Forks who had beaten the boy when he had worked for him stopping to get some feed. The boy refusing and the old man saying he would beat him again. The boy got the rifle from the kitchen and shot him when he tried to come [169/170] *into the barn and when they came back to the ranch he'd been dead a week, frozen in the corral, and the dogs had eaten part of him. But what was left you packed on a sled wrapped in a*

blanket and roped on and you got the boy to help you haul it, and the two of you took it out over the road on skis, and sixty miles down to town to turn the boy over. He having no idea that he would be arrested. Thinking he had done his duty and that you were his friend and he would be rewarded. He'd helped to haul the old man in so everybody could know how bad the old man had been and how he'd tried to steal some feed that didn't belong to him, and when the sheriff put the handcuffs on the boy he couldn't believe it. Then he'd started to cry. That was one story he had saved to write. He knew at least twenty good stories from out there and he had never written one. Why?

"You tell them why," he said.

"Why what, dear?"

"Why nothing."

She didn't drink so much, now, since she had him. But if he lived he would never write about her, he knew that now. Nor about any of them. The rich were dull and they drank too much, or they played too much backgammon. They were dull and they were repetitious. He remembered poor Julian and his romantic awe of them and how he had started a story once that began, "The very rich are different from you and me." And how some one had said to Julian, Yes, they have more money. But that was not humorous to Julian. He thought they were a special glamourous race and when he found they weren't it wrecked him just as much as any other thing that wrecked him.

He had been contemptuous of those who wrecked. You did not have to like it because you understood it. He could beat anything, he thought, because no thing could hurt him if he did not care.

All right. Now he would not care for death. One thing he [170/171] had always dreaded was the pain. He could stand pain as well as any man, until it went on too long, and wore him out, but here he had something that had hurt frightfully and just when he had felt it breaking him, the pain had stopped.

He remembered long ago when Williamson, the bombing officer, had been hit by a stick bomb some one in a German patrol had thrown as he was coming in through the wire that night and, screaming, had begged every one to kill him. He was a fat man, very brave, and a good officer, although addicted to fantastic shows. But that night he was caught in the wire, with a flare lighting him up and his bowels spilled out into the wire, so when they brought him in, alive, they had to cut him loose. Shoot me, Harry. For Christ sake shoot me. They had had an argument one time about our Lord never sending you anything you could not bear and some one's theory had been that meant that at a certain time the pain passed you out automatically. But he had always remembered Williamson, that night. Nothing passed out Williamson until he gave him all his morphine tablets that he had always saved to use himself and then they did not work right away.

Still this now, that he had, was very easy; and if it was no worse as it went on there was nothing to worry about. Except that he would rather be in better company.

He thought a little about the company that he would like to have.

No, he thought, when everything you do, you do too long, and do too late, you can't expect to find the people still there. The people all are gone. The party's over and you are with your hostess now.

I'm getting as bored with dying as with everything else, he thought.

"It's a bore," he said out loud.

"What is, my dear?"

"Anything you do too bloody long." [171/172]

He looked at her face between him and the fire. She was leaning back in the chair and the firelight shone on her pleasantly lined face and he could see that she was sleepy. He heard the hyena make a noise just outside the range of the fire.

"I've been writing," he said. "But I got tired."

"Do you think you will be able to sleep?"

"Pretty sure. Why don't you turn in?"

"I like to sit here with you."

"Do you feel anything strange?" he asked her.

"No. Just a little sleepy."

"I do," he said.

He had just felt death come by again.

"You know the only thing I've never lost is curiosity," he said to her.

"You've never lost anything. You're the most complete man I've ever known."

"Christ," he said. "How little a woman knows. What is that? Your intuition?"

Because, just then, death had come and rested its head on the foot of the cot and he could smell its breath.

"Never believe any of that about a scythe and a skull," he told her. "It can be two bicycle policemen as easily, or be a bird. Or it can have a wide snout like a hyena."

It had moved up on him now, but it had no shape any more. It simply occupied space.

"Tell it to go away."

It did not go away but moved a little closer.

"You've got a hell of a breath," he told it. "You stinking bastard."

It moved up closer to him still and now he could not speak to it, and when it saw he could not speak it came a little closer, and now he tried to send it away without speaking, but it moved in on him so its weight was all upon his chest, and while it crouched there and he could not move, or speak, he heard the woman say, "Bwana is asleep now. Take the cot up very gently and carry it into the tent." [172/173]

He could not speak to tell her to make it go away and it crouched now, heavier, so he could not breathe. And then, while they lifted the cot, suddenly it was all right and the weight went from his chest.

It was morning and had been morning for some time and he heard the plane. It showed very tiny and then made a wide circle and the boys ran out and lit the fires, using kerosene, and piled on grass so there were two big smudges at each end of the level place and the morning breeze blew them toward the camp and the plane circled twice more, low this time, and then glided down and levelled off and landed smoothly and, coming walking toward him, was old Compton in slacks, a tweed jacket and a brown felt hat.

"What's the matter, old cock?" Compton said.

"Bad leg," he told him. "Will you have some breakfast?"

"Thanks. I'll just have some tea. It's the Puss Moth you know. I won't be able to take the Memsahib. There's only room for one. Your lorry is on the way."

Helen had taken Compton aside and was speaking to him. Compton came back more cheery than ever.

"We'll get you right in," he said. "I'll be back for the Mem. Now I'm afraid I'll have to stop at Arusha to refuel. We'd better get going."

"What about the tea?"

"I don't really care about it you know."

The boys had picked up the cot and carried it around the green tents and down along the rock and out onto the plain and along past the smudges that were burning brightly now, the grass all consumed, and the wind fanning the fire, to the little plane. It was difficult getting him in, but once in he lay back in the leather seat, and the leg was stuck straight out to one side of the seat where Compton sat. Compton started the motor and got in. He waved to Helen and to the boys and, as the clatter moved into the old familiar roar, they swung around with Compie watching for wart-hog holes and roared, bump- [173/174] ing, along the stretch between the fires and with the last bump rose and he saw them all standing below, waving, and the camp beside the hill, flattening now, and the plain spreading, clumps of trees, and the bush flattening, while the game trails ran now smoothly to the dry waterholes, and there was a new water that he had never known of. The zebra, small rounded backs now, and the

wildebeeste, big-headed dots seeming to climb as they moved in long fingers across the plain, now scattering as the shadow came toward them, they were tiny now, and the movement had no gallop, and the plain as far as you could see, gray-yellow now and ahead old Compie's tweed back and the brown felt hat. Then they were over the first hills and the wildebeeste were trailing up them, and then they were over mountains with sudden depths of green-rising forest and the solid bamboo slopes, and then the heavy forest again, sculptured into peaks and hollows until they crossed, and hills sloped down and then another plain, hot now, and purple brown, bumpy with heat and Compie looking back to see how he was riding. Then there were other mountains dark ahead.

And then instead of going on to Arusha they turned left, he evidently figured that they had the gas, and looking down he saw a pink sifting cloud, moving over the ground, and in the air, like the first snow in a blizzard, that comes from nowhere, and he knew the locusts were coming up from the South. Then they began to climb and they were going to the East it seemed, and then it darkened and they were in a storm, the rain so thick it seemed like flying through a waterfall, and then they were out and Compie turned his head and grinned and pointed and there, ahead, all he could see, as wide as all the world, great, high, and unbelievably white in the sun, was the square top of Kilimanjaro. And then he knew that there was where he was going.

Just then the hyena stopped whimpering in the night and started to make a strange, human, almost crying sound. The woman heard it and stirred uneasily. She did not wake. In her [174/175] dream she was at the house on Long Island and it was the night before her daughter's début. Somehow her father was there and he had been very rude. Then the noise the hyena made was so loud she woke and for a moment she did not know where she was and she was very afraid. Then she took the flashlight and shone it on the other cot that they had carried in after Harry had gone to sleep. She could see his bulk under the mosquito bar but somehow he had gotten his leg out and it hung down alongside the cot. The dressings had all come down and she could not look at it.

"Molo," she called, "Molo! Molo!"

Then she said, "Harry, Harry!" Then her voice rising, "Harry! Please, Oh Harry!"

There was no answer and she could not hear him breathing.

Outside the tent the hyena made the same strange noise that had awakened her. But she did not hear him for the beating of her heart.

PART TWO

THEORY

A writer's job is to tell the truth. His standard of fidelity to the truth should be so high that his invention, out of his experience, should produce a truer account than anything factual can be. For facts can be observed badly; but when a good writer is creating something, he has time and scope to make it of an absolute truth.*

* Ernest Hemingway, from "Introduction," *Men at War* (New York: Crown Publishers, 1942), p. xv. Copyright © 1942 by Crown Publishers, Inc. Used with the permission of Crown Publishers, Inc.

["There is a fourth and fifth dimension that can be gotten."] *

ERNEST HEMINGWAY sailed for Africa from Marseilles in November, 1933, and returned to America in April, 1934. He began *Green Hills of Africa* shortly after his return. The book focuses on his hunting in the highlands of Tanganyika between January 21 and February 20, 1934. Though writing what he called a "true book" rather than a novel, he does, however, introduce in flashback events from his hunting on the Serengetti Plain prior to January 16, when he was flown to Nairobi, Kenya (by way of Arusha and Mount Kilimanjaro) for medical treatment. Accompanying him on safari were his wife, Pauline (called "P.O.M." or "poor old mama"); a friend from Key West, Charles Thompson (called "Karl"); and Philip Percival, a professional hunter (called "Jackson Phillip" or "Pop"). The person asking questions in the excerpt reprinted here was an expatriate Austrian named Kandisky; he appears in this chapter only. *Green Hills of Africa* was first serialized in *Scribner's Magazine,* starting in May, 1935; then published as a book on October 25, 1935.

CHAPTER I

... "We do not have great writers," I said. "Something happens to our good writers at a certain age. I can explain but it is quite long and may bore you."

"Please explain," he said. "This is what I enjoy. This is the best part of life. The life of the mind. This is not killing kudu."

"You haven't heard it yet," I said.

"Ah, but I can see it coming. You must take more beer to loosen your tongue."

"It's loose," I told him. "It's always too bloody loose. But *you* don't drink anything."

"No, I never drink. It is not good for the mind. It is unnecessary. But tell me. Please tell me." [19/20]

"Well," I said, "we have had, in America, skillful writers. Poe is a skillful writer. It is skillful, marvellously constructed, and it is dead. We have had writers of rhetoric who had the good fortune to find a little, in a chronicle of another man and from voyaging, of how things, actual things, can be, whales for instance, and this knowledge is wrapped in the rhetoric like plums in a pudding. Occasionally it is there, alone, unwrapped in pudding, and it is good. This is Melville. But the people who praise it, praise it for the rhetoric which is not important. They put a mystery in which is not there."

"Yes," he said. "I see. But it is the mind working, its ability to work, which makes the rhetoric. Rhetoric is the blue sparks from the dynamo."

"Sometimes. And sometimes it is only blue sparks and what is the dynamo driving?"

"So. Go on."

"I've forgotten."

"No. Go on. Do not pretend to be stupid."

"Did you ever get up before daylight——"

"Every morning," he said. "Go on."

"All right. There were others who wrote like exiled English colonials from an England of which they were never a part to a newer England that they were making. Very good men with the small, dried, and excellent wisdom of Unitarians; men of letters; Quakers with a sense of humor."

"Who were these?" **[20/21]**

"Emerson, Hawthorne, Whittier, and Company. All our early classics who did not know that a new classic does not bear any resemblance to the classics that have preceded it. It can steal from anything that it is better than, anything that is not a classic, all classics do that. Some writers are only born to help another writer to write one sentence. But it cannot derive from or resemble a previous classic. Also all these men were gentlemen, or wished to be. They were all very respectable. They did not use the words that people always have used in speech, the words that survive in language. Nor would you gather that they had bodies. They had minds, yes. Nice, dry, clean minds. This is all very dull, I would not state it except that you ask for it."

"Go on."

"There is one at that time that is supposed to be really good, Thoreau. I cannot tell you about it because I have not yet been able to read it. But that means nothing because I cannot read other naturalists unless they are being extremely accurate and not literary. Naturalists should all work alone and some one else should correlate their findings for them. Writers should work alone. They should see each other only after their work is done, and not too often then. Otherwise they become like writers in New York. All angleworms in a bottle, trying to derive knowledge and nourishment from their own contact and from the bottle. Sometimes the bottle is shaped art, sometimes economics, sometimes economic- **[21/22]** religion. But once they are in the bottle they stay there. They are lonesome outside of the bottle. They do not want to be lonesome. They are afraid to be alone in their beliefs and no woman would love any of them enough so that they could kill their lonesomeness in that woman, or pool it with hers, or make something with her that makes the rest unimportant."

"But what about Thoreau?"

"You'll have to read him. Maybe I'll be able to later. I can do nearly everything later."

"Better have some more beer, Papa."

"All right."

"What about the good writers?"

"The good writers are Henry James, Stephen Crane, and Mark Twain. That's not the order they're good in. There is no order for good writers."

"Mark Twain is a humorist. The others I do not know."

"All modern American literature comes from one book by Mark Twain called *Huckleberry Finn*. If you read it you must stop where the Nigger Jim is stolen from the boys. That is the real end. The rest is just cheating. But it's the best book we've had. All American writing comes from that. There was nothing before. There has been nothing as good since."

"What about the others?"

"Crane wrote two fine stories. *The Open Boat* and *The Blue Hotel*. The last one is the best." **[22/23]**

"And what happened to him?"

"He died. That's simple. He was dying from the start."

"But the other two?"

"They both lived to be old men but they did not get any wiser as they got older. I don't know what they really wanted. You see we make our writers into something very strange."

"I do not understand."

"We destroy them in many ways. First, economically. They make money. It is only by hazard that a writer makes money although good books always make money eventually. Then our writers when they have made some money increase their standard of living and they are caught. They have to write to keep up their establishments, their wives, and so on, and they write slop. It is slop not on purpose but because it is hurried. Because they write when there is nothing to say or no water in the well. Because they are ambitious. Then, once they have betrayed themselves, they justify it and you get more slop. Or else they read the critics. If they believe the critics when they say they are great then they must believe them when they say they are rotten and they lose confidence. At present we have two good writers who cannot write because they have lost confidence through reading critics. If they wrote, sometimes it would be good and sometimes not so good and sometimes it would be quite bad, but the good would get out. But they have [23/24] read the critics and they must write masterpieces. The masterpieces the critics said they wrote. They weren't masterpieces, of course. They were just quite good books. So now they cannot write at all. The critics have made them impotent.

"Who are these writers?"

"Their names would mean nothing to you and by now they may have written, become frightened, and be impotent again."

"But what is it that happens to American writers? Be definite."

"I was not here in the old days so I cannot tell you about them, but now there are various things. At a certain age the men writers change into Old Mother Hubbard. The women writers become Joan of Arc without the fighting. They become leaders. It doesn't matter who they lead. If they do not have followers they invent them. It is useless for those selected as followers to protest. They are accused of disloyalty. Oh, hell. There are too many things happen to them. That is one thing. The others try to save their souls with what they write. That is an easy way out. Others are ruined by the first money, the first praise, the first attack, the first time they find they cannot write, or the first time they cannot do anything else, or else they get frightened and join organizations

that do their thinking for them. Or they do not know what they want. Henry James wanted to make money. He never did, of course." [24/25]

"And you?"

"I am interested in other things. I have a good life but I must write because if I do not write a certain amount I do not enjoy the rest of my life."

"And what do you want?"

"To write as well as I can and learn as I go along. At the same time I have my life which I enjoy and which is a damned good life."

"Hunting kudu?"

"Yes. Hunting kudu and many other things."

"What other things?"

"Plenty of other things."

"And you know what you want?"

"Yes."

"You really like to do this, what you do now, this silliness of kudu?"

"Just as much as I like to be in the Prado."

"One is not better than the other?"

"One is as necessary as the other. There are other things, too."

"Naturally. There must be. But this sort of thing means something to you, really?"

"Truly."

"And you know what you want?"

"Absolutely, and I get it all the time."

"But it takes money."

"I could always make money and besides I have been very lucky." [25/26]

"Then you are happy?"

"Except when I think of other people."

"Then you think of other people?"

"Oh, yes."

"But you do nothing for them?"

"No."

"Nothing?"

"Maybe a little."

"Do you think your writing is worth doing—as an end in itself?"

"Oh, yes."

"You are sure?"

"Very sure."

"That must be very pleasant."

"It is," I said. "It is the one altogether pleasant thing about it."

"This is getting awfully serious," my wife said.

"It's a damned serious subject."

"You see, he is really serious about something," Kandisky said. "I knew he must be serious on something besides kudu."

"The reason every one now tries to avoid it, to deny that it is important, to make it seem vain to try to do it, is because it is so difficult. Too many factors must combine to make it possible."

"What is this now?"

"The kind of writing that can be done. How far prose can be carried if any one is serious enough and has luck. [26/27] There is a fourth and fifth dimension that can be gotten."

"You believe it?"

"I know it."

"And if a writer can get this?"

"Then nothing else matters. It is more important than anything he can do. The chances are, of course, that he will fail. But there is a chance that he succeeds."

"But that is poetry you are talking about."

"No. It is much more difficult than poetry. It is a prose that has never been written. But it can be written, without tricks and without cheating. With nothing that will go bad afterwards."

"And why has it not been written?"

"Because there are too many factors. First, there must be talent, much talent. Talent such as Kipling had. Then there must be discipline. The discipline of Flaubert. Then there must be the conception of what it can be and an absolute conscience as unchanging as the standard meter in Paris, to prevent faking. Then the writer must be intelligent and disinterested and above all he must survive. Try to get all these in one person and have him come through all the influences that press on a writer. The hardest thing, because time is so short, is for him to survive and get his work done. But I would like us to have such a writer and to read what he would write. What do you say? Should we talk about something else?" . . .

["Write the truest sentence that you know."] *

ERNEST HEMINGWAY disliked most cities, but he never ceased to love Paris. As he says in the epigraph to *A Moveable Feast*, "If you are lucky enough to have lived in Paris as a young man, then wherever you go for the rest of your life, it stays with you, for Paris is a moveable feast." He began the book in Cuba in the fall, 1957 and, after numerous interruptions, made his final revisions in the fall, 1960 in Ketchum, Idaho.

. . . Up in the room I had a bottle of kirsch that we had brought back from the mountains and I took a drink of kirsch when I would get toward the end of a story or toward the end of the day's work. When I was through working for the day I put away the notebook, or the paper, in the drawer of the table and put any mandarines that were left in my pocket. They would freeze if they were left in the room at night.

It was wonderful to walk down the long flights of stairs knowing that I'd had good luck working. I always worked until I had something done and I always stopped when I knew what was going to happen next. That way I could be sure of going on the next day. But sometimes when I was starting a new story and I could not get it going, I would sit in front of the fire and squeeze the peel of the little oranges into the edge of the flame and watch the sputter of blue that they made. I would stand and look out over the roofs of Paris and think, "Do not worry. You have always written before and you will write now. All you have to do is write one true sentence. Write the truest sentence that you know." So finally I would write one true sentence, and then go on from there. It was easy then because there was always one true sentence that I knew or had seen or had heard someone say. If I started to

write elaborately, or like someone introducing or presenting something, I found that I could cut that scrollwork or ornament out and throw it away and start with the first true simple declarative sentence I had written. Up in that room I decided that I would write one story about each thing that I knew about. I was trying to do this all the time I was writing, and it was good and severe discipline. [12/13]

It was in that room too that I learned not to think about anything that I was writing from the time I stopped writing until I started again the next day. That way my subconscious would be working on it and at the same time I would be listening to other people and noticing everything, I hoped; learning, I hoped; and I would read so that I would not think about my work and make myself impotent to do it. Going down the stairs when I had worked well, and that needed luck as well as discipline, was a wonderful feeling and I was free then to walk anywhere in Paris.

If I walked down by different streets to the Jardin du Luxembourg in the afternoon I could walk through the gardens and then go to the Musée du Luxembourg where the great paintings were that have now mostly been transferred to the Louvre and the Jeu de Paume. I went there nearly every day for the Cézannes and to see the

Manets and the Monets and the other Impressionists that I had first come to know about in the Art Institute at Chicago. I was learning something from the painting of Cézanne that made writing simple true sentences far from enough to make the stories have the dimensions that I was trying to put in them. I was learning very much from him but I was not articulate enough to explain it to anyone. Besides it was a secret. But if the light was gone in the Luxembourg I would walk up through the gardens and stop in at the studio apartment where Gertrude Stein lived at 27 rue de Fleurus. . . .

Monologue to the Maestro: A High Seas Letter *

ERNEST HEMINGWAY contributed twenty-five articles to *Esquire* between the Autumn issue of 1933 and the May issue of 1936. Most of these brief articles, or "letters," were about various sporting and hunting activities —often in a "how to do it" vein. In "Monologue to the Maestro" Hemingway takes the same approach to writing.

About a year and a half ago a young man came to the front door of the house in Key West and said that he had hitch-hiked down from upper Minnesota to ask your correspondent a few questions about writing. Arrived that day from Cuba, having to see some good friends off on the train in an hour, and to write some letters in the meantime, your correspondent, both flattered and appalled at the prospect of the questioning, told the young man to come around the next afternoon. He was a tall, very serious young man with very big feet and hands and a porcupine haircut.

It seemed that all his life he had wanted to be a writer. Brought up on a farm he had gone through high school and the University of Minnesota, had worked as a newspaper man, a rough carpenter, a harvest hand, a day laborer, and had bummed his way across America twice. He wanted to be a writer and he had good stories to write. He told them very badly but you could see that there was something there if he could get it out. He was so entirely serious about writing that it seemed that seriousness would overcome all obstacles. He had lived by himself for a year in a cabin he had built in North Dakota and written all that year. He did not show me anything that he had written then. It was all bad, he said.

I thought, perhaps, that this was modesty until he showed me a piece he had published in one of the Minneapolis papers. It was abominably written. Still, I thought, many other people write badly at the start and this boy is so extremely serious that he must have something; real seriousness in regard to writing being one of the two absolute necessities. The other, unfortunately, is talent.

Besides writing this young man had one other obsession. He had always wanted to go to sea. So, to shorten this account, we gave him a job as night watchman on the boat which furnished him a place to sleep and work and gave him two or three hours' work each day at cleaning up and a half of each day free to do his writing. To fulfill his desire to go to sea, we promised to take him to Cuba when we went across.

He was an excellent night watchman and worked hard on the boat and at his writing but at sea he was a calamity; slow where he should be agile, seeming sometimes to have four feet instead of two feet and two hands, nervous under excitement, and with an incurable tendency toward sea-sickness and a peasant reluctance to take orders. Yet he was always willing and hard working if given plenty of time to work in.

We called him the Maestro because he played the violin, this name was eventually

*Ernest Hemingway, "Monologue to the Maestro: A High Seas Letter," Esquire, IV (October 1935), 21, 174A, 174B. (Copyright 1935 Ernest Hemingway; renewal copyright © 1963 Mary Hemingway.) Reprinted in By-Line: Ernest Hemingway, ed. William White (New York: Charles Scribner's Sons, 1967), pp. 213–220.

shortened to the Mice, and a big breeze would so effectually slow up his co-ordination that your correspondent once remarked to him, "Mice, you certainly must be going to be a hell of a good writer because you certainly aren't worth a damn at anything else."

On the other hand his writing improved steadily. He may yet be a writer. But your correspondent, who sometimes has an evil temper, is never going to ship another hand who is an aspirant writer; nor go through another summer off the Cuban or any other coast accompanied by questions and answers on the practice of letters. If any more aspirant writers come on board the Pilar let them be females, let them be very beautiful, and let them bring champagne.

Your correspondent takes the practice of letters, as distinct from the writing of these monthly letters, very seriously; but dislikes intensely talking about it with almost anyone alive. Having had to mouth about many aspects of it during a period of one hundred and ten days with the good old Maestro, during much of which time your correspondent had to conquer an urge to throw a bottle at the Mice whenever he would open his mouth and pronounce the word writing, he hereby presents some of these mouthings written down.

If they can deter anyone from writing he should be deterred. If they can be of use to anyone your correspondent is pleased. If they bore you there are plenty of pictures in the magazine that you may turn to.

Your correspondent's excuse for presenting them is that some of the information contained would have been worth fifty cents to him when he was twenty-one.

Mice: What do you mean by good writing as opposed to bad writing?

Your correspondent: Good writing is true writing. If a man is making a story up it will be true in proportion to the amount of knowledge of life that he has and how conscientious he is; so that when he makes something up it is as it would truly be. If

he doesn't know how many people work in their minds and actions his luck may save him for a while, or he may write fantasy. But if he continues to write about what he does not know about he will find himself faking. After he fakes a few times he cannot write honestly any more.

Mice: Then what about imagination?

Y.C.: Nobody knows a damned thing about it except that it is what we get for nothing. It may be racial experience. I think that is quite possible. It is the one thing beside honesty that a good writer must have. The more he learns from experience the more truly he can imagine. If he gets so he can imagine truly enough people will think that the things he relates all really happened and that he is just reporting.

Mice: Where will it differ from reporting?

Y.C.: If it was reporting they would not remember it. When you describe something that has happened that day the timeliness makes people see it in their own imaginations. A month later that element of time is gone and your account would be flat and they would not see it in their minds nor remember it. But if you make it up instead of describe it you can make it round and whole and solid and give it life. You create it, for good or bad. It is made; not described. It is just as true as the extent of your ability to make it and the knowledge you put into it. Do you follow me?

Mice: Not always.

Y.C. (crabbily): Well for chrisake let's talk about something else then. [21/174A]

Mice (undeterred): Tell me some more about the mechanics of writing.

Y.C.: What do you mean? Like pencil or typewriter? For chrisake.

Mice: Yes.

Y.C.: Listen. When you start to write you get all the kick and the reader gets none. So you might as well use a typewriter because it is that much easier and you enjoy it that much more. After you learn to write your whole object is to convey everything, every sensation, sight, feeling, place and emotion to the reader. To do this you have to work over what you write. If you write with a pencil you get three different sights at it to see if the reader is getting what you want him to. First when you read it over; then when it is typed you get another chance to improve it, and again in the proof. Writing it first in pencil gives you one-third more chance to improve it. That is .333 which is a damned good average for a hitter. It also keeps it fluid longer so that you can better it easier.

Mice: How much should you write a day?

Y.C.: The best way is always to stop when you are going good and when you know what will happen next. If you do that every day when you are writing a novel you will never be stuck. That is the most valuable thing I can tell you so try to remember it.

Mice: All right.

Y.C.: Always stop while you are going good and don't think about it or worry about it until you start to write the next day. That way your subconscious will work on it all the time. But if you think about it consciously or worry about it you will kill it and your brain will be tired before you start. Once you are into the novel it is as cowardly to worry about whether you can go on the next day as to worry about having to go into inevitable action. You *have* to go on. So there is no sense to worry. You have to learn that to write a novel. The hard part about a novel is to finish it.

Mice: How can you learn not to worry?

Y.C.: By not thinking about it. As soon as you start to think about it stop it. Think about something else. You have to learn that.

Mice: How much do you read over every day before you start to write?

Y.C.: The best way is to read it all every day from the start, correcting as you go along, then go on from where you stopped the day before. When it gets so long that you can't do this every day read back two or three chapters each day; then each week read it all from the start. That's how you make it all of one piece. And remember to stop while you are still going good. That keeps it moving instead of having it die whenever you go on and write yourself out. When you do that you find that the next day you are pooped and can't go on.

Mice: Do you do the same on a story?

Y.C.: Yes, only sometimes you can write a story in a day.

Mice: Do you know what is going to happen when you write a story?

Y.C.: Almost never. I start to make it up and have happen what would have to happen as it goes along.

Mice: That isn't the way they teach you to write in college.

Y.C.: I don't know about that. I never went to college. If any sonofabitch could write he wouldn't have to teach writing in college.

Mice: You're teaching me.

Y.C.: I'm crazy. Besides this is a boat, not a college.

Mice: What books should a writer have to read?

Y.C.: He should have read everything so he knows what he has to beat.

Mice: He can't have read everything.

Y.C.: I don't say what he can. I say what he should. Of course he can't.

Mice: Well what books are necessary?

Y.C.: He should have read *War and Peace* and *Anna Karenina* by Tolstoi, *Midshipman Easy, Frank Mildmay* and *Peter Simple* by Captain Marryat, *Madame Bovary* and *L'Education Sentimentale* by Flaubert, *Buddenbrooks* by [**174A/ 174B**] Thomas Mann, Joyce's *Dubliners, Portrait of the Artist* and *Ulysses, Tom Jones* and *Joseph Andrews* by Fielding, *Le Rouge et le Noir* and *La Chartreuse de Parme* by Stendhal, *The Brothers Karamazov* and any two other Dostoevskis, *Huckleberry Finn* by Mark Twain, *The Open Boat* and *The Blue Hotel* by Stephen Crane, *Hail and Farewell* by George Moore, Yeats's *Autobiographies,* all the good De Maupassant, all the good Kipling, all of Turgenev, *Far Away and Long*

Ago by W. H. Hudson, Henry James's short stories,—especially *Madame de Mauves,* and *The Turn of the Screw, The Portrait of a Lady, The American*—

Mice: I can't write them down that fast. How many more are there?

Y.C.: I'll give you the rest another day. There are about three times that many.

Mice: Should a writer have read all of those?

Y.C.: All of those and plenty more. Otherwise he doesn't know what he has to beat.

Mice: What do you mean "has to beat"?

Y.C.: Listen. There is no use writing anything that has been written before unless you can beat it. What a writer in our time has to do is write what hasn't been written before or beat dead men at what they have done. The only way he can tell how he is going is to compete with dead men. Most live writers do not exist. Their fame is created by critics who always need a genius of the season, someone they understand completely and feel safe in praising, but when these fabricated geniuses are dead they will not exist. The only people for a serious writer to compete with are the dead that he knows are good. It is like a miler running against the clock rather than simply trying to beat whoever is in the race with him. Unless he runs against time he will never know what he is capable of attaining.

Mice: But reading all the good writers might discourage you.

Y.C.: Then you ought to be discouraged.

Mice: What is the best early training for a writer?

Y.C.: An unhappy childhood.

Mice: Do you think Thomas Mann is a great writer?

Y.C.: He would be a great writer if he had never written another thing than *Buddenbrooks.*

Mice: How can a writer train himself?

Y.C.: Watch what happens today. If we get into a fish see exactly what it is that everyone does. If you get a kick out of it while he is jumping remember back until you see exactly what the action was that gave you the emotion. Whether it was the rising of the line from the water and the way it tightened like a fiddle string until drops started from it, or the way he smashed and threw water when he jumped. Remember what the noises were and what was said. Find what gave you the emotion; what the action was that gave you the excitement. Then write it down making it clear so the reader will see it too and have the same feeling that you had. That's a five finger exercise.

Mice: All right.

Y.C.: Then get in somebody else's head for a change. If I bawl you out try to figure what I'm thinking about as well as how you feel about it. If Carlos curses Juan think what both their sides of it are. Don't just think who is right. As a man things are as they should or shouldn't be. As a man you know who is right and who is wrong. You have to make decisions and enforce them. As a writer you should not judge. You should understand.

Mice: All right.

Y.C.: Listen *now.* When people talk listen completely. Don't be thinking what you're going to say. Most peo₁le never listen. Nor do they observe. You should be able to go into a room and when you come out know everything that you saw there and not only that. If that room gave you any feeling you should know exactly what it was that gave you that feeling. Try that for practice. When you're in town stand outside the theatre and see how the people differ in the way they get out of taxis or motor cars. There are a thousand ways to practice. And always think of other people.

Mice: Do you think I will be a writer?

Y.C.: How the hell should I know? Maybe you have no talent. Maybe you can't feel for other people. You've got some good stories if you can write them.

Mice: How can I tell?

Y.C.: Write. If you work at it five years and you find you're no good you can just as well shoot yourself then as now.

Mice: I wouldn't shoot myself.

Y.C.: Come around then and I'll shoot you.

Mice: Thanks.

Y.C.: Perfectly welcome, Mice. Now should we talk about something else?

Mice: What else?

Y.C.: Anything else, Mice, old timer, anything else at all.

Mice: All right. But—

Y.C.: No but. Finish. Talk about writing finish. No more. All gone for today. Store all close up. Boss he go home.

Mice: All right then. But tomorrow I've got some things to ask you.

Y.C.: I'll bet you'll have fun writing after you know just how it's done.

Mice: What do you mean?

Y.C.: You know. Fun. Good times. Jolly. Dashing off an old masterpiece.

Mice: Tell me—

Y.C.: Stop it.

Mice: All right. But tomorrow—

Y.C.: Yes. All right. Sure. But tomorrow.

["The dignity of movement of an ice-berg. . . ."] *

ERNEST HEMINGWAY researched and wrote *Death in the Afternoon* over a period of almost three years, from the summer, 1929 to January, 1932. Generally considered one of the best treatises on bullfighting ever written, it is also one of the best sources for students of Hemingway's artistic theory. Nowhere else does Hemingway state so clearly either his esthetic of violence or his theory of writing.

. . . I remember saying that I did not like the bullfights because of the poor horses. I was trying to write then and I found the greatest difficulty, aside from knowing truly what you really felt, rather than what you were supposed to feel, and had been taught to feel, was to put down what really happened in action; what the actual things were which produced the emotion that you experienced. In writing for a newspaper you told what happened and, with one trick and another, you communicated the emotion aided by the element of timeliness which gives a certain emotion to any account of something that has happened on that day; but the real thing, the sequence of motion and fact which made the emotion and which would be as valid in a year or in ten years or, with luck and if you stated it purely enough, always, was beyond me and I was working very hard to try to get it. The only place where you could see life and death, *i.e.,* violent death now that the wars were over, was in the bull ring and I wanted very much to go to Spain where I could study it. I was trying to learn to write, commencing with the simplest things, and one of the simplest things of all and the most fundamental is violent death. It has none of the complications of death by disease, or so-called natural death, or the death of a friend or some one you have loved or have hated, but it is death nevertheless, one of the subjects that a man may write of. I had read many books in which, when the author tried to convey it, he only produced a blur, and I decided that this was because either the author had never seen it clearly or at the moment of it, he had physically or mentally shut his eyes, as one might do if he saw a child that he could not possibly reach or aid, about to be struck by a **[2/3]** train. In such a case I suppose he would probably be justified in shutting his eyes as the mere fact of the child being about to be struck by the train was all that he could convey, the actual striking would be an anti-climax, so that the moment before striking might be as far as he could represent. But in the case of an execution by a firing squad, or a hanging, this is not true, and if these very simple things were to be made permanent, as, say, Goya tried to make them in *Los Desastros de la Guerra,* it could not be done with any shutting of the eyes. I had seen certain things, certain simple things of this sort that I remembered, but through taking part in them, or, in other cases, having to write of them immediately after and consequently noticing the things I needed for instant recording, I had never been able to study them as a man might, for instance, study the death of his father or the hanging of

*Ernest Hemingway, from *Death in the Afternoon* (New York: Charles Scribner's Sons, 1932), pp. 2–3; 191–192. (Copyright 1932 Charles Scribner's Sons; renewal copyright © 1960 Ernest Hemingway.)

some one, say, that he did not know and would not have to write of immediately after for the first edition of an afternoon newspaper.

So I went to Spain to see bullfights and to try to write about them for myself. I thought they would be simple and barbarous and cruel and that I would not like them, but that I would see certain definite action which would give me the feeling of life and death that I was working for. I found the definite action; but the bullfight was so far from simple and I liked it so much that it was much too complicated for my then equipment for writing to deal with and, aside from four very short sketches, I was not able to write anything about it for five years—and I wish I would have waited ten. [3/191]

* * * * *

When writing a novel a writer should create living people; people not characters. A *character* is a caricature. If a writer can make people live there may be no great characters in his book, but it is possible that his book will remain as a whole; as an entity; as a novel. If the people the writer is making talk of old masters; of music; of modern painting; of letters; or of science then they should talk of those subjects in the novel. If they do not talk of those subjects and the writer makes them talk of them he is a faker, and if he talks about them himself to show how much he knows then he is showing off. No matter how good a phrase or a simile he may have if he puts it in where it is not absolutely necessary and irreplaceable he is spoiling his work for egotism. Prose is architecture, not interior decoration, and the Baroque is over. For a writer to put his own intellectual musings, which he might sell for a low price as essays, into the mouths of artificially constructed characters which are more remunerative when issued as people in a novel is good economics, perhaps, but does not make literature. People in a novel, not skillfully constructed *characters,* must be projected from the writer's assimilated experience, from his knowledge, from his head, from his heart and from all there is of him. If he ever has luck as well as seriousness and gets them out entire they will have more than one dimension and they will last a long time. A good writer should know as near everything as possible. Naturally he will not. A great enough writer seems to be born with knowledge. But he really is not; he has only been born with the ability to learn in a quicker ratio to the passage of time than other men and without conscious application, and with an intelligence to accept or reject what is already pre- [191/192] sented as knowledge. There are some things which cannot be learned quickly and time, which is all we have, must be paid heavily for their acquiring. They are the very simplest things and because it takes a man's life to know them the little new that each man gets from life is very costly and the only heritage he has to leave. Every novel which is truly written contributes to the total of knowledge which is there at the disposal of the next writer who comes, but the next writer must pay, always, a certain nominal percentage in experience to be able to understand and assimilate what is available as his birthright and what he must, in turn, take his departure from. If a writer of prose knows enough about what he is writing about he may omit things that he knows and the reader, if the writer is writing truly enough, will have a feeling of those things as strongly as though the writer had stated them. The dignity of movement of an ice-berg is due to only one-eighth of it being above water. A writer who omits things because he does not know them only makes hollow places in his writing. A writer who appreciates the seriousness of writing so little that he is anxious to make people see he is formally educated, cultured or well-bred is merely a popinjay. And this too remember; a serious writer is not to be confounded with a solemn writer. A serious writer may be a hawk or a buzzard or even a popinjay, but a solemn writer is always a bloody owl. . . .

PART THREE

EXPERIENCE

The *Green Hills of Africa* is not a novel but was written in an attempt to write an absolutely true book to see whether the shape of a country and the pattern of a month's action could, if truly presented, compete with a work of the imagination. After I had written it I wrote two short stories, "The Snows of Kilimanjaro" and "The Short Happy Life of Francis Macomber." These were stories which I invented from the knowledge and experience acquired on the same long hunting trip one month of which I had tried to write a truthful account of in the *Green Hills.*—Ernest Hemingway, from "The Art of Fiction XXI: Ernest Hemingway," *The Paris Review,* xviii (Spring 1958), 80–81.*

* Reprinted with the permission of The Viking Press Inc., from *Writers at Work: The Paris Review Interviews,* Second Series.

The Slopes of Kilimanjaro *

CARLOS BAKER (1909–   ), Woodrow Wilson Professor of Literature at Princeton University, is the author of *Hemingway: The Writer as Artist* (1952, 1956, 1963) of *Ernest Hemingway: A Life Story* (1969), of a critical study of Shelley, and of two novels, *A Friend in Power* (1958) and *The Land of Rumbelow* (1963), and has published editions of Fielding, Keats, Wordsworth, and Shelley.

In August, 1935, Ernest Hemingway completed the first draft of a story about a writer who died of gangrene on a hunting trip in what was then Tanganyika. The nonfiction "novel," *Green Hills of Africa,* was already in press and due for publication in October. But the book had not used up all the material which Hemingway had accumulated in the course of his shooting safari of January and February, 1934. The new story was an attempt to present some more of what he knew, or could imagine, in fictional form. As was his custom, he put the handwritten sheets away in his desk to settle and objectify. Eight months later, on a fishing trip to Cuba, he re-examined his first draft, modified it somewhat, got it typed, and gave the typescript one final working over. Then he mailed it to Arnold Gingrich for publication in *Esquire* magazine in August, 1936, exactly a year after its inception. Although he had sweated mightily over the title, as he commonly did with all his titles, his ultimate choice displayed the true romantic luminosity. It was called "The Snows of Kilimanjaro."

The new story was curiously and subtly connected with Henry David Thoreau's *Walden.* Thoreau had lately been in Hemingway's consciousness. "There is one [author] at that time [of the nineteenth century] that is supposed to be really good," he had asserted in *Green Hills of Africa.* "I cannot tell you about it [*Walden*] because I have not yet been able to read it. But that means nothing because I cannot read other naturalists unless they are being extremely accurate and not literary. . . . Maybe I'll be able to [read it] later."

If he ever read the second chapter of *Walden,* "Where I Lived and What I Lived For," Hemingway would certainly have been struck by Thoreau's statement about his reasons for the sojourn at Walden Pond. He took to the woods in order "to live deliberately, to front only the essential facts of life." He wanted to learn the lore of nature as early as pos- **[40/42]** sible so that he would not reach the point of dying only to discover that he "had not lived" in any real sense at all. It is of course a far cry from Thoreau's asceticism to Hemingway's aggressive hedonism. Yet the passage from *Walden,* slightly modified, embodies the theme of "The Snows of Kilimanjaro." For Hemingway's protagonist, Harry, dying of an infection on the plains of Africa, is made to reflect bitterly upon his failure to set down the results of his experience of life in the forms of fiction. Although Hemingway wisely changed his mind before the story appeared, it is a

*Carlos Baker, "The Slopes of Kilimanjaro," *American Heritage Magazine,* XIX, No. 5 (August 1968), 40, 42, 43, 90, 91. First published in slightly different form as "The Slopes of Kilimanjaro: A Biographical Perspective," *Novel: A Forum on Fiction,* I (Fall 1967), 19–23. Copyright © 1967 Carlos Baker. Reprinted with the permission of the author.

curious fact that his original name for the dying writer in "The Snows" was Henry Walden.

The revised typescript of the story was garnished with a pair of epigraphs, neither of them from Thoreau, but both from "other naturalists." One was drawn from a remarkable book called *Speak to the Earth: Wanderings and Reflections among Elephants and Mountains* (1935). Its author was a naturalized Englishwoman named Vivienne de Watteville, an exact contemporary of Hemingway's, a friend of Edith Wharton's, and a Fellow of the Royal Geographical Society. She was the daughter of Bernard de Watteville, a distinguished Swiss naturalist from Berne. She had been orphaned at the age of twenty-four when her father was mauled to death by an African lion. She had been with him when he died and subsequently wrote a book called *Out in the Blue,* based on her diaries from that safari. She returned to Africa again four years later, recording her adventures in a second volume, *Speak to the Earth.* There Miss de Watteville wrote of her determination to climb Mount Kilimanjaro. An adviser who had already made the ascent drew her a rough map of the trail up the mountain and told her that she "could pick up a guide and porters at Moshi." "This," she said, "fired me more than ever to make the attempt. I had, of course, no climbing outfit with me; but the difficulties, he said, were not in the actual climbing. It was a long grind, and success depended not on skill but on one's ability to withstand the high altitude. His parting words were that I must make the attempt soon, before there was any risk of the rains setting in."

Hemingway's other epigraph, composed by himself, stated simply that "Kilimanjaro is a snow-covered mountain 19,710 feet high, and is said to be the highest mountain in Africa. Its western summit is called the Masai 'Ngàje Ngài,' The House of God. Close to the western summit there is the dried and frozen carcass of a leopard. No one has explained what the leopard was seeking at that altitude." Hemingway had gleaned his facts from the guidebooks he had used in preparing for his trip to Kenya and Tanganyika. He had heard the story of the leopard (whose carcass was still there in 1967) from Philip Percival, his white hunter, during an evening's conversation on safari in 1934.

The two epigraphs had in common the idea of immense height. Both Miss de Watteville's anonymous adviser and the example of the dead leopard indicated that the chief problem for the mountaineer on Kibo Peak of Kilimanjaro was "one's ability to withstand the high altitude." In the story, Hemingway's hero was obliged to confront the fact that never in his life had he attempted to climb that high. His bitterness arose from the realization that he was now literally rotting to death without ever having attained the heights of literary achievement to which he had once aspired. In the end, Ernest deleted the epigraph from Vivienne de Watteville, retaining the one he had himself composed.

Harry tries to assuage his bitterness by making a scapegoat of his pleasant wife, Helen. He blames her wealth for his own aesthetic decay. Because of it he has followed a life of ease and sloth instead of realizing his former ambition to be a great writer. More than twenty years after the story first appeared, Hemingway explained how he had arrived at his portraits of Helen and Harry and his conception of the central theme. "If you are interested in how you get the idea for a story," he wrote, "this is how it was." On returning to New York after the African trip early in April, 1934, he was met at the pier by ship news reporters who queried him about his future plans. He told them that he was going to work until he had accumulated enough money to go back to Africa. When the story appeared in the newspapers next morning, "a really nice and really fine and really rich woman" invited him to tea. After "a few drinks," she said that she "had read in the papers about the [42/43] project." She was unable to see any reason for delay. "She and my wife [Pauline] and I could go to Africa any time and money was only something to be used intelligently for the best enjoyment of good people." The offer struck Ernest as "sincere and fine and good," and he liked the lady "very much." But for various reasons he felt obliged to decline her invitation.

Back in Key West he began to reflect upon what might have happened to someone like himself, whose defects he knew, if he had accepted the offer. Out of these reflections gradually arose a portrait of the lady, whom he named Helen, and one of Harry, the dying writer, to whom she was married. To describe the dying part was no problem to Hemingway. He had been through all that, said he, early, middle, and late. So he invented someone who could not sue him, which was himself, speculated on how he would have turned out under the circumstances, and then put into one short story the material of four novels. He made up the man and the woman, loaded his story with personal and imagined memoirs, and found that even with this load (the heaviest, he thought, that any short story had ever carried) the story still managed to take off and fly. As for the leopard, he was part of the metaphysics. Hemingway did not propose to explain that or a lot of other matters connected with the story. While he knew what they were, he was under no obligation to tell anyone about them.

Among the other matters that Hemingway felt no obligation to explain was the fact that Helen was a composite of at least two women. One, if we can trust the story, was the munificent lady in New York. The other was his own second wife, Pauline. He had seen her in action during the recent safari, and he could not forget that her father was among the wealthiest citizens of northeastern Arkansas or that her paternal uncle, Gustavus Adolphus Pfeiffer, was a millionaire who had generously underwritten the trip to Africa with a grant-in-aid of twenty-five thousand dollars. While Hemingway had not by any means surrendered his integrity as a writer

in the presence of riches, and while he often complained at this period about his shrunken bank balance, he knew very well that among his "defects" was a liking for the pleasures wealth could buy. The dying writer in his story was an image of himself as he might have been if the temptation to lead the life of the very rich had ever overcome his determination to continue his career as a writer.

A similar mixture of "true stuff" and invention appears in the stream-of-consciousness monologues which periodically interrupt the surface movement of the story. These represent Harry's memories of his past life, and many of them, naturally enough, are Hemingway's own. It is only by knowing the course of his life in some detail that one can sort out truth from fiction. As in any process of free association of ideas and scenes, the episodes Harry recalls ignore strict chronology. Yet if they are arranged in historical sequence, they provide a rough running account of scenes from the life of the author. The earliest of Harry's internal landscapes reveals "a log house, chinked white with mortar, on a hill above the lake." The lake is Walloon, nine miles from Petoskey, Michigan, where Hemingway spent the seventeen summers of his boyhood, beginning in 1900. The house is that of Grandpa Bacon, an aged patriarch with a red beard who was still alive when the Hemingway children were growing up. References to the First World War are brief. There is one to the fighting around Monte Corvo on the Italian-Austrian front, a passage at arms that Hemingway had heard of but not seen, and another about trench warfare, presumably in France, in which an officer named Williamson is disembowelled by a German stick-bomb in the tangled barbed wire of no man's land.

Hemingway returns to his own experience with a graphic cityscape—the hilltop on the Left Bank in Paris where he lived with his first wife, Hadley, in a walk-up flat in the rue du Cardinal Lemoine from the spring of 1922 until they left for

Toronto in the summer of 1923. It is a part of Paris that has changed relatively little in forty-odd years, and although Hemingway undoubtedly invented touches here and there, the *quartier* is still recognizable from his description. The allusion to the *femme de ménage* and her views on the disadvantages of the eight-hour working day is [**43/90**] a direct quotation from Madame Marie Rohrbach, who was in service to Ernest and Hadley during most of their time in Paris.

There is also a reminiscence of a fishing vacation in the Black Forest of Germany in August, 1922. Hemingway romanticizes and fictionizes his trip to Constantinople and Adrianople to cover the Greco-Turkish War as correspondent for the Toronto *Star*. He also goes out of his way to insult the Left Bank literati by retailing a trivial incident connected with Harry's homecoming from the Middle East. On the way back to his apartment the day of his return, Harry passes a café and glances inside. There sits "Malcolm Cowley with a pile of saucers in front of him and a stupid look on his face talking about the Dada movement with . . . Tristan Tzara." Hemingway deleted Cowley's name before the story appeared. Harry's wife forgives him for going to Constantinople, just as Hadley forgave Ernest that October morning in 1922, though she had refused to speak to him for three days before his departure because she was afraid to be left alone in the rough neighborhood of the rue du Cardinal Lemoine and the Place Contrescarpe. Hemingway seems to have invented the episode in which Harry's first wife discovers a love letter from another girl in the morning mail, though something not unlike this may have happened while Ernest was conducting a surreptitious liaison with Pauline Pfeiffer before she became his second wife.

The apartment in the rue Notre Dame des Champs, where Ernest, Hadley, and their infant son, John, lived after their return from Toronto, does not figure in this story because Hemingway had already

used it in [**90/91**] a flashback *in Green Hills of Africa.* But it was from this apartment, in the early winters of 1924–25 and 1925–26, that the Hemingways twice left for the village of Schruns in the Austrian Voralberg so that Ernest could write and ski in comparative peace. Harry is made to recall the village and to use the actual name of Walther Lent, who operated a ski school in Schruns and played poker with Ernest at the Madlenerhaus, an Alpine hut high in the Silvretta Range. Another of Hemingway's favorite locales which comes into Harry's mind is the valley of the Clarks Fork branch of the Yellowstone River in Wyoming. Harry is made to remember "the silvered gray of the sage brush, the quick, clear water in the irrigation ditches, and the heavy green of the alfalfa." The violent anecdote of the halfwit chore boy who murdered his cantankerous employer is largely though not entirely an invention of Hemingway's, based on a real-life story dating from 1912 that he had overheard during one of his visits to Wyoming. This brings to an end the pastiche of truth and fiction which courses through Harry's memory as he lies dying, full of vain regret that he has not used enough of what he knows in what he has written.

For the climactic scene of his story, Hemingway drew upon yet another autobiographical episode. Though actually on the very brink of death, Harry is made to imagine that an airplane has arrived to carry him back to the hospital in Nairobi. Hemingway was flown out of the plains country to Nairobi on January 16, 1934, in a Puss Moth biplane for treatment of a severe case of amoebic dysentery. Harry recalls in detail the arrival of the plane, the appearance of the bush pilot, the look of the land, and the behavior of the grazing animals as the plane takes off for the long flight to the north, passing on the way the enormous snow-capped western summit of Kilimanjaro. This was where the adventurous leopard had succumbed to the altitude, only to lie preserved forever in his "metaphysical" fastness. But Harry has died without having attained a similar height.

One of Hemingway's recurrent motivations to literary creativity throughout his life was the conviction that he might soon be going to die without having completed his work or fulfilled his unwritten promise to his talents. At the time when he wrote this story he knew very well that he had climbed no farther than the lower slopes of his personal Kilimanjaro. It is at least a legitimate speculation that he read the passage in Vivienne de Watteville in a symbolic as well as a literal sense. Certainly he must have been struck by the statement that success depended "on one's ability to withstand the high altitude" as well as the warning that the attempt must be made "soon, before there was any risk of the rains setting in" to destroy his plans. This was one of the things he knew but felt "no obligation to tell" as he stood poised upon the slopes of the mountain in the midst of his career.

Asia Minor *

CHARLES A. FENTON (1919–1960) was a professor of English at Duke University and the author of *The Apprenticeship of Ernest Hemingway* (1954) and *Stephen Vincent Benét; the life and times of an American, 1898–1943* (1958).

I

. . . Hemingway's six Constantinople stories had touched on almost every element in the explosive, varied situation. He [**178/179**] had defined the nature of the Turkish position, with particular emphasis on the all-important French and Russian alliances. He had attempted an analysis of the composition of the Kemalist group, and its prospects for continued unity. He had given a vivid base to the articles through the portrait of the city, and his sketch of Hamid Bey supplied a glimpse of Turkish leadership and a foreshadowing of what a Turkish occupation of Constantinople could imply. The essay on Afghanistan had reminded his readers of the fragility of European peace. He had cabled and mailed John Bone a comprehensive feature treatment of the assignment. Hemingway's reservations about newspaper work have always been sound ones, but during this entire period as a foreign correspondent in 1922 he had on the whole the sort of duties, and gave to them the kind of treatment, which reduced some of the dangers, creatively speaking, of a journalistic apprenticeship. He had, above all, done a minimum of spot news reporting.

"When you describe something that has happened that day," he wrote in 1935, "the timeliness makes people see it in their own imaginations. A month later that element of time is gone and your account would be flat and they would not see in their minds nor remember it." [12]

Hemingway, at least until he covered the Lausanne Conference late in 1922, was able to give to his journalism ingredients which to a degree replaced the false strength of timeliness. "But if you make it up instead of describe it," he continued on that same occasion in the 1930's, once again paraphrasing Miss Stein's lessons, "you can make it round and whole and solid and give it life. You create it, for good or bad. It is made; not described." Hemingway had not made up his Constantinople dispatches, but neither had he been imprisoned within the restrictions of topical reporting. He could have remained indefinitely in the city, finding other ramifications of the broad outline he had already [**179/180**] written. Constantinople was exciting and turbulent, full of drama and romance and excess, and never more so than in October, 1922. Years later Hemingway wrote a little of it into the introspection of the writer dying in the shadow of Kilimanjaro, as Harry remembers that in Constantinople, after a night of violence and brawling, he "drove out to Rimmily Hissa along the Bosphorus." [13]

The instinct that made Hemingway a good reporter eventually eclipsed the charm of the gay, reckless life, with its echoes of 1918 moods. When he had filed his Afghanistan dispatch he left Constantinople and went after what was for him a story more important than even the political and diplomatic realities. He moved southward and followed the Greek army as it evacuated Eastern Thrace. He had missed the climactic fighting in August and September; he had no intention of missing this later phase. From Italian soldiers and officers in 1918, and from other wounded men in the Milan hospital, Hemingway had heard the stories about Caporetto; now, four years later, he was about to see his own variation of the Italian retreat. [**180/181**]

II

. . . Hemingway's primary concern, though he was acutely aware of the tactics and strategy of withdrawal, was with the individual Greek soldier. "Even in the evacuation," he wrote, "the Greek soldiers looked like good troops." Hemingway learned a great deal from an English captain, a cavalryman from the Indian Army. Captain Wittal was one of the two officers attached to the Greeks as an observer during the fighting around Angora in the late summer. Hemingway tried hard to put the idiom and inflection of the English officer's speech into the article's dialogue. " 'In the one show in Anatolia,' Captain Wittal said, 'the Greek infantry were doing an absolutely magnificent attack and their artillery was doing them in.' " Wittal also told Hemingway about Major Johnson, the other English observer, an experienced gunner who was so shocked by the unprofessional spectacle that he " 'cried at what those gunners were doing to their infantry.' " Years later this became another of the fragments of memory in "The Snows of Kilimanjaro"; Harry remembers "where they had made the attack with the newly arrived Con-

stantine officers, that did not know a goddamned thing, and the artillery had fired [**181/182**] into the troops and the British observer had cried like a child." Hemingway's last sentences in the 1922 dispatch were clear and bitter, testimony to his imaginative involvement in the scene.

All day I have been passing them, dirty, tired, unshaven, wind-bitten soldiers hiking along the trails across the brown, rolling, barren Thracian country. No bands, no relief organizations, no leave areas, nothing but lice, dirty blankets, and mosquitoes at night. They are the last of the glory that was Greece. This is the end of their second siege of Troy.

Hemingway learned other things about a retreat, things he didn't mail to Toronto but saved for the long Caporetto passages he wrote in 1929 for *A Farewell to Arms.* He had other stories, too, from Captain Wittal and from Major Johnson; the latter had become press liaison officer in Constantinople. Once again Hemingway saved them for Harry's dying monologue. "That was the day he'd first seen dead men wearing white ballet skirts and upturned shoes with pompons on them . . . he and the British observer had run . . . until his lungs ached and his mouth was full of the taste of pennies and they stopped behind some rocks and there were the Turks coming as lumpily as ever." In 1922, however, Hemingway filed no further details on the military aspects of the evacuation. He moved north toward the vast civilian exodus from Western Thrace. He stopped briefly in Constantinople,[15] and then on October 20, now many miles north of the city, he cabled from Adrianople a fine story of the refugees who were moving out of Eastern Thrace.[16] It was harsh and compressed, a vivid recapitulation of civilian tragedy. In 1922 its horror had not become a global commonplace; Hemingway saw it with a fresh, shocked awareness. [**182/183**]

In a never-ending, staggering march the Christian population of Eastern Thrace is jamming the roads towards Macedonia. The main column crossing the Maritza River at Adrianople is twenty miles long. Twenty miles of carts drawn by cows, bullocks and muddy-flanked water buffalo, with exhausted, staggering men, women, and children, blankets over their heads, walking blindly in the rain beside their wordly goods.

This spectacle of refugee misery, beyond all the rest of what he saw in Asia Minor, left the most permanent scar on Hemingway. In his creative work he made far more use of what he learned from the military catastrophe; he told Malcolm Cowley, in fact, that he "really learned about war" in the Near East.[17] The civilian suffering, however, gave a new dimension to his determination to be a writer. He has always been generous and quick in his response to grief. His ready, decent anger had already been displayed in his indignation about Italian fascism. His susceptibilities once caused him to explain that "I cannot see a horse down in the street without having it make me feel a necessity for helping the horse, and I have spread sacking, unbuckled harness and dodged shod hoofs many times and will again if they have

horses on city streets in wet and icy weather. . . ."[18] Hemingway had neither seen nor imagined such human suffering as he saw in October, 1922, along the road to Adrianople.

When he got back to France after finishing his Greco-Turk assignment, he made on the basis of it a decision about his career. "I remember," he said thirty years later, "coming home from the Near East . . . absolutely heartbroken at what was going on and in Paris trying to decide whether I would put my whole life into trying to do something about it or to be a writer." His indignation made the decision a difficult one; he had been raised, after all, in the [183/184] decent world of Oak Park, with its middle-class, nineteenth-century heritage of New England humanitarianism. "I decided," he said in 1951, "cold as a snake, to be a writer and to write as truly as I could all my life."[19] [184/280]

· · · · ·

NOTES

· · · · ·

[12] *Ibid.*, [i.e., in "Monologue to the Maestro: A High Seas Letter"], 21.

[13] Ernest Hemingway, "The Snows of Kilimanjaro," *Esquire*, VI (August, 1936), 197.

· · · · ·

[15] Hemingway mailed from Constantinople on October 18 a long article which was the least impressive of his Near East dispatches. It was published in the DS [*Toronto Daily Star*] on November 10, on page 12, but in treatment it was an uncharacteristic return to his loose, SW [*Toronto Star Weekly*] approach. He presented a grab bag of material whose various sections were held together only by their common connection with naval episodes in the Bosphorus. Its appeal for a Canadian audience was in its obvious admiration for the Royal Navy. Its paragraphs were hearty and British, and a reminder that Hemingway was accustomed to being paid

by the word. It was also mildly corrupt as a piece of journalism, since at no point did he fulfill in any complete way his avowed, censor-free exposure of naval activities.

[16] DS [*Toronto Daily Star*], October 20, 1922, 1 (Second Section).

[17] Malcolm Cowley, "A Portrait of Mister Papa," *Ernest Hemingway: The Man and His Work*, ed. John K. M. McCaffery (World, 1950), 49.

[18] DITA [*Death in the Afternoon*], 4.

[19] EH [Ernest Hemingway] to CAF [Charles A. Fenton], September 23, 1951. In 1934, in an angry denunciation of the complacent indignation of literary critics about the depression, Hemingway defined his position similarly when he declared that "things were in just as bad shape, and worse, as far as vileness, injustice and rottenness are concerned, in 1921, '22 and '23 as they are now. . . ." "Old Newsman Writes," 25.

["You belong to me and all Paris belongs to me. . . ."] *

ERNEST HEMINGWAY. For information about *A Moveable Feast,* see p. 43.

Then there was the bad weather. It would come in one day when the fall was over. We would have to shut the windows in the night against the rain and the cold wind would strip the leaves from the trees in the Place Contrescarpe. The leaves lay sodden in the rain and the wind drove the rain against the big green autobus at the terminal and the Café des Amateurs was crowded and the windows misted over from the heat and the smoke inside. It was a sad, evilly run café where the drunkards of the quarter crowded together and I kept away from it because of the smell of dirty bodies and the sour smell of drunkenness. The men and women who frequented the Amateurs stayed drunk all of the time, or all of the time they could afford it, mostly on wine which they bought by the half-liter or liter. Many strangely named apéritifs were advertised, but few people could afford them except as a foundation to build their wine drunks on. The women drunkards were called *poivrottes* which meant female rummies.

The Café des Amateurs was the cesspool of the rue Mouffetard, that wonderful narrow crowded market street which led into the Place Contrescarpe. The squat toilets of the old apartment houses, one by the side of the stairs on each floor with the two cleated cement shoe-shaped elevations on each side of the aperture so a *locataire* would not slip, emptied into cesspools which were emptied by pumping into horse-drawn tank wagons at night. In the summer time, with all windows [3/4] open, we would hear the pumping and the odor was very strong. The tank wagons were painted brown and saffron color and in the moonlight when they worked the rue Cardinal Lemoine their wheeled, horse-drawn cylinders looked like Braque paintings. No one emptied the Café des Amateurs though, and its yellowed poster stating the terms and penalties of the law against public drunkenness was as flyblown and disregarded as its clients were constant and ill-smelling.

All of the sadness of the city came suddenly with the first cold rains of winter, and there were no more tops to the high white houses as you walked but only the wet blackness of the street and the closed doors of the small shops, the herb sellers, the stationery and the newspaper shops, the midwife—second class—and the hotel where Verlaine had died where I had a room on the top floor where I worked.

It was either six or eight flights up to the top floor and it was very cold and I knew how much it would cost for a bundle of small twigs, three wire-wrapped packets of short, half-pencil length pieces of split pine to catch fire from the twigs, and then the bundle of half-dried lengths of hard wood that I must buy to make a fire that would warm the room. So I went to the far side of the street to look up at the roof in the rain and see if any chimneys were going, and how the smoke blew. There was no smoke and I thought about how the chimney would be cold and might not draw and of the room possibly filling with smoke, and the fuel wasted, and the money gone with it, and I walked on in the rain.

I walked down past the Lycée Henri Quatre and the ancient church of St.-Étienne-du-Mont and the windswept Place du Panthéon and cut in for shelter to the right and finally came out on the lee side of the [4/5] Boulevard St.-Michel and worked on down it past the Cluny and the Boulevard St.-Germain until I came to a good café that I knew on the Place St.-Michel.

It was a pleasant café, warm and clean and friendly, and I hung up my old waterproof on the coat rack to dry and put my worn and weathered felt hat on the rack above the bench and ordered a *café au lait*. The waiter brought it and I took out a notebook from the pocket of the coat and a pencil and started to write. I was writing about up in Michigan and since it was a wild, cold, blowing day it was that sort of day in the story. I had already seen the end of fall come through boyhood, youth and young manhood, and in one place you could write about it better than in another. That was called transplanting yourself, I thought, and it could be as necessary with people as with other sorts of growing things. But in the story the boys were drinking and this made me thirsty and I ordered a rum St. James. This tasted wonderful on the cold day and I kept on writing, feeling very well and feeling the good Martinique rum warm me all through my body and my spirit.

A girl came in the café and sat by herself at a table near the window. She was very pretty with a face fresh as a newly minted coin if they minted coins in smooth flesh with rain-freshened skin, and her hair was black as a crow's wing and cut sharply and diagonally across her cheek.

I looked at her and she disturbed me and made me very excited. I wished I could put her in the story, or anywhere, but she had placed herself so she could watch the street and the entry and I knew she was waiting for someone. So I went on writing. [5/6]

The story was writing itself and I was having a hard time keeping up with it. I ordered another rum St. James and I watched the girl whenever I looked up, or when I sharpened the pencil with a pencil sharpener with the shavings curling into the saucer under my drink.

I've seen you, beauty, and you belong to me now, whoever you are waiting for and if I never see you again, I thought. You belong to me and all Paris belongs to me and I belong to this notebook and this pencil.

Then I went back to writing and I entered far into the story and was lost in it. I was writing it now and it was not writing itself and I did not look up nor know anything about the time nor think where I was nor order any more rum St. James. I was tired of rum St. James without thinking about it. Then the story was finished and I was very tired. I read the last paragraph and then I looked up and looked for the girl and she had gone. I hope she's gone with a good man, I thought. But I felt sad.

I closed up the story in the notebook and put it in my inside pocket and I asked the waiter for a dozen *portugaises* and a half-carafe of the dry white wine they had there. After writing a story I was always empty and both sad and happy, as though I had made love, and I was sure this was a very good story although I would not know truly how good until I read it over the next day.

As I ate the oysters with their strong taste of the sea and their faint metallic taste that the cold white wine washed away, leaving only the sea taste and the succulent texture, and as I drank their cold liquid from each shell and washed it down with the crisp taste of the wine, I lost the empty feeling and began to be happy and to make plans. [6/7]

Now that the bad weather had come, we could leave Paris for a while for a place where this rain would be snow coming down through the pines and covering the road and the high hillsides and at an altitude where we would hear it creak as we walked home at night. Below Les Avants there was a chalet where the pension was wonderful and where we would be together and have our books and at night be warm in bed together with the windows open and the stars bright. That was where we could go. Traveling third class on the train was not expensive. The pension cost very little more than we spent in Paris.

I would give up the room in the hotel where I wrote and there was only the rent of 74 rue Cardinal Lemoine which was nominal. I had written journalism for Toronto and the checks for that were due. I could write that anywhere under any circumstances and we had money to make the trip.

Maybe away from Paris I could write about Paris as in Paris I could write about Michigan. I did not know it was too early for that because I did not know Paris well enough. But that was how it worked out eventually. Anyway we would go if my wife wanted to, and I finished the oysters and the wine and paid my score in the café and made it the shortest way back up the Montaigne Ste. Geneviève through the rain, that was now only local weather and not something that changed your life, to the flat at the top of the hill.

"I think it would be wonderful, Tatie," my wife said. She had a gently modeled face and her eyes and her smile lighted up at decisions as though they were rich presents. "When should we leave?"

"Whenever you want."

"Oh, I want to right away. Didn't you know?" [7/8]

"Maybe it will be fine and clear when we come back. It can be very fine when it is clear and cold."

"I'm sure it will be," she said. "Weren't you good to think of going, too."

["The truly great killer must have a sense of honor. . . ."] *

ERNEST HEMINGWAY. For information about *Death in the Afternoon*, see p. 50.

CHAPTER NINETEEN

There are only two proper ways to kill bulls with the sword and muleta and as both of them deliberately invoke a moment in which there is unavoidable goring for the man if the bull does not follow the cloth properly, matadors have steadily tricked this finest part of the fight until ninety of one hundred bulls that you will see killed will be put to death in a manner that is only a parody of the true way to kill. One reason for this is that rarely will a great artist with the cape and muleta be a killer. A great killer must love to kill; unless he feels it is the best thing he can do, unless he is conscious of its dignity and feels that it is its own reward, he will be incapable of the abnegation that is necessary in real killing. The truly great killer must have a sense of honor and a sense of glory far beyond that of the ordinary bullfighter. In other words he must be a simpler man. Also he must take pleasure in it, not simply as a trick of wrist, eye, and managing of his left hand that he does better than other men, which is the simplest form of that pride and which he will naturally have as a simple man, but he must have a spiritual enjoyment of the moment of killing. Killing cleanly and in a way which gives you aesthetic pleasure and pride has always been one of the greatest enjoyments of a part of the human race. Because the other part, which does not enjoy killing, has always been the more articulate and has furnished most of the good writers we have had a very few statements of the true enjoyment of killing. One of its greatest pleasures, aside from the purely aesthetic ones, [**232/233**] such as wing shooting, and the ones of pride, such as difficult game stalking, where it is the disproportionately increased importance of the fraction of a moment that it takes for the shot that furnishes the emotion, is the feeling of rebellion against death which comes from its administering. Once you accept the rule of death thou shalt not kill is an easily and a naturally obeyed commandment. But when a man is still in rebellion against death he has pleasure in taking to himself one of the Godlike attributes; that of giving it. This is one of the most profound feelings in those men who enjoy killing. These things are done in pride and pride, of course, is a Christian sin, and a pagan virtue. But it is pride which makes the bullfight and true enjoyment of killing which makes the great matador. . . .

Three Tanganyika Letters

ERNEST HEMINGWAY published his three Tanganyika "letters" in proximate issues of *Esquire*, beginning with the April issue, 1934. He wrote the first letter in a Nairobi hospital, where he was being treated for amoebic dysentery. He wrote the last letter while on a ship returning home. They portray his first reactions to his African experience.

A.D. IN AFRICA:
A TANGANYIKA LETTER *

To write this sort of thing you need a typewriter. To describe, to narrate, to make funny cracks you need a typewriter. To fake along, to stall, to make light reading, to write a good piece, you need luck, two or more drinks and a typewriter. Gentlemen, there is no typewriter.

The air-mail leaves tomorrow night. Your amoebic dysentery correspondent is in bed, fully injected with emetine, having flown four hundred miles to Nairobi via Arusha from where the outfit is camped on the Serenea river on the far side of the Serengeti plain. Cause of flight, a. d. Cause of a. d. unknown. Symptoms of a. d. run from weakly insidious through spectacular to phenomenal. I believe the record is held by a Mr. McDonald with 232 movements in the twenty-four hours although many old a. d. men claim the McDonald record was never properly audited.

According to Dr. Anderson the difficulty about a. d. is to diagnose it. My own diagnosis was certainly faulty. Leaning against a tree two days ago shooting flighting sand-grouse as they came into a water hole near camp after ten days of what Dr. Anderson says was a. d. all the time, I became convinced that though an unbeliever I had been chosen as the one to bear our Lord Buddha when he should be born again on earth. While flattered at this, and wondering how much Buddha at that age would resemble Gertrude Stein, I found the imminence of the event made it difficult to take high incoming birds and finally compromised by reclining against the tree and only accepting crossing shots. This, the coming-of-Buddha symptom, Dr. Anderson describes as prolapsus.

Anyway, no matter how you get it, it is very easily cured. You feel the good effects of the emetine within six hours and the remedy, continued, kills the amoeba the way quinine kills the malarial parasite. Three days from now we'll fly back to join the outfit in the country to the south of Ngocongoro where we are going to hunt greater Kudu. But, as stated, there is no typewriter; they won't let you drink with this; and if the reader finds this letter more dysenteric than the usual flow, lay it to the combination of circumstances.

The general run of this highland country is the finest I have ever seen. When there has been rain the plains roll green against the blue hills the way the western end of Nebraska lifts as you approach Wyoming when it has gone too long without rain. It is a brown land like Wyoming and Montana but with greater roll and

distance. Much of the upland bush country that you hunt through looks exactly
like an abandoned New England orchard
until you top a hill and see the orchard
runs on for fifty miles. Nothing that I have
ever read has given any idea of the beauty
of the country or the still remaining quantity of game.

On the Serengeti we struck the great
migration of the wildebeeste. Where they
were grazing the plain was green after a
nine months' drought and it was black
with the bison shaped antelope as far as
you could see in all directions during a full
day in the truck. The Game Department
of Tanganyika estimates the herd at three
million. Following them and living on
the fringe of the herd were the lions, the
spotted hyenas and the jackals.

Going out at sunrise every morning we
would locate lions by the vultures circling
above a kill. Approaching you would see
the jackals trotting away and hyenas going
off in that drag belly obscene gallop, looking back as they ran. If the birds were on
the ground you knew the lions were gone.

Sometimes we met them in the open
plain on their way toward a gully or shallow water course to lie up for the day.
Sometimes we saw them on a high knoll in
the plain with the herd grazing not half
a mile away, lying sleepy and contempu-
ous looking over the country. More often
we saw them under the shade of a tree or
saw their great round heads lift up out of
the grass of a shallow donga as they heard
the noise of the truck. In two weeks and
three days in lion country we saw 84 lions
and lionesses. Of these twenty were maned
lions.

We shot the twenty-third, the forty-
seventh, the sixty-fourth and the seventy-
ninth. All were shot on foot, three were

killed in bush country to the west of the
Serengeti and one on the plain itself.
Three were full black maned lions and
one was a lioness. She was in heat and
when the big lion she was with was hit and
had gotten into cover the lioness took up
her position outside the thick bush. She
wanted to charge and it was impossible to
go after the lion without killing [**19/146**]
her first. I broke her neck with a 220
grain .30-06 solid at thirty yards.

At this point Dr. Anderson just came in
and administered another injection of
emetine and offered the information that
when you take emetine you can't think
coherently. So this may be a good place
to knock off. Had been feeling that too for
some time.

In the next letter I will attempt to discuss whether lion shooting in Tanganyika
is a sport or not; go into the difference between lion and leopard hunting, have a
few remarks on the buffalo and try to get
in a lot of facts. This letter has been pretty
well emetined.

As far as bag goes, if anyone is interested, we have good heads of Eland,
Waterbuck, Grant Robertsi and other
gazelles. A fine roan antelope, two big
leopard, and excellent, if not record, im-
palla; also the limit all around on cheetah.
They are much too nice an animal to
shoot and I will never kill another.

On the other hand we shot thirty-five
hyena out of the lot that follow the wildebeeste migration to keep after the cows
that are about to calve and wish we had
ammunition to kill a hundred.

In three days we start out for rhino,
buffalo again, lesser and greater Kudu,
and sable antelope.

Dr. Anderson, a little emetine please.

Nairobi, January 18, 1934

SHOOTISM VERSUS SPORT:
THE SECOND TANGANYIKA LETTER *

There are two ways to murder a lion. One is to shoot him from a motor car, the other, to shoot him at night with a flashlight from a platform or the shelter of a thorn boma, or blind, as he comes to feed on a bait placed by the shootist or his guide. (Tourists who shoot in Africa are called shootists to distinguish them from sportsmen.) These two ways to murder lion rank, as sport, with dynamiting trout or harpooning swordfish. Yet many men who go to Africa and return to think of themselves as sportsmen and big game hunters, have killed lions from motor cars or from blinds.

The Serengeti plain is the great lion country of present day Africa and the Serengeti is a motor car proposition. The distances between water are too great for it to have been reached and hunted in the old foot safari days, and that was what preserved it. The game migrations, which are determined by the food which is produced by an often casual and unpredictable rainfall, are movements over hundreds of miles, and you may drive seventy-five or a hundred miles over a brown, dry, parched, dusty waste without seeing a head of game, to come suddenly onto a rise of green horizon broken and edged with the black of wildebeeste as far as you can see. It is because of these distances that you must use the motor car in hunting the Serengeti, since your camp must be on a water hole and the game may be over half a day's march away on the plain.

Now a lion, when you locate him in the morning after he has fed, will have only one idea if he sees a man, to get away into cover where the man will not trouble him. Until he is wounded, that lion will not be dangerous unless you come on him unexpectedly, so closely that you startle him, or unless he is on a kill and does not want to leave it.

If you approach the lion in a motor car, the lion will not see you. His eyes can only distinguish the outline or silhouette of objects, and, because it is illegal to shoot from a motor car, this object means nothing to him. If anything, since the practice of shooting a zebra and dragging it on a rope behind the motor car as a bait for lion in order to take photographs, the motor car may seem a friendly object. For a man to shoot at a lion from the protection of a motor car, where the lion cannot even see what it is that is attacking him, is not only illegal but is a cowardly way to assassinate one of the finest of all game animals.

But supposing, unexpectedly, as you are crossing the country, you see a lion and a lioness say a hundred yards from the car. They are under a thorn tree and a hundred yards behind them is a deep donga, or dry, reed-filled water course, that winds across the plain for perhaps ten miles and gives perfect cover in the daytime to all the beasts of prey that follow the game herds.

You sight the lions from the car; you look the male over and decide he is shootable. You have never killed a lion. You are allowed to kill only two lions on the Serengeti and you want a lion with a full mane, as black as possible. The white hunter says quietly:

"I believe I'd take him. We might beat him but he's a damned fine lion."

You look at the lion under the tree. He looks very close, very calm, very, very big and proudly beautiful. The lioness has flattened down on the yellow grass and is swinging her tail parallel to the ground.

"All right," says the white hunter.

You step out of the car from beside the driver on the side away from the lion, and the white hunter gets out on the same side from the seat behind you.

*Ernest Hemingway, "Shootism vs. Sport: The Second Tanganyika Letter," *Esquire*, II (June 1934), 19, 150. (Copyright 1934 Ernest Hemingway; renewal copyright © 1962 Mary Hemingway.) Reprinted in *By-Line: Ernest Hemingway*, ed. William White (New York: Charles Scribner's Sons, 1967), pp. 162–166.

"Better sit down," he says. You both sit down and the car drives away. As the car starts to move off you have a very different feeling about lions than you have ever had when you saw them from the motor car.

As the end of the car is past, you see that the lioness has risen and is standing so that you cannot see the lion clearly.

"Can't see him," you whisper. As you say it you see that the lions have seen you. He has turned away and is trotting off and she is still standing, the tail swinging wide.

"He'll be in the donga," the white hunter says.

You stand up to shoot and the lioness turns. The lion stops and looks back. You see his great head swing toward you, his mouth wide open and his mane blowing in the wind. You hold on his shoulder, start to flinch, correct, hold your breath and squeeze off. You don't hear the gun go off but you hear a crack like the sound of a policeman's club on a rioter's head and the lion is down.

"You've got him. Watch the lioness."

She has flattened down facing you so that you see her head, the ears back, the long yellow of her is flat out along the ground and her tail is now flailing straight up and down.

"I think she's going to come," the white hunter says. "If she comes, sit down to shoot."

"Should I bust her?" you say.

"No. Maybe she won't come. Wait till she starts to come."

You stand still and see her and beyond her the bulk of the big lion, on his side now, and finally she turns slowly and goes off and out of sight into the donga.

"In the old days," the white hunter said, "the rule was to shoot the lioness first. Damned sensible rule."

The two of you walk toward the lion with your guns ready. The car comes up and the gunbearers join you. One of them throws a [19/150] stone at the lion. He doesn't move. You lower the guns and go up to him.

"You got him in the neck," the white hunter says. "Damned good shooting." There is blood coming from the thick hair of his mane where the camel flies are crawling. You regret the camel flies.

"It was a lucky one," you say.

You say nothing about having squeezed off from his shoulder, and then, suddenly, a strain is over and people are shaking your hand.

"Better keep an eye out for the old lady," the white hunter says. "Don't wander over too far that way."

You are looking at the dead lion; at his wide head and the dark shag of his mane and the long, smooth, yellow sheathed body, the muscles still twitching and running minutely under the skin. He is a fine hide and all that but he was a damned wonderful looking animal when he was alive—it was a shame he should always have had the camel flies, you think.

All right. That is the nearest to a sporting way to use a motor car after lion. Once you are on the ground and the car is gone, lion hunting is the same as it always was. If you wound the lion in any but a vital spot he will make for the shelter of the donga and then you will have to go after him. At the start, if you can shoot carefully and accurately and know where to shoot, the odds are ten to one in your favor against anything untoward happening, provided you do not have to take a running shot at first. If you wound the lion and he gets into cover it is even money you will be mauled when you go in after him. A lion can still cover one hundred yards so fast toward you that there is barely time for two aimed shots before he is on you. After he has the first bullet, there is no nervous shock to further wounds, and you have to kill him stone dead or he will keep coming.

If you shoot as you should on the Serengeti, having the car drive off as you get out, the chances are that the first shot will be a moving shot, as the lions will move off when they see the man on foot. That means that unless you are a good or a very lucky shot there will be a wounded lion and a possible charge. So do not let anyone tell you that lion shooting, if you hunt big maned lions, who, being super-fine trophies, will obviously have been hunted before and be adept at saving their hides, is no longer a sporting show. It will be exactly as dangerous as you choose to make it. The only way the danger can be removed or mitigated is by your ability to shoot, and that is as it should be. You are out to kill a lion, on foot and cleanly, not to be mauled. But you will be more of a sportsman to come back from Africa without a lion than to shoot one from the protection of a motor car, or from a blind at night when the lion is blinded by a light and cannot see his assailant.

(Next month—more lion and leopard—ethics of dangerous game.)

NOTES ON DANGEROUS GAME: THE THIRD TANGANYIKA LETTER *

In the ethics of shooting dangerous game is the premise that the trouble you shoot yourself into you must be prepared to shoot yourself out of. Since a man making his first African shoot will have a white hunter, as a non-native guide is called, to counsel him and aid him when he is after dangerous animals, and since the white hunter has the responsibility of protecting him no matter what trouble he gets into, the shooter should do exactly what the white hunter tells him to do.

If you make a fool of yourself all that you get is mauled but the white hunter who has a client wounded or killed loses, or seriously impairs, his livelihood. So when the white hunter begins to trust you and let you take chances, that is a mark of confidence and you should not abuse it. For any good man would rather take chances any day with his life than his livelihood and that is the main point about professionals that amateurs seem never to appreciate.

There are two white hunters in Africa who not only have never had a client mauled—there are many such, but these two have never been mauled themselves; and there are very few of these. It is true that Philip Percival had a buffalo die with his head in the now ample Percival lap, and that Baron von Blixen, if there were any justice for elephants, would have been trampled to death at least twice. But the point is that they do not get mauled and that their clients get record heads, record tusks and super lions year after year. They simply happen to be super hunters and super shots. *(There are too many supers in these last two sentences. Re-write them yourselves lads and see how easy it is to do better than Papa. Thank you. Exhilarating feeling, isn't it?)*

Both mask their phenomenal skill under a pose of nervous incapacity which serves as an effective insulation and cover for their truly great pride in the reserve of deadliness that they live by. *(All right now, better that one. Getting harder, what? Not too hard you say? Good. Perhaps you're right.)* Blix, who can shoot partridges flying with a .450 No. 2 Express rifle will say, "I use the hair trigger because my hand is always shaking so, what?" Or, stopping a charging rhino at ten yards, remarking apologetically to his client who happened to have his rifle already started back to camp by the gunbearer, "I could not let him come forever, what?"

(You see, this is where Papa scores. Just as you learn to better one of those awful sentences, with too many supers or too many verys in it and you think he's gone wa-wa on you, you find that it is the thing he is writing about that is interesting. Not the way it's written. Any of you lads can go out there and write twice as good a piece, what?)

*Ernest Hemingway, "Notes on Dangerous Game: The Third Tanganyika Letter," *Esquire,* II (July 1934), 19, 94. (Copyright 1934 Ernest Hemingway; renewal copyright © 1962 Mary Hemingway.) Reprinted in *By-Line: Ernest Hemingway,* ed. William White (New York: Charles Scribner's Sons, 1967), pp. 167–171.

Philip, who swears by the .450 No. 2 as the only, or at least lightest, stopper for a man to use on animals that will "come," killed all his own lions with a .256 Mannlicher when he had only his own life to look after. I have seen him, careful, cautious, as [19/94] wary about procedure as Saleri, Marcial Lalanda, or any of the old masters of chance controlling, light up like a schoolboy at the approach of vacation, when all the safe and sane methods were finally exhausted or rendered impractical and there was no choice but to go in after him as he went in after them in the old days before it was a matter of the safety of the client. (*Excuse me, Mr. P. You see I do this for a living. We all have to do a lot of things for a living. But we're still drinking their whiskey, aren't we?*)

Many people want not to shoot but to have shot dangerous game. These people, regardless of their means, usually make the African shoot only once, and their white hunter usually fires as many or more shots than his client does. A very good standard by which to judge your real effectiveness against buffalo, rhino, elephant, lion and leopard is to keep track of how many times your white hunter shot on the safari. (*You shot twice, Mr. P. Correct me if I'm wrong. Once at that leopard's mate when she broke back and you spun her over like a rabbit, and the other time when we caught the bull in the open and had two down and the third bull with four solids in him going at that same gallop, all one solid piece, the neck a part of the shoulders, dusty black and the horns blacker, the head not tossing in the gallop. You figured he would make the bush so you shot and the gallop changed into a long slide forward on his nose.*)

Philip Percival ranks leopard as more dangerous than lion for these reasons. They are nearly always met unexpectedly, usually when you are hunting impala or buck. They usually give you only a running shot which means more of a chance of wounding than killing. They will charge nine times out of ten when wounded, and they come so fast that no man can be sure of stopping them with a rifle. They use their claws, both fore and hind when mauling and make for the face so that the eyes are endangered, whereas the lion grabs with the claws and bites, usually for the arm, shoulders or thigh. The most effective stopper for a leopard is a shotgun and you should not fire until the animal is within ten yards. It does not matter what size shot is used at that range. Birdshot is even more effective than buckshot as it hangs together to blow a solid hole. (*Mr. P. took the top of the head off one once with a load of number sevens and the leopard came right on by and on for fifteen yards. Didn't know he was dead it seems. Tripped on a blade of grass or something finally.*)

Personally, so far, and it is from a very minute quantity of experience indeed—the killing of four of them—I cannot see the buffalo as comparing in dangerous possibilities to either lion or leopard. We twice saw lion catch and kill wildebeeste. This is a very rare thing. Philip Percival had seen lion kill only once before in all his years of hunting. It was while he was out with Mr. Prentice Gray, who recorded the occurrence, I believe. The sight of that speed, that unbelievable smooth rush the lioness made to close the gap between herself and the fast galloping, though ungainly, antelope made me see what a charge from a slightly wounded lion could be if allowed to get under way. The buffalo, on the other hand, seemed unbelievably slow compared to a Spanish fighting bull, and I see no reason why a man who could wait for him as he came could not be sure of blowing the front of his head in if he let him get close and shot carefully with a heavy enough rifle. Certainly a tunnel in thick bush, or high reeds, or any dense cover can make the wounded buffalo dangerous, but that is a case of circumstances rather than the animal, and in the same circumstances a lion would be much more deadly. In the open a lion or leopard is a hundred times more dangerous.

The buffalo has courage, vindictiveness

and an incredible ability to absorb punishment but I believe that in the bull ring he would be more like the big truck that comes charging in during the intermission to water the dusty sand than like the light hoofed, quick whirling, fast charging fighting bull.

Of course, he is not an animal of the open and you must take him where you find him and follow him where he goes, and he goes into bad places, but the point was to compare the inherent danger in the actual animals on an equal terrain—not in the peculiar circumstances under which he must be dealt with. *(There won't be any more asides you will be glad to hear. Am going to write Mr. P. a letter instead. The asides were put in when I read this over on the boat. Got to missing him.)*

To me, also, and the experience it must be again stated is profoundly limited, the rhino is a joke. He may be a bad joke, too, but his atrociously poor eyesight gives the hunter an advantage over him that his bulk, his really remarkable speed and agility, and his sometimes idiotic pugnacity cannot overcome unless aided by advantage of terrain. Many times the rhino will have this advantage which will usually consist in encountering him on one of the paths or tunnels he has made through otherwise impossible tall grass and bush, and then he is as dangerous as a vindictive, horned, locomotive. He is, too, very fast. I believe he is faster than a buffalo. But fundamentally, to me, he seems a dangerous practical joke let loose by nature and armed with a horn which the Chinese pay high prices for to grind up and use as an aphrodisiac, and the pursuit of which by white and native hunters has made him shy and furtive in his habits and driven him from the plains to the broken hills and high mountain forests—

where he can grow his horn and browse in peace, and where, incidentally, he is much better hunting.

Elephant I have never shot so I cannot write of them even to give the questionable impressions of the greenhorn. We plan to go out again to Kenya for six months next year to try to get a really good one, to hunt buffalo and rhino, and to see how far wrong first impressions of these were, and to try to get a good bull sable. Meantime, I know nothing about elephant from personal experience, and since notes on dangerous game by a man who has never hunted elephant are like campaign impressions of a bloke who has never seen a major engagement, that is the sort of notes these notes will have to be.

(There turns out to be one more of these. One night when we were eating supper at Mombasa after fishing, A. V. and Mr. P. and I were talking about writing these letters and I suggested Alfred write one about hunting elephant with Blix before he started to write on racing. I was writing on rhino and buffalo, etc., I said. Mr. P., who was on his first deep sea fishing trip, didn't say much, but the next day we got into a big school of large dophin and caught about 15 before the lousy boat broke down. Mr. P. got so excited that his legs shook, he screwed the reel brake backwards until it stuck, he had dolphin jumping into, out of, and over the boat. Sometimes he jerked the bait out of their mouths; occasionally he let them swallow it, but always he had a dolphin jumping on his line.

"How do you like it, Pop?" I asked him.

"God," he said, "I haven't had so much fun since the day you shot the buffalo." Then, a little later, "I'm going to write an article on it for Esquire. Call it Dolphin Fishing by One Who Knows.")

In *Green Hills of Africa* *

ERNEST HEMINGWAY. For information about *Green Hills of Africa,* see p. 39.

CHAPTER II

We were out from under the shade of camp and along the sandy river of a road, driving into the western sun, the bush thick to the edge of the sand, solid as a thicket, the little hills rising above it, and all along the road we passed groups of people making their way to the westward. Some were naked except for a greasy cloth knotted over one shoulder, and carried bows and sealed quivers of arrows. Others carried spears. The wealthy carried umbrellas and wore draped white cloth and their women walked behind them, with their pots and pans. Bundles and loads of skins were scattered along ahead on the heads of other natives. All were travelling away [34/35] from the famine. And in the heat, my feet out over the side of the car to keep them away from the heat of the engine, hat low over the eyes against the sun, watching the road, the people, and all clearings in the bush for game, we drove to the westward.

Once we saw three lesser kudu cows in an open place of broken bush. Gray, big bellied, long necked, small headed, and with big ears, they moved quickly into the woods and were gone. We left the car and tracked them but there was no bull track.

A little beyond there a flock of guineas quick-legged across the road running steady-headed with the motion [35/36] of trotters. As I jumped from the car and sprinted after them they rocketed up, their legs tucked close beneath them, heavy-bodied, short wings drumming, cackling, to go over the trees ahead. I dropped two that thumped hard when they fell and as they lay, wings beating, Abdullah cut their heads off so they would be legal eating. He put them in the car where M'Cola sat laughing; his old man's healthy laugh, his making-fun-of-me laugh, his bird-shooting laugh that dated from a streak of raging misses one time that had delighted him. Now when I killed, it was a joke as when we shot a hyena; the funniest joke of all. He laughed always to see the birds tumble and when I missed he roared and shook his head again and again.

"Ask him what the hell he's laughing about?" I asked Pop once.

"At B'wana," M'Cola said, and shook his head, "at the little birds."

"He thinks you're funny," Pop said.

"Goddam it. I am funny. But the hell with him."

"He thinks you're very funny," Pop said. "Now the Memsahib and I would never laugh."

"Shoot them yourself."

"No, you're the bird shot. The self-confessed bird shot," she said.

So bird shooting became this marvellous joke. If I killed, the joke was on the birds and M'Cola would shake his head and laugh and make his hands go round [36/37] and round to show how the bird turned over in the air. And if I missed, I was the clown of the piece and he would

*Ernest Hemingway, from *Green Hills of Africa* (New York: Charles Scribner's Sons, 1935), pp. 34–43; 64–66; 68–73; 96–107; 111–118; 148–150; 283–285. Copyright 1935 Charles Scribner's Sons; renewal copyright © 1963 Mary Hemingway.

look at me and shake with laughing. Only the hyenas were funnier.

Highly humorous was the hyena obscenely loping, full belly dragging, at daylight on the plain, who, shot from the stern, skittered on into speed to tumble end over end. Mirth provoking was the hyena that stopped out of range by an alkali lake to look back and, hit in the chest, went over on his back, his four feet and his full belly in the air. Nothing could be more jolly than the hyena coming suddenly wedge-headed and stinking out of high grass by a *donga,* hit at ten yards, who raced his tail in three narrowing, scampering circles until he died.

It was funny to M'Cola to see a hyena shot at close range. There was that comic slap of the bullet and the hyena's agitated surprise to find death inside of him. It was funnier to see a hyena shot at a great distance, in the heat shimmer of the plain, to see him go over backwards, to see him start that frantic circle, to see that electric speed that meant that he was racing the little nickelled death inside him. But the great joke of all, the thing M'Cola waved his hands across his face about, and turned away and shook his head and laughed, ashamed even of the hyena; the pinnacle of hyenic humor, was the hyena, the classic hyena, that hit too far back while running, would circle madly, snapping and tearing at himself until he pulled his own intestines out, and [37/38] then stood there, jerking them out and eating them with relish.

"*Fisi,*" M'Cola would say and shake his head in delighted sorrow at there being such an awful beast. Fisi, the hyena, hermaphroditic, self-eating devourer of the dead, trailer of calving cows, ham-stringer, potential biter-off of your face at night while you slept, sad yowler, camp-follower, stinking, foul, with jaws that crack the bones the lion leaves, belly dragging, loping away on the brown plain, looking back, mongrel dog-smart in the face; whack from the little Mannlicher and then the horrid circle starting. "*Fisi,*" M'Cola laughed, ashamed of him, shaking his bald black head. "*Fisi.* Eats himself. *Fisi.*"

The hyena was a dirty joke but bird shooting was a clean joke. My whiskey was a clean joke. There were many variations of that joke. Some we come to later. The Mohammedans and all religions were a joke. A joke on all the people who had them. Charo, the other gun bearer, was short, very serious and highly religious. All Ramadan he never swallowed his saliva until sunset and when the sun was almost down I'd see him watching nervously. He had a bottle with him of some sort of tea and he would finger it and watch the sun and I would see M'Cola watching him and pretending not to see. This was not outrightly funny to him. This was something that he could not laugh about openly but that he felt superior to and wondered at the silliness of it. The Mohammedan religion was very fashionable and [38/39] all the higher social grades among the boys were Mohammedans. It was something that gave caste, something to believe in, something fashionable and god-giving to suffer a little for each year, something that made you superior to other people, something that gave you more complicated habits of eating, something that I understood and M'Cola did not understand, nor care about, and he watched Charo watch for the sun to set with that blank look on his face that it put on about all things that he was not a part of. Charo was deadly thirsty and truly devout and the sun set very slowly. I looked at it, red over the trees, nudged him and he grinned. M'Cola offered me the water bottle solemnly. I shook my head and Charo grinned again. M'Cola looked blank. Then the sun was down and Charo had the bottle tilted up, his Adam's apple rising and falling greedily and M'Cola looking at him and then looking away.

In the early days, before we became good friends, he did not trust me at all. When anything came up he went into this blankness. I liked Charo much better then. We understood each other on the question of religion and Charo admired my shooting and always shook hands and smiled when we had killed anything particularly good. This was flattering and pleasing. M'Cola looked on all this early shooting as a series of lucky accidents. We were supposed to shoot. We had not yet shot anything that amounted to anything and he was not really my gun bearer. He was Mr. Jackson Phillip's gun bearer [**39/40**] and he had been loaned to me. I meant nothing to him. He did not like me nor dislike me. He was politely contemptuous of Karl. Who he liked was Mama.

The evening we killed the first lion it was dark when we came in sight of camp. The killing of the lion had been confused and unsatisfactory. It was agreed beforehand that P. O. M. should have the first shot but since it was the first lion any of us had ever shot at, and it was very late in the day, really too late to take the lion on, once he was hit we were to make a dog-fight of it and any one was free to get him. This was a good plan as it was nearly sundown and if the lion got into cover, wounded, it would be too dark to do anything about it without a mess. I remember seeing the lion looking yellow and heavy-headed and enormous against a scrubby-looking tree in a patch of orchard bush and P. O. M. kneeling to shoot and wanting to tell her to sit down and make sure of him. Then there was the short-barrelled explosion of the Mannlicher and the lion was going to the left on a run, a strange, heavy-shouldered, foot-swinging, cat run. I hit him with the Springfield and he went down and spun over and I shot again, too quickly, and threw a cloud of dirt over him. But there he was, stretched out, on his belly, and, with the sun just over the top of the trees, and the grass very green, we walked up on him like a posse, or a gang of Black and Tans, guns ready and cocked, not knowing whether he was stunned or dead. When we were close M'Cola threw a [**40/41**] stone at him. It hit him in the flank and from the way it hit you could tell he was a dead animal. I was sure P. O. M. had hit him but there

was only one bullet hole, well back, just below the spine and ranging forward to come to the surface under the skin of the chest. You could feel the bullet under the skin and M'Cola made a slit and cut it out. It was a 220-grain solid bullet from the Springfield and it had raked him, going through lungs and heart.

I was so surprised by the way he had rolled over dead from the shot after we had been prepared for a charge, for heroics, and for drama, that I felt more let down than pleased. It was our first lion and we were very ignorant and this was not what we had paid to see. Charo and M'Cola both shook P. O. M.'s hand and then Charo came over and shook hands with me.

"Good shot, B'wana," he said in Swahili. *"Piga m'uzuri."*

"Did you shoot, Karl?" I asked.

"No. I was just going to when you shot."

"You didn't shoot him, Pop?"

"No. You'd have heard it." He opened the breech and took out the two big .450 No. 2's.

"I'm sure I missed him," P. O. M. said.

"I was sure you hit him. I still think you hit him," I said.

"Mama hit," M'Cola said.

"Where?" Charo asked. [**41/42**]

"Hit," said M'Cola. "Hit."

"You rolled him over," Pop said to me. "God, he went over like a rabbit."

"I couldn't believe it."

"Mama *piga*," M'Cola said. *"Piga Simba."*

As we saw the camp fire in the dark ahead of us, coming in that night, M'Cola suddenly commenced to shout a stream of high-pitched, rapid, singing words in Wakamba ending in the word *"Simba."* Some one at the camp shouted back one word.

"Mama!" M'Cola shouted. Then another long stream. Then "Mama! Mama!"

Through the dark came all the porters, the cook, the skinner, the boys, and the headman.

"Mama!" M'Cola shouted. "Mama *piga Simba.*"

The boys came dancing, crowding, and beating time and chanting something from down in their chests that started like a cough and sounded like *"Hey la Mama! Hay la Mama! Hey la Mama!"*

The rolling-eyed skinner picked P.O.M. up, the big cook and the boys held her, and the others pressing forward to lift, and if not to lift to touch and hold, they danced and sang through the dark, around the fire and to our tent.

"Hey la Mama! huh! huh! huh! Hay la Mama! huh! huh! huh!" they sang the lion dance with that deep, lion asthmatic cough in it. Then at the tent they put her down and every one, very shyly, shook hands, the boys [**42/43**] saying *"m'uzuri, Memsahib,"* and M'Cola and the porters all saying *"m'uzuri, Mama"* with much feeling in the accenting of the word "Mama."

Afterwards in the chairs in front of the fire, sitting with the drinks, Pop said, "You shot it. M'Cola would kill any one who said you didn't."

"You know, I feel as though I did shoot it," P. O. M. said. "I don't believe I'd be able to stand it if I really had shot it. I'd be too proud. Isn't triumph marvellous?"

"Good old Mama," Karl said.

"I believe you did shoot him," I said.

"Oh, let's not go into that," P. O. M. said. "I feel so wonderful about just being supposed to have killed him. You know people never used to carry me on their shoulders much at home."

"No one knows how to behave in America," Pop said. "Most uncivilized."

"We'll carry you in Key West," Karl said. "Poor old Mama."

"Let's not talk about it," P. O. M. said. "I like it too much. Shouldn't I maybe distribute largess?"

"They didn't do it for that," Pop said. "But it is all right to give something to celebrate."

"Oh, I want to give them all a great deal of money," P. O. M. said. "Isn't triumph simply marvellous?"

"Good old Mama," I said. "You killed him."

"No I didn't. Don't lie to me. Just let me enjoy my triumph." . . .

CHAPTER III

. . . We went out that afternoon and glassed the country from the hills and never saw a thing. That night after supper we were in the tent. P. O. M. disliked intensely being compared to a little terrier. If she must be like any dog, and she did not wish to be, she would prefer a wolf-hound, something lean, racy, long-legged and ornamental. Her courage was so automatic and so much a simple state of being that she never thought of danger; then, too, danger was in the hands of Pop and for Pop she had a complete, clear-seeing, absolutely trusting adoration. Pop was her ideal of how a man should be, brave, gentle, comic, never losing his temper, never bragging, never complaining except in a joke, tolerant, understanding, intelligent, drinking a little too much as a good man should, and, to her eyes, very handsome.

"Don't you think Pop's handsome?"

"No," I said. "Droopy's handsome."

"Droopy's *beautiful*. But don't you *really* think Pop's handsome?" [**64/65**]

"Hell, no. I like him as well as any man I've ever known, but I'm damned if he's handsome."

"I think he's lovely looking. But you understand about how I feel about him, don't you?"

"Sure. I'm as fond of the bastard myself."

"But *don't* you think he's handsome, really?"

"Nope."

Then, a little later:

"Well, who's handsome to you?"

"Belmonte and Pop. And you."

"Don't be patriotic," I said. "Who's a beautiful woman?"

"Garbo."

"Not any more. Josie is. Margot is."

"Yes, they are. I know I'm not."

"You're lovely."

"Let's talk about Mr. J. P. I don't like you to call him Pop. It's not dignified."

"He and I aren't dignified together."

"Yes, but I'm dignified with him. Don't you think he's wonderful?"

"Yes, and he doesn't have to read books written by some female he's tried to help get published saying how he's yellow."

"She's just jealous and malicious. You never should have helped her. Some people never forgive that."

"It's a damned shame, though, with all that talent gone [65/66] to malice and nonsense and self-praise. It's a god-damned shame, really. It's a shame you never knew her before she went to pot. You know a funny thing; she never could write dialogue. It was terrible. She learned how to do it from my stuff and used it in that book. She had never written like that before. She never could forgive learning that and she was afraid people would notice it, where she'd learned it, so she had to attack me. It's a funny racket, really. But I swear she was damned nice before she got ambitious. You would have liked her then, really."

"Maybe, but I don't think so," said P.O.M. "We have fun though, don't we? Without all those people."

"God damn it if we don't. I've had a better time every year since I can remember."

"But isn't Mr. J. P. wonderful? Really?"

"Yes. He's wonderful."

"Oh, you're nice to say it. Poor Karl."

"Why?"

"Without his wife."

"Yes," I said. "Poor Karl." [66/68 (page 67 is blank)]

CHAPTER IV

So in the morning, again, we started ahead of the porters and went down and across the hills and through a deeply forested valley and then up and across a long rise of country with high grass that made the walking difficult and on and up and across, resting sometimes in the shade of a tree, and then on and up and down and across, all in high grass, now, that you had to break a trail in, and the sun was very hot. The five of us in single file, Droop and M'Cola with a big gun apiece, hung with musettes and water bottles and the cameras, we all sweating in the sun, Pop and I with guns and the Memsahib trying to walk like Droopy, her Stetson tilted [68/69] on one side, happy to be on a trip, pleased about how comfortable her boots were, we came finally to a thicket of thorn trees over a ravine that ran down from the side of a ridge to the water and we leaned the guns against the trees and went in under the close shade and lay on the ground. P. O. M. got the books out of one of the musettes and she and Pop read while I followed the ravine down to the little stream that came out of the mountain side, and found a fresh lion track and many rhino tunnels in the tall grass that came higher than your head. It was very hot climbing back up the sandy ravine and I was glad to lean my back against the tree [69/70] trunk and read in Tolstoi's *Sevastopol*. It was a very young book and had one fine description of fighting in it, where the French take the redoubt and I thought about Tolstoi and about what a great advantage an experience of war was to a writer. It was one of the major subjects and certainly one of the hardest to write truly of and those writers who had not seen it were always very jealous and tried to make it seem unimportant, or abnormal, or a disease as a subject, while, really, it was just something quite irreplaceable that they had missed. Then Sevastopol made me think of the Boulevard Sevastopol in Paris, about riding a bicycle down it in the rain on the way home from Strassburg and the slipperiness of the rails of the tram cars and the feeling of riding on greasy, slippery asphalt and cobble stones in traffic in the rain, and how we had nearly lived on the Boulevard du Temple that time, and I remembered the look of that apartment, how it was arranged, and the wall paper, and instead we had taken the upstairs of the pavilion in Notre Dame des Champs in the court-yard with the sawmill (*and the sudden whine of the saw, the smell of sawdust and the chestnut tree over the roof with a mad woman downstairs*) and the year worrying about money (*all of the stories back in the mail that came in through a slit in the saw-mill door, with notes of rejection that would never call them stories, but always anecdotes, sketches, contes, etc. They did not want them, and we lived on poireaux and drank cahors and water*) and how [**70/71**] fine the fountains were at the Place de L'Observatoire (*water sheen rippling on the bronze of horses' manes, bronze beasts and shoulders, green under thin-flowing water*) and when they put up the bust of Flaubert in the Luxembourg on the short cut through the gardens on the way to the rue Soufflot (*one that we believed in, loved without criticism, heavy now in stone as an idol should be*). He had not seen war but he had seen a revolution and the Commune and a revolution is much the best if you do not become bigoted because every one speaks the same language. Just as civil war is the best war for a writer, the most complete. Stendhal had seen a war and Napoleon taught him to write. He was teaching everybody then; but no one else learned. Dostoevsky was made by being sent to Siberia. Writers are forged in injustice as a sword is forged. I wondered if it would make a writer of him, give him the necessary shock to cut the over-flow of words and give him a sense of proportion, if they sent Tom Wolfe to Siberia or to the Dry Tortugas. Maybe it would and maybe it wouldn't. He seemed sad, really, like Carnera. Tolstoi was a small man. Joyce was of medium height and he wore his eyes out. And that last night, drunk, with Joyce and the thing he kept quoting from Edgar Quinet, "Fraîche et rose comme au jour de la bataille." I didn't have it right I knew. And when you saw him he would take up a conversation interrupted three years before. It was nice to see a great writer in our time. [**71/72**]

What I had to do was work. I did not care, particularly, how it all came out. I did not take my own life seriously any more, any one else's life, yes, but not mine. They all wanted something that I did not want and I would get it without wanting it, if I worked. To work was the only thing, it was the one thing that always made you feel good, and in the meantime it was my own damned life and I would lead it where and how I pleased. And where I had led it now pleased me very much. This was a better sky than Italy. The hell it was. The best sky was in Italy and Spain and Northern Michigan in the fall and in the fall in the Gulf off Cuba. You could beat this sky; but not the country.

All I wanted to do now was get back to Africa. We had not left it, yet, but when I would wake in the night I would lie, listening, homesick for it already.

Now, looking out the tunnel of trees over the ravine at the sky with white clouds moving across in the wind, I loved the country so that I was happy as you are after you have been with a woman that you really love, when, empty, you feel it welling up again and there it is and you can never have it all and yet what there is, now, you can have, and you want more and more, to have, and be, and live in, to possess now again for always, for that long, sudden-ended always; making time stand still, sometimes so very still that afterwards you wait to hear it move, and it is slow in starting. But you are not alone, because if you have ever really loved her happy and un- [**72/73**] tragic, she loves you always; no matter whom she loves nor where she goes she loves you more. So if you have loved some woman and some country you are very fortunate and, if you die afterwards it makes no difference. Now, being in Africa, I was hungry for more of it, the changes of the seasons, the rains with no need to travel, the discomforts that you paid to make it real, the names of the trees, of the small animals, and all the birds, to know the language and have time to be in it and to move slowly. I had loved country all my life; the

country was always better than the people.
I could only care about people a very few
at a time.

P.O.M. was sleeping. She was always
lovely to look at asleep, sleeping quietly,
close curled like an animal, with nothing
of the being dead look that Karl had
asleep. Pop slept quietly too, you could
see his soul was close in his body. His body
no longer housed him fittingly. It had
gone on and changed, thickening here,
losing its lines, bloating a little there, but
inside he was young and lean and tall and
hard as when he galloped lion on the
plain below Wami, and the pouches under
his eyes were all outside, so that now I
saw him asleep the way P. O. M. saw him
always. M'Cola was an old man asleep,
without history and without mystery.
Droopy did not sleep. He sat on his heels
and watched for the safari. . . .

CHAPTER V

. . . We stood now in the shade of trees
with great smooth trunks, circled at their
base with the line of roots that showed in
rounded ridges up the trunks like arteries;
the trunks the yellow green of a French
forest on a day in winter after rain. But
these trees had a great spread of branches
and were in leaf and below them, in the
stream bed in the sun, reeds like papyrus
grass grew thick as wheat and twelve feet
tall. There was a game trail through the
grass along the stream and Droopy was
bent down looking at it. M'Cola went over
and looked and they both followed it a
little way, stooped close over it, then came
back to us.

"Nyati," M'Cola whispered. "Buffalo."
Droopy whispered to Pop and then Pop
said, softly in his throaty, whiskey whisper,
"They're buff gone down the river. Droop
says there are some big bulls. They haven't
come back."

"Let's follow them," I said. "I'd rather
get another buff than rhino."

"It's as good a chance as any for rhino,
too," Pop said.

"By God, isn't it a great looking country?" I said.

"Splendid," Pop said. "Who would have
imagined it?"

"The trees are like André's pictures,"
P. O. M. said. "It's simply beautiful. Look
at that green. It's Masson. Why can't a
good painter see this country?"

"How are your boots?"

"Fine."

As we trailed the buffalo we went very
slowly and [96/97] quietly. There was no
wind and we knew that when the breeze
came up it would be from the east and
blow up the canyon toward us. We followed the game trail down the river-bed
and as we went the grass was much higher.
Twice we had to get down to crawl and
the reeds were so thick you could not see
two feet into them. Droop found a fresh
rhino track, too, in the mud. I began to
think about what would happen if a rhino
came barging along this tunnel and who
would do what. It was exciting but I did
not like it. It was too much like being in
a trap and there was P. O. M. to think
about. Then as the stream made a bend
and we came out of the high grass to the
bank I smelled game very distinctly. I do
not smoke, and hunting at home I have
several times smelled elk in the rutting
season before I have seen them and I can
smell clearly where an old bull has lain in
the forest. The bull elk has a strong musky
smell. It is a strong but pleasant odor and
I know it well, but this smell I did not
know.

"I can smell them," I whispered to Pop.
He believed me.

"What is it?"

"I don't know but it's plenty strong.
Can't you?"

"No."

"Ask Droop."

Droopy nodded and grinned.

"They take snuff," Pop said. "I don't
know whether they can scent or not."
[97/98]

We went on into another bed of reeds
that were high over our heads, putting
each foot down silently before lifting the
other, walking as quietly as in a dream or

a slow motion picture. I could smell whatever it was clearly now, all of the time,
sometimes stronger than at others. I did
not like it at all. We were close to the bank
now, and, ahead the game trail went
straight out into a long slough of higher
reeds than any we had come through.

"I can smell them close as hell," I whispered to Pop. "No kidding. Really."

"I believe you," Pop said. "Should we
get up here onto the bank and skirt this
bit? We'll be above it."

"Good." Then, when we were up, I
said, "That tall stuff had me spooked. I
wouldn't like to hunt in that."

"How'd you like to hunt elephant in
that?" Pop whispered.

"I wouldn't do it."

"Do you really hunt elephant in grass
like that?" P. O. M. asked.

"Yes," Pop said. "Get up on somebody's
shoulders to shoot."

Better men than I am do it, I thought.
I wouldn't do it.

We went along the grassy right bank,
on a sort of shelf, now in the open, skirt-
ing a slough of high dry reeds. Beyond on
the opposite bank were the heavy trees
and above them the steep bank of the
canyon. You could not see the stream.
Above us, on the right, were the hills,
wooded in patches of orchard bush.
Ahead, at the end **[98/99]** of the slough
of reeds the banks narrowed and the
branches of the big trees almost covered
the stream. Suddenly Droopy grabbed me
and we both crouched down. He put the
big gun in my hand and took the Springfield. He pointed and around a curve in
the bank I saw the head of a rhino with
a long, wonderful-looking horn. The head
was swaying and I could see the ears forward and twitching, and see the little pig
eyes. I slipped the safety catch and motioned Droopy down. Then I heard
M'Cola saying, "Toto! Toto!" and he
grabbed my arm. Droopy was whispering,
"Manamouki! Manamouki! Manamouki!"
very fast and he and M'Cola were frantic
that I should not shoot. It was a cow rhino
with a calf and as I lowered the gun, she
gave a snort, crashed in the reeds, and was

gone. I never saw the calf. We could see
the reeds swaying where the two of them
were moving and then it was all quiet.

"Damn shame," Pop whispered. "She
had a beautiful horn."

"I was all set to bust her," I said. "I
couldn't tell she was a cow."

"M'Cola saw the calf."

M'Cola was whispering to Pop and
nodding his head emphatically.

"He says there's another rhino in there,"
Pop said. "That he heard him snort."

"Let's get higher, where we can see them
if they break, and throw something in," I
said. **[99/100]**

"Good idea," Pop agreed. "Maybe the
bull's there."

We went a little higher up the bank
where we could look out over the lake of
high reeds and, with Pop holding his big
gun ready and I with the safety off mine,
M'Cola threw a club into the reeds where
he had heard the snort. There was a
wooshing snort and no movement, not a
stir in the reeds. Then there was a crashing further away and we could see the
reeds swaying with the rush of something
through them toward the opposite bank,
but could not see what was making the
movement. Then I saw the black back, the
wide-swept, point-lifted horns and then
the quick-moving, climbing rush of a buffalo up the other bank. He went up, his
neck up and out, his head horn-heavy, his
withers rounded like a fighting bull, in fast
strong-legged climb. I was holding on the
point where his neck joined his shoulder
when Pop stopped me.

"He's not a big one," he said softly. "I
wouldn't take him unless you want him
for meat."

He looked big to me and now he stood,
his head up, broadside, his head swung
toward us.

"I've got three more on the license and
we're leaving their country," I said.

"It's awfully good meat," Pop whispered. "Go ahead then. Bust him. But be
ready for the rhino after you shoot."

I sat down, the big gun feeling heavy
and unfamiliar, held on the buff's shoulder, squeezed off and flinched **[100/101]**

without firing. Instead of the sweet clean pull of the Springfield with the smooth, unhesitant release at the end, this trigger came to what, in a squeeze, seemed metal stuck against metal. It was like when you shoot in a nightmare. I couldn't squeeze it and I corrected from my flinch, held my breath, and pulled the trigger. It pulled off with a jerk and the big gun made a rocking explosion out of which I came, seeing the buffalo still on his feet, and going out of sight to the left in a climbing run, to let off the second barrel and throw a burst of rock dust and dirt over his hind quarters. He was out of shot before I could reload the double-barrelled .470 and we had all heard the snorting and the crashing of another rhino that had gone out of the lower end of the reeds and on under the heavy trees on our side without showing more than a glimpse of his bulk in the reeds.

"It was the bull," Pop said. "He's gone down the stream."

"N'Dio. Doumi! Doumi!" Droopy insisted it was a bull.

"I hit the damned buff," I said. "God knows where. To hell with those heavy guns. The trigger pull put me off."

"You'd have killed him with the Springfield," Pop said.

"I'd know where I hit him anyway. I thought with the four-seventy I'd kill him or miss him," I said. "Instead, now we've got him wounded." [101/102]

"He'll keep," Pop said. "We want to give him plenty of time."

"I'm afraid I gut-shot him."

"You can't tell. Going off fast like that he might be dead in a hundred yards."

"The hell with that four-seventy," I said. "I can't shoot it. The trigger's like the last turn of the key opening a sardine can."

"Come on," Pop said. "We've got God knows how many rhino scattered about here."

"What about the buff?"

"Plenty of time for him later. We must let him stiffen up. Let him get sick."

"Suppose we'd been down in there with all that stuff coming out."

"Yes," said Pop.

All this in whispers. I looked at P. O. M. She was like some one enjoying a good musical show.

"Did you see where it hit him?"

"I couldn't tell," she whispered. "Do you suppose there are any more in there?"

"Thousands," I said. "What do we do, Pop?"

"That bull may be just around the bend," Pop said. "Come on."

We went along the bank, our nerves cocked, and as we came to the narrow end of the reeds there was another rush of something heavy through the tall stalks. I had the gun up waiting for whatever it was to show. But [102/103] there was only the waving of the reeds. M'Cola signalled with his hand not to shoot.

"The goddamned calf," Pop said. "Must have been two of them. Where's the bloody bull?"

"How the hell do you see them?"

"Tell by the size."

Then we were standing looking down into the stream bed, into the shadows under the branches of the big trees, and off ahead down the stream when M'Cola pointed up the hill on our right.

"Faro," he whispered and reached me the glasses.

There on the hillside, head-on, wide, black, looking straight toward us, ears twitching and head lifted, swaying as the nose searched for the wind, was another rhino. He looked huge in the glasses. Pop was studying him with his binoculars.

"He's no better than what you have," he said softly.

"I can bust him right in the sticking place," I whispered.

"You only have one more," Pop whispered. "You want a good one."

I offered the glasses to P. O. M.

"I can see him without," she said. "He's huge."

"He may charge," Pop said. "Then you'll have to take him."

Then, as we watched, another rhino came into sight from behind a wide feathery-topped tree. He was quite a bit smaller. [103/104]

"By God, it's a calf," Pop said. "That one's a cow. Good thing you didn't shoot her. She bloody well *may* charge too."

"Is it the same cow?" I whispered.

"No. That other one had a hell of a horn."

We all had the nervous exhilaration, like a laughing drunk, that a sudden over-abundance, idiotic abundance of game makes. It is a feeling that can come from any sort of game or fish that is ordinarily rare and that, suddenly, you find in a ridiculously unbelievable abundance.

"Look at her. She knows there's something wrong. But she can't see us or smell us."

"She heard the shots."

"She knows we're here. But she can't make it out."

The rhino looked so huge, so ridiculous, and so fine to see, and I sighted on her chest.

"It's a nice shot."

"Perfect," Pop said.

"What are we going to do?" P. O. M. said. She was practical.

"We'll work around her," Pop said.

"If we keep low I don't believe our scent will carry up there once we're past."

"You can't tell," Pop said. "We don't want her to charge."

She did not charge, but dropped her head, finally, and worked up the hill followed by the nearly full-grown calf. [**104/ 105**]

"Now," said Pop, "we'll let Droop go ahead and see if he can find the bull's tracks. We might as well sit down."

We sat in the shade and Droopy went up one side of the stream and the local guide the other. They came back and said the bull had gone on down.

"Did any one ever see what sort of horn he had?" I asked.

"Droop said he was good."

M'Cola had gone up the hill a little way. Now he crouched and beckoned.

"Nyati," he said with his hand up to his face.

"Where?" Pop asked him. He pointed, crouched down, and as we crawled up to him he handed me the glasses. They were a long way away on the jutting ridge of one of the steep hillsides on the far side of the canyon, well down the stream. We could see six, then eight, buffalo, black, heavy necked, the horns shining, standing on the point of a ridge. Some were grazing and others stood, their heads up, watching.

"That one's a bull," Pop said, looking through the glasses.

"Which one?"

"Second from the right."

"They all look like bulls to me."

"They're a long way away. That one's a good bull. Now we've got to cross the stream and work down toward them and try to get above them."

"Will they stay there?" [**105/106**]

"'No. Probably they'll work down into this stream bed as soon as it's hot."

"Let's go."

We crossed the stream on a log and then another log and on the other side, half way up the hillside, there was a deeply worn game trail that graded along the bank under the heavily leafed branches of the trees. We went along quite fast, but walking carefully, and below us, now, the stream bed was covered solidly with foliage. It was still early in the morning but the breeze was rising and the leaves stirred over our heads. We crossed one ravine that came down to the stream, going into the thick bush to be out of sight and stooping as we crossed behind trees in the small open place, then, using the shoulder of the ravine as protection, we climbed so that we might get high up the hillside above the buffalo and work down to them. We stopped in the shelter of the ridge, me sweating heavily and fixing a handkerchief inside the sweatband of my Stetson, and sent Droop ahead to look. He came back to say they were gone. From above we could see nothing of them, so we cut across the ravine and the hillside thinking we might intercept them on their way down into the river bed. The next hillside had been burned and at the bottom of the hill there was a burned area of bush. In the ash dust were the tracks of the buffalo as they came down and into the thick jungle of the stream bed. Here it was too overgrown and there were too many vines to follow them. There were no tracks [**106/107**] going down the stream so we knew they were down in that part of the stream bed we had looked down on from the game trail. Pop said there was nothing to do about them in there. It was so thick that if we jumped them we could not get a shot. You could not tell one from another, he said. All you would see would be a rush of black. An old bull would be gray but a good herd bull might be as black as a cow. It wasn't any good to jump them like that.

It was ten o'clock now and very hot in the open, the sun pegged and the breeze lifted the ashes of the burned-over ground as we walked. Everything would be in the thick cover now. We decided to find a shady place and lie down and read in the cool; to have lunch and kill the hot part of the day.

* * * * *

When they woke up we had lunch of cold sliced tenderloin, bread, and mustard, and a can of plums, and drank the third, and last, bottle of beer. Then we read again and all went to sleep. I woke thirsty and was unscrewing the top from a water bottle when I heard a rhino snort and crash in the brush of the river bed. Pop was awake and heard it too and we took our guns, without speaking, and started toward where the noise had come from. M'Cola found the tracks. The rhino had come up the stream, evidently he had winded us when he was only about thirty yards away, and had gone on up. We could not follow the tracks the way the wind was blowing so we circled away from the stream and back to the edge of the burned place to get above him and then hunted very carefully against the wind along the stream through very thick bush, but we did not find him. Finally Droopy found where he had gone up the other side and on into [**111/112**] the hills. From the tracks it did not seem a particularly large one.

We were a long way from camp, at least

four hours as we had come, and much of it up-hill going back, certainly there would be that long climb out of the canyon; we had a wounded buffalo to deal with, and when we came out on the edge of the burned country again, we agreed that we should get P. O. M. and get started. It was still hot, but the sun was on its way down and for a good way we would be on the heavily shaded game trail on the high bank above the stream. When we found P. O. M. she pretended to be indignant at our going off and leaving her alone but she was only teasing us.

We started off, Droop and his spearsman in the lead, walking along the shadow of the trail that was broken by the sun through the leaves. Instead of the cool early morning smell of the forest there was a nasty stink like the mess cats make.

"What makes the stink?" I whispered to Pop.

"Baboons," he said.

A whole tribe of them had gone on just ahead of us and their droppings were everywhere. We came up to the place where the rhinos and the buff had come out of the reeds and I located where I thought the buff had been when I shot. M'Cola and Droopy were casting about like hounds and I thought they were at least fifty yards too high up the bank when Droop held up a leaf.

"He's got blood," Pop said. We went up to them. [**112/113**] There was a great quantity of blood, black now on the grass, and the trail was easy to follow. Droop and M'Cola trailed one on each side, leaving the trail between them, pointing to each blood spot formally with a long stem of grass. I always thought it would be better for one to trail slowly and the other cast ahead but this was the way they trailed, stooped heads, pointing each dried splash with their grass stems and occasionally, when they picked up the tracks after losing them, stooping to pluck a grass blade or a leaf that had the black stain on it. I followed them with the Springfield, then came˙Pop, with P. O. M. behind him. Droop carried my big gun and Pop had his. M'Cola had P. O. M.'s Mannlicher slung over his shoulder. None of us spoke and every one seemed to regard it as a pretty serious business. In some high grass we found blood, at a pretty good height on the grass leaves on both sides of the trail where the buff had gone through the grass. That meant he was shot clean through. You could not tell the original color of the blood now, but I had a moment of hoping he might be shot through the lungs. But further on we came on some droppings in the rocks with blood in them and then for a while he had dropped dung wherever he climbed and all of it was blood-spotted. It looked, now, like a gut shot or one through the paunch. I was more ashamed of it all the time.

"If he comes don't worry about Droopy or the others," Pop whispered. "They'll get out of his way. Stop him."

"Right up the nose," I said. **[113/114]**

"Don't try anything fancy," Pop said. The trail climbed steadily, then twice looped back on itself and for a time seemed to wander, without plan, among some rocks, Once it led down to the stream, crossed a rivulet of it and then came back up on the same bank, grading up through the trees.

"I think we'll find him dead," I whispered to Pop. That aimless turn had made me see him, slow and hard hit, getting ready to go down.

"I hope so," Pop said.

But the trail went on, where there was little grass now, and trailing was much slower and more difficult. There were no tracks now that I could see, only the probable line he would take, verified by a shiny dark splatter of dried blood on a stone. Several times we lost it entirely and, the three of us making casts, one would find it, point and whisper "Damu," and we would go on again. Finally it led down from a rocky hillside with the last of the sun on it, down into the stream bed where there was a long, wide patch of the highest dead reeds that we had seen. These were higher and thicker even than the slough the buff had come out of in the morning

and there were several game trails that went into them.

"Not good enough to take the little Memsahib in there," Pop said.

"Let her stay here with M'Cola," I said.

"It's not good enough for the little Memsahib," Pop repeated. "I don't know why we let her come." **[114/115]**

"She can wait here. Droop wants to go on."

"Right you are. We'll have a look."

"You wait here with M'Cola," I whispered over my shoulder.

We followed Droopy into the thick, tall grass that was five feet above our heads, walking carefully on the game trail, stooping forward, trying to make no noise breathing. I was thinking of the buff the way I had seen them when we had gotten the three that time, how the old bull had come out of the bush, groggy as he was, and I could see the horns, the boss coming far down, the muzzle out, the little eyes, the roll of fat and muscle on his thin-haired, gray, scaly-hided neck, the heavy power and the rage in him, and I admired him and respected him, but he was slow, and all the while we shot I felt that it was fixed and that we had him. This was different, this was no rapid fire, no pouring it on him as he comes groggy into the open, if he comes now I must be quiet inside and put it down his nose as he comes with the head out. He will have to put the head down to hook, like any bull, and that will uncover the old place the boys wet their knuckles on and I will get one in there and then must go sideways into the grass and he would be Pop's from then on unless I could keep the rifle when I jumped. I was sure I could get that one in and jump if I could wait and watch his head come down. I knew I could do that and that the shot would kill him but how long would it take? That was the whole thing. How long would it take? Now, going for- **[115/116]** ward, sure he was in here, I felt the elation, the best elation of all, of certain action to come, action in which you had something to do, in which you can kill and come out of it, doing something you are ignorant about and so not scared, no one to worry about and no responsibility except to perform something you feel sure you can perform, and I was walking softly ahead watching Droopy's back and remembering to keep the sweat out of my glasses when I heard a noise behind us and turned my head. It was P. O. M. with M'Cola coming on our tracks.

"For God's sake," Pop said. He was furious.

We got her back out of the grass and up onto the bank and made her realize that she must stay there. She had not understood that she was to stay behind. She had heard me whisper something but thought it was for her to come behind M'Cola.

"That spooked me," I said to Pop.

"She's like a little terrier," he said. "But it's not good enough."

We were looking out over that grass.

"Droop wants to go still," I said. I'll go as far as he will. When he says no that lets us out. After all, I gut-shot the son of a bitch."

"Mustn't do anything silly, though."

"I can kill the son of a bitch if I get a shot at him. If he comes he's got to give me a shot."

The fright P. O. M. had given us about herself had made me noisy. [116/117]

"Come on," said Pop. We followed Droopy back in and it got worse and worse and I do not know about Pop but about half way I changed to the big gun and kept the safety off and my hand over the trigger guard and I was plenty nervous by the time Droopy stopped and shook his head and whispered "Hapana." It had gotten so you could not see a foot ahead and it was all turns and twists. It was really bad and the sun was only on the hillside now. We both felt good because we had made Droopy do the calling off and I was relieved as well. What we had followed him into had made my fancy shooting plans seem very silly and I knew all we had in there was Pop to blast him over with the four-fifty number two after I'd maybe miss him with that lousy four-

seventy. I had no confidence in anything but its noise any more.

We were back trailing when we heard the porters on the hillside shout and we ran crashing through the grass to try to get to a high enough place to see to shoot. They waved their arms and shouted that the buffalo had come out of the reeds and gone past them and then M'Cola and Droopy were pointing and Pop had me by the sleeve trying to pull me to where I could see them and then, in the sunlight, high up on the hillside against the rocks I saw two buffalo. They shone very black in the sun and one was much bigger than the other and I remember thinking this was our bull and that he had picked up a cow and she had made the pace and kept him going. Droop had handed me the Springfield and I slipped my [117/118] arm through the sling and sighting, the buff now all seen through the aperture, I froze myself inside and held the bead on the top of his shoulder and as I started to squeeze he started running and I swung ahead of him and loosed off. I saw him lower his head and jump like a bucking horse as he comes out of the chutes and as I threw the shell, slammed the bolt forward and shot again, behind him as he went out of sight, I knew I had him. Droopy and I started to run and as we were running I heard a low bellow. I stopped and yelled at Pop, "Hear him? I've got him, I tell you!"

"You hit him," said Pop. "Yes."

"Goddamn it, I killed him. Didn't you hear him bellow?"

"No."

"Listen!" We stood listening and there it came, clear, a long, moaning, unmistakable bellow.

"By God," Pop said. It was a very sad noise.

M'Cola grabbed my hand and Droopy slapped my back and all laughing we started on a running scramble, sweating, rushing, up the ridge through the trees and over rocks. I had to stop for breath, my heart pounding, and wiped the sweat off my face and cleaned my glasses.

"Kufa!" M'Cola said, making the word for dead almost explosive in its force. "N'Dio! Kufa!"

"Kufa!" Droopy said grinning.

"Kufa!" M'Cola repeated and we shook hands again before we went on climbing. . . .

CHAPTER VIII

. . . I did nothing that had not been done to me. I had been shot and I had been crippled and gotten away. I expected, always, to be killed by one thing or another and I, truly, did not mind that any more. Since I still loved to hunt I resolved that I would only shoot as long as I could kill cleanly and as soon as I lost that ability I would stop.

If you serve time for society, democracy, and the other things quite young, and declining any further enlistment make yourself responsible only to yourself, you exchange the pleasant, comforting stench of comrades for something you can never feel in any other way than by yourself. That something I cannot yet define completely but the feeling comes when you write well and truly of something and [148/149] know impersonally you have written in that way and those who are paid to read it and report on it do not like the subject so they say it is all a fake, yet you know its value absolutely; or when you do something which people do not consider a serious occupation and yet you know, truly, that it is as important and has always been as important as all the things that are in fashion, and when, on the sea, you are alone with it and know that this Gulf Stream you are living with, knowing, learning about, and loving, has moved, as it moves, since before man, and that it has gone by the shoreline of that long, beautiful, unhappy island since before Columbus sighted it and that the things you find out about it, and those that have always lived in it are permanent and of value because that stream will flow, as it has flowed, after the Indians, after the Span-

iards, after the British, after the Americans and after all the Cubans and all the systems of governments, the richness, the poverty, the martyrdom, the sacrifice and the venality and the cruelty are all gone as the high-piled scow of garbage, bright-colored, white-flecked, ill-smelling, now tilted on its side, spills off its load into the blue water, turning it a pale green to a depth of four or five fathoms as the load spreads across the surface, the sinkable part going down and the flotsam of palm fronds, corks, bottles, and used electric light globes, seasoned with an occasional condom or a deep floating corset, the torn leaves of a student's exercise book, a well-inflated dog, the occasional rat, the no-longer-distinguished cat; all [149/150] this well shepherded by the boats of the garbage pickers who pluck their prizes with long poles, as interested, as intelligent, and as accurate as historians; they have the viewpoint; the stream, with no visible flow, takes five loads of this a day when things are going well in La Habana and in ten miles along the coast it is as clear and blue and unimpressed as it was ever before the tug hauled out the scow; and the palm fronds of our victories, the worn light bulbs of our discoveries and the empty condoms of our great loves float with no significance against one single, lasting thing—the stream. [150/283]

* * * * *

Sure, you couldn't make a living. Every one had explained that. The locusts came and ate your crops and the monsoon failed, and the rains did not come, and everything dried up and died. There were ticks and fly to kill the stock, and the mosquitoes gave you fever and maybe you got blackwater. Your cattle would die and you would get no price for your coffee. It took an Indian to make money from sisal and on the coast every cocoanut plantation meant a man ruined by the idea or making money from copra. A white hunter worked three months out of the year and drank for twelve and the Government was ruining the country for the benefit of the

Hindu and the natives. That was what they told you. Sure. But I did not want to make money. All I wanted was to live in it and have time to hunt. Already I had had one of the diseases and had experienced the necessity of washing a three-inch bit of my large intestine with soap and water and tucking it back where it belonged an unnumbered amount of times a day. There were remedies which cured this and it was well worth going through for what I had seen and where I had been. Besides I caught that on the dirty boat out from Marseilles. P. O. M. hadn't been ill a day. Neither had Karl. I [**283/284**] loved this country and I felt at home and where a man feels at home, outside of where he's born, is where he's meant to go. Then, in my grandfather's time, Michigan was a malaria ridden state. They called it fever and ague. And in Tortugas, where I'd spent months, a thousand men once died of yellow fever. New continents and islands try to frighten you with disease as a snake hisses. The snake may be poisonous too. You kill them off. Hell, what I had a month ago would have killed me in the old days before they invented the remedies. Maybe it would and maybe I would have gotten well.

It is easier to keep well in a good country by taking simple precautions than to pretend that a country which is finished is still good.

A continent ages quickly once we come. The natives live in harmony with it. But the foreigner destroys, cuts down the trees, drains the water, so that the water supply is altered and in a short time the soil, once the sod is turned under, is cropped out and, next, it starts to blow away as it has blown away in every old country and as I had seen it start to blow in Canada. The earth gets tired of being exploited. A country wears out quickly unless man puts back in it all his residue and that of all his beasts. When he quits using beasts and uses machines, the earth defeats him quickly. The machine can't reproduce, nor does it fertilize the soil, and it eats what he cannot raise. A country was made to be as we found it. We are the intruders and after we are dead we may [**284/285**] have ruined it but it will still be there and we don't know what the next changes are. I suppose they all end up like Mongolia.

I would come back to Africa but not to make a living from it. I could do that with two pencils and a few hundred sheets of the cheapest paper. But I would come back to where it pleased me to live; to really live. Not just let my life pass. Our people went to America because that was the place to go then. It had been a good country and we had made a bloody mess of it and I would go, now, somewhere else as we had always had the right to go somewhere else and as we had always gone. You could always come back. Let the others come to America who did not know that they had come too late. Our people had seen it at its best and fought for it when it was well worth fighting for. Now I would go somewhere else. We always went in the old days and there were still good places to go.

I knew a good country when I saw one. Here there was game, plenty of birds, and I liked the natives. Here I could shoot and fish. That, and writing, and reading, and seeing pictures was all I cared about doing. And I could remember all the pictures. Other things I liked to watch but they were what I liked to do. That and ski-ing. But my legs were bad now and it was not worth the time you spent hunting good snow any more. You saw too many people, ski-ing now. . . .

[". . . A man can die but once. . . ."] *

ERNEST HEMINGWAY selected eighty-two war stories for reprinting in *Men at War*, including three selections from his own work. In his introduction to this volume, published in October, 1942, a time when America's future was very much at stake, Hemingway makes it clear that this volume is his own personal battle cry.

. . . When you go to war as a boy you have a great illusion of immortality. Other people get killed; not you. It can happen to other people; but not to you. Then when you are badly wounded the first time you lose that illusion and you know it can happen to you. After being severely wounded two weeks before my nineteenth birthday I had a bad time until I figured it out that nothing could happen [xiii/xiv] to me that had not happened to all men before me. Whatever I had to do men had always done. If they had done it then I could do it too and the best thing was not to worry about it.

I was very ignorant at nineteen and had read little and I remember the sudden happiness and the feeling of having a permanent protecting talisman when a young British officer I met when in the hospital first wrote out for me, so that I could remember them, these lines:

"By my troth, I care not: a man can die but once; we owe God a death . . . and let it go which way it will, he that dies this year is quit for the next."

That is probably the best thing that is written in this book and, with nothing else, a man can get along all right on that. [xiv/xxvii]

* * * * *

A good soldier does not worry. He knows that nothing happens until it actually happens and you live your life up until then. Danger only exists at the moment of danger. To live properly in war, the individual eliminates all such things as potential danger. Then a thing is only bad when it is bad. It is neither bad before nor after. Cowardice, as distinguished from panic, is almost always simply a lack of ability to suspend the functioning of the imagination. Learning to suspend your imagination and live completely in the very second of the present minute with no before and no after is the greatest gift a soldier can acquire. It, naturally, is the opposite of all those gifts a writer should have. That is what makes good writing by good soldiers such a rare thing and why it is so prized when we have it. . . .

PART FOUR

CONTEXT

AFRICA

MT. RUWENZORI

UGANDA

LAKE
VICTORIA

MT. KENYA

KENYA

SERENGETI PLAIN

Nairobi

SERENEA (SERONERA) RIVER

RIFT VALLEY

MT. KILIMANJARO

NGORONGORO CRATER

Arusha

LAKE EYASI

LAKE MANYARA

Mombasa

CONGO

TANGANYIKA

INDIAN OCEAN

RHODESIA

MILES

0   100   200   300

MOZAMBIQUE

Hemingway's Riddle of Kilimanjaro: Idea and Image *

ROBERT O. STEPHENS (1928–   ) is a professor of English at the University of North Carolina at Greensboro and the author of *Hemingway's Nonfiction: The Public Voice* (1968).

The connection between Hemingway's riddle at the opening of "The Snows of Kilimanjaro" and the story itself is tenuous at best. Nowhere in the story does author or character mention the mysterious leopard carcass which, set in such a significant place, seems to offer some key to Harry's predicament. Rather, the riddle itself states a predicament: "Kilimanjaro is a snow covered mountain 19,710 feet high, and is said to be the highest mountain in Africa. Its western summit is called the Masai 'Ngaje Ngai,' the House of God. Close to the western summit there is the dried and frozen carcass of a leopard. No one has explained what the leopard was seeking at that altitude." The closest the bedridden Harry comes to either the mountain or the carcass is in his imaginary flight on the rescue plane to Arusha.

The connection between riddle and story becomes more apparent, however, in light of Hemingway's probable source for the riddle. We know of his interest in travel books: he deals sympathetically with Kandisky's note-taking on the country and natives in *Green Hills of Africa*, and in "A Natural History of the Dead" he cites the [84/85] travels and researches of W. H. Hudson, Bishop Stanley, and Mungo Park. In a travel book by the German geographer Hans Meyer, Hemingway found the raw material for the riddle of Kilimanjaro. The first European to climb the peak of Kilimanjaro, Meyer recorded in *Across East African Glaciers* a discovery he made while approaching the crest:

We were about half-way through this terrific bit of work when we came upon what was perhaps as wonderful a discovery as any we made on Kilimanjaro. It almost savours of the fabulous, but here in this stern frostbound region, at the very summit of a mountain 20,000 feet high, we lighted on the dead body of an antelope—one of the small species we had noticed on the pasturelands below. How the animal came there it is impossible to say. In all probability it had made its way upward by the same path as ourselves at a time when the ice was covered with its winter coating of snow, and, overtaken in these lofty solitudes by the fury of a mountain-storm, had paid with its life the penalty of its adventurous curiosity.[1]

The phrasing and the discovery itself are too similar to Hemingway's to ignore.

In the book Meyer also accounts for the religious names for Kilimanjaro. To the Swahili the name means "Mountain of the spirit Njaro," a male spirit said to inhabit another mountain also known as "Kilimanjaro." The Wajagga inhabitants of the greater Kilimanjaro "have no name for the mountain as a whole, but call the ice-covered western peak 'Kibo' (the bright), and the dark rocky eastern peak 'Mawenzi' (the dark)." [2] Hemingway juxtaposes the quest of the animal and the religious significance of the mountain to imply a connection between them. The leopard approaches the bright "House of God" just as Harry approaches the "great, high, and unbelievably white . . . square top of Kilimanjaro."

[1] *Across East African Glaciers: An Account of the First Ascent of Kilimanjaro* (London, 1891), pp. 183–184.
[2] *Ibid.*, p. 297.

*Robert O. Stephens, "Hemingway's Riddle of Kilimanjaro: Idea and Image," *American Literature*, XXXII (March 1960), 84–87. Reprinted with the permission of Duke University Press and the author.

Meyer's reason for the animal's presence makes more explicit the connection between riddle and story: man's attempt to transcend his animal nature and to reach a spiritual plane of existence, no matter what the cost. Use of the thematic idea couched in the riddle, moreover, extends beyond the single story. If Hemingway anticipates the conflict of man and his animal nature in the bull fights of *The Sun* [**85/86**] *Also Rises* and *Death in the Afternoon,* he uses it most philosophically in *The Old Man and the Sea.*

Significantly also, there is a chronological correlation between the germinal ideas of the sea novel and "The Snows of Kilimanjaro." The African story was published in the August, 1936, issue of *Esquire* and was written out of Hemingway's African experience of two years before. In the May, 1936, *Esquire* Hemingway recounted the story that later became *The Old Man and the Sea:*

Another time an old man fishing alone in a skiff out of Cabanas hooked a great marlin that, on the heavy sash cord handline, pulled the skiff far out to sea. Two days later the old man was picked up by fishermen sixty miles to the eastward, the head and forward part of the marlin lashed alongside. What was left of the fish, less than half, weighed eight hundred pounds. The old man had stayed with him a day, a night, a day and another night while the fish swam deep and pulled the boat. When he had come up the old man had pulled the boat upon him and harpooned him. Lashed alongside the sharks had hit him and the old man had fought them out alone in the Gulf Stream in a skiff, clubbing them, stabbing at them, lunging at them with an oar until he was exhausted and the sharks had eaten all they could hold. He was crying in the boat when the fishermen picked him up, half crazy from his loss, and the sharks were still circling the boat.[3]

Hemingway filled out this account of man against animal instinct with the motifs of fateful choice and of search beyond ordinary limits, both implicit in the Kili-

[3] "On the Blue Water," *Esquire,* V, 184 (April, 1936).

manjaro riddle. In *The Old Man and the Sea* Santiago comes to identify himself with the great fish and observes, "His choice had been to stay in the deep dark water far out beyond all snares and traps and treacheries. My choice was to go there to find him beyond all people. Beyond all people in the world. Now we are joined together and have been since noon." And after the sharks leave only the carcass of the marlin, Santiago notes that their choice to go far out ruined them both: "You violated your luck when you went too far outside." [4]

Hemingway's reason for changing the antelope into a leopard appears outside the story. In *Green Hills of Africa* Hemingway and his gun bearer M'Cola work out an intuitive ranking of the hunted animals into the noble and the obscene. The prehistoric rhinoceros [**86/87**] and the hermaphroditic hyena are obscene; the lion, leopard, kudu, and water buffalo are noble. Also the Masai tribesmen, in whose terms the religious name of Kilimanjaro is stated in the riddle, are among the naturally noble.[5] The association of the noble felines with the extraordinary experience recurs in the sea novel as Santiago finally wants to think only of the young lions playing on the African beaches. And in "The Snows of Kilimanjaro" animal death appears as a stinking hyena at the foot of Harry's cot.

Hemingway's handling of the riddle of Kilimanjaro is significant, we see, in two respects: first, his translation of mundane fact into mythical import and, second, his extension of the myth idea while transmuting the terms of presentation for other narrative uses. The riddle serves as an index to Hemingway's craftsmanship in idea and image.

[4] *The Old Man and the Sea* (New York, 1952), pp. 55, 128.
[5] *Green Hills of Africa* (New York, 1935), pp. 37–39, 79, 221.

Across East African Glaciers: An Account of the First Ascent of Kilimanjaro *

HANS MEYER (1858–1929) was a professor of colonial geography in Leipzig, and the author of numerous books on climbing expeditions and travels in Asia, America, and Africa. In addition to *Across East African Glaciers,* he published two other books about Kilimanjaro: *To the Snow-Dome of Kilimanjaro* (1888) and *Kilimanjaro* (1900).

... A bitterly cold wind was blowing from the north, and we availed ourselves of the friendly shelter of a neighbouring rock to snatch a much-needed rest of half-an-hour. Here we watched the sun as he leaped up triumphantly from behind the rocky pinnacles of Mawenzi. The plains below were hidden by a thick layer of heavy cumulus clouds, high above which, in the south, floated distinctly marked dark flecks of cirrus, moving slowly towards the southwest. Kibo above, the plateau beneath, and Mawenzi facing us, shone grey and brown and red in the rays of the morning sun.

We continued our way upwards along ridges of weathered lava and obsidian, displaying all the colours of the rainbow in marvellously beautiful combinations. Slowly but surely we approached the ice-cap, and at last, at half-past seven, arrived at its lower limit at an altitude of 18,910 feet. Immediately above us was the great notch on the eastern side of the crater; to the left, 600 or 700 feet below, was the wall of ice which had effectually barred my progress in my former attempt to reach the summit from this side. To the right the ice extended in an unbroken line towards the north, [**182/183**] presenting a slightly overhanging series of massive cliffs of nearly uniform height.

Pausing only to get our ice-tackle in order, we commenced the ascent of the ice-cap, which at first proved so slippery and so steep that once more we were obliged to have recourse to the tedious process of hewing steps. About ten minutes of this work brought us to the notch, whence, from a different standpoint, we again had a full view of the crater. Here projecting points and bosses of rock were visible through the ice, and everything seemed to promise such easy progress that Purtscheller gave it as his opinion we should reach the cone at the bottom in an hour, and be back in camp by mid-day. A little experience of the *nieve penitente* surface of the ice ahead soon caused us to modify our sanguine expectations, and presently we were beset by a series of obstacles which sufficiently proved the wisdom of the pithy adage which forbids the counting of chickens before they are hatched.

The ice-sheet stretched in a compact mass to the foot of the small central cone below, and its surface was tremendously weathered by sun and wind. Without wasting much time in reflection, we plunged into our difficulties forthwith, and soon became involved in a chaos of ruts and rents and jagged points, amid which it was next to impossible to find a footing. Often, when we thought we had succeeded in doing so, the brittle crust

*Hans Meyer, from *Across East African Glaciers: An Account of the First Ascent of Kilimanjaro,* tr. E. H. S. Calder (London: George Philip & Son, Limited, 1891), pp. 182–184; 273; 297. Reprinted with the permission of George Philip & Son, Limited.

gave way beneath us, and we found ourselves up to the armpits, struggling to extricate ourselves from the jaws of a crevasse. Needless to say, our hands were soon bruised and bleeding, and, in spite of warm gloves, our fingers were perfectly benumbed.

We were about half-way through this terrific bit of work when we came upon what was perhaps as wonderful a discovery as any we made on Kilimanjaro. It almost savours of the fabulous, but here in this stern frost-bound region, at [183/184] the very summit of a mountain 20,000 feet high, we lighted on the dead body of an antelope—one of the small species we had noticed on the pasture-lands below. How the animal came there it is impossible to say. In all probability it had made its way upward by the same path as ourselves at a time when the ice was covered with its winter coating of snow, and, overtaken in these lofty solitudes by the fury of a mountain-storm, had paid with its life the penalty of its adventurous curiosity. [184/273]

*   *   *   *   *

Our next day's tramp of four hours, through the luxuriant valley of the Matate to the mountain of Javia, was almost like a pleasant constitutional, compared with the trying marches which had preceded it. It was more enjoyable to the booted Europeans than to the porters, however, for many of the latter were suffering from blistered feet, and limped painfully along over the rocky débris which strewed the path.

As I turned to take a farewell look backwards in the direction of the Taita wilderness, a scene of unexpected loveliness met my eye. High above the masses of cumulous clouds which drifted slowly over the steppes rose the snowy dome of Kibo, solitary, serene, majestic, yet soft and shadowy as a mirage. Involuntarily the Masai name of *Ngaje Ngai* (the house of God) rose to my lips, as I gazed in rapture on the phantom shape hanging thus suspended in mid-air. [273/297]

*   *   *   *   *

In Africa, as in other parts of the world, the greatest manifestations of volcanic activity are to be met with near the equator. There we have Kenia (18,400 feet, according to Von Höhnel), Ruwenzori (18,500 feet, according to Stanley), and Kilimanjaro (19,700 feet)—all of them close upon the average volcanic maximum, for there is no volcanic mountain on the earth's surface which attains a greater elevation than 23,000 feet. According to these figures, Kilimanjaro is the highest volcano in Africa.

"Kilimanjaro" is the name given to the mountain by the Swahili, and means "Mountain of the spirit Njaro." Njaro is a male spirit, a sort of African "Rübezahl," who also inhabits another mountain in Bondei, which is likewise called "Kilimanjaro." The inhabitants of Kilimanjaro, the Wajagga, have no name for the mountain as a whole, but call the ice-covered western peak "Kibo" (the bright), and the dark rocky eastern peak "Mawenzi" (the dark). The Swahili have adopted the name Kibo, but, following the analogy in Ki-bo and Ki-limanjaro, Mawenzi has become corrupted into Ki-mawenzi. . . .

Snows on the Equator *

H. W. TILMAN (1898–   ) served with the Royal Artillery in both World Wars. It was during his years as a farmer in Kenya, from 1919 to 1933, that he made his climbing expeditions to Mts. Kilimanjaro, Kenya, and Ruwenzori. Later in the thirties he made and wrote of similar expeditions to Mts. Everest and Nanda Devi. Since World War II, he has published numerous accounts of his travels in China, Patagonia, Antarctica, and Greenland.

. . . It was first seen in 1848 by the two missionaries Rebmann and Krapf, and was climbed for the first time by Hans Mayer and Ludwig Purtscheller in 1889. High though it is and capped with ice and snow descending as low as 16,000 feet on the south-west and to 18,500 feet on the north side, the great bulk of the mountain is more impressive than its height, for to travel round the base would involve a journey on foot of several days. The enormous base detracts from the apparent height, and this detraction is accentuated by the squat, pudding-like dome of Kibo, the highest summit. In fine weather Kibo can be seen from Nairobi, when the haze rising from the hot intervening plains blots out the lower slopes, leaving the white dome suspended in mid-air like a cloud. The Masai, who inhabit the plains between Nairobi and the mountain, call Kibo 'Ngaje Ngai'—the House of God. [42/171]

* * * * *

Looking at the two peaks of Kibo and Mawenzi and recalling our visit of 1930, I was amazed to see the very striking difference in conditions which now prevailed. [171/172] The present year of 1933 had been an exceptionally dry one throughout East Africa, so that the snow on Kibo scarcely descended further than Leopard's Point, just below the lip of the crater. Mawenzi was completely bare of snow. The steep snow gully up which we had kicked steps was rust-red rock, with the result that neither as a climb nor as a peak did it look so attractive as when draped in snow and ice.

* * * * *

The unusual absence of snow on the lower slopes made it difficult to find water. I had to search in nooks and crannies of the rocks above the caves before I could scrape together enough old snow for my wants. Next morning, carrying a light load consisting of sleeping-bag and two days' food, I started for the top before sunrise —at about half past five. In normal years the snow lies as low as 17,000 feet, but now I toiled up loose scree until Leopard's Point, just below the crater [172/173] rim, was reached. Leopard's Point is a little rocky knoll on top of which lies the desiccated remains of a leopard. I have never heard any explanation of how it came to be there, but presumably it went up of its own volition. A similar curiosity is the buffalo skeleton high up on Kenya, but that lies at a place nearly 3,000 feet lower than the leopard on Kibo.

It was delightful weather here, clear,

*H. W. Tilman, from Snows on the Equator (New York: The Macmillan Company, 1938), pp. 42, 171–173; 176–177. Reprinted with the permission of the author.

[First suggested as a source by Barney Childs, "Hemingway and the Leopard of Kilimanjaro," American Notes and Queries, II (September 1963), 3.]

sunny, windless. Below, at the 12,000 feet level, was a billowing sea of cloud which broke against the mountain, sending up wisps of mist like spray, which were in turn quickly dispersed by the sun. I seemed to be alone on an island detached from the world, floating in space on a sea of cloud. [**173/176**]

*   *   *   *   *

Romping down the slope from Leopard's Point was a pleasant change, and, arriving at the top hut about eight, I had breakfast there before pushing on to Peters's [hut], where the night was spent. Lunch next day was eaten at Marungu with mine host, who was with [**176/177**] difficulty convinced of the fact that thirty hours ago I had been on the summit.

Hoping to reach Nairobi in the day, I made an early start, and, soon after leaving Marungu, passed my stranded motorist of Namanga. He was still on his way to the coast to enjoy the three remaining days of his fortnight's holiday.

I failed to reach Nairobi, and spent the night in the car in the middle of the Game Reserve. As I sat at dusk by my fire, listening to the mournful cry of a hyena, the rays of a sun, which for me had already set, picked out, high up in a darkening sky, Kibo's snowy dome. . . .

[The Leopard of Kilimanjaro: Dr. Richard Reusch's Letter to the Editor] *

RICHARD REUSCH, D.D. (1891–   ), soldier, historian, missionary, and mountaineer, taught at the University of Dorpat and served in the war of Independence of Estonia and Finland. In 1922, he founded the Lutheran Church of Northern Tanganyika and served for many years as President of the Federation of Mission Churches. In 1954 he left Tanganyika to join the faculty of Gustavus Adolphus College, in St. Peter, Minnesota, from which he retired in 1966. Among his many books are: in German, The Messianic Prophecies of Micah (1921) and The Islam in East Africa and Its Secret Societies (1931); in English, History of East Africa (1954) and World Religions (1955); and, in Kiswahili, Introduction into the New Testament (1929), Introduction into the Old Testament (1933), and Commentary on Matthew (1937).

Dear Professor Howell:

. . . When I went up in September, 1926, for the first time, I found the leopard curled up and dead on the ice a few feet below the Leopard Point. On the glacier nearby I found a frozen mountain goat. Apparently the leopard followed the goat, trying to catch it. A snow storm developed, accompanied by a heavy fog. According to the habit of the leopards, he curled up to keep himself warm and to wait for the fog to disappear. The goat, pursued by him, went to the Ratzel glacier and froze there, some 300 feet away from the leopard.

I put the dead leopard on a small rock, looking down into the crater. In July, 1927, on my return from my second ascent, I cut one of his ears off to show to my friends. We called the point "Leopard Point." This name was accepted by the East African Mountain Club, which I founded a short time later, as the official name of the place. About 18 years later, during my 50th climb to the very top (Kaiser Wilhelm Point) of the mountain, I found only his skeleton and pieces of skin. The leopard had dried up in the high altitude. The last time, when I made my 65th ascent to the top in 1954, I found only a few scattered bones.

A legend developed among the Wachaga and Masai concerning this leopard. There is a glacier resembling an ice-dome inside the southern crater of Kibo, the higher peak of Kilimanjaro. The Abyssinians believe that their great King Menelik I, the son of Solomon and the Queen of Sheba, was buried under this ice-dome. After having conquered Kenya, Somaliland, and Northern Tanganyika, he felt that he must die. On his way back to Abyssinia he climbed Kibo with his treasures and some slaves, died on its top and sleeps there, until the old glory of Abyssinia is restored. The ice-dome is supposed to be his last resting place. The

Editor's note: I learned, in reading a note by R. W. Bevis, M. A. J. Smith, Jr., and G. Brose, "Leopard Tracks in 'The Snows . . . ' " in American Notes & Queries, VI (April 1968), 115, that Dr. Reusch had mentioned the leopard in an article entitled "Mt. Kilimanjaro and Its Ascent," first published in 1928, but recently reprinted in Tanganyika Notes and Records, No. 64 (March 1965). I wrote Dr. Reusch, asking for additional information about the leopard. This is an excerpt from his reply.

*Richard Reusch. Printed here for the first time with the permission of Dr. Richard Reusch.

Abyssinian Emperors traditionally kept tame lions in their palace gardens, but Menelik I also had tame leopards. One of them, his master's pet, supposedly followed his master to the crater and died there, guarding the entrance to the burial place of the dead king. When I told this story to the Wachaga and Masai, they asked me whether I found some traces of the dead king. I told them that I found no traces of him, but that I found a frozen leopard at the entrance of the crater. They apparently identified the frozen leopard with the pet leopard of Menelik I. . . .

With my best compliments I am, Professor Howell,

Most sincerely yours,
Dr. R. Reusch

Vivienne de Watteville, Hemingway's Companion on Kilimanjaro *

ROBERT W. LEWIS, JR. (1930–   ) is an assistant professor of English at the University of Texas and the author of *Hemingway on Love* (1965).

. . . Two books that he [Hemingway] almost certainly read were Vivienne de Watteville's *Speak to the Earth* and Hans Meyer's *Across East African Glaciers*. In "Hemingway's Riddle of Kilimanjaro: Idea and Image" (*American Literature*, 32, March, 1960), Robert O. Stephens has pointed out that the epigraph about the frozen leopard is a version of an anecdote in Meyer's book. Evidence in the University of Texas manuscript of "The Snows" indicates that Hemingway must also have read the Watteville book shortly after its publication in 1935 and at the very time he was working on his own African book and stories. Not only was he interested in the subjects of East Africa and big game from a sportsman's point of view, but he was first of all a writer, and Africa was something he knew; it was, in a sense, new "material." And from that material he was shaping *Green Hills of Africa* and two great short stories. He would be interested in professionally useful information that he himself, after all, might have overlooked or not known of during his relatively short sojourn. Furthermore, *Speak to the Earth* was published with a preface by Edith Wharton, a first-rate American writer and, like Hemingway, also a Scribners author. It is conceivable that Maxwell Perkins, Hemingway's editor at Scribners, who regularly obtained books of interest for his authors, had sent Hemingway volumes relevant to work-in-progress.

But the specific reason for examining *Speak to the Earth* is the nearly conclusive evidence of the Texas manuscript with an epigraph from that book. Immediately after the title of the Texas manuscript is the well known "riddle" paragraph about the frozen leopard. Immediately following that epigraph is this quotation:

> "The difficulites, he said, were not in the actual climbing. It was a long grind, and success depended not on skill, but on one's ability to withstand the high altitude. His parting words were that I must make the attempt soon, before there was any risk of the rains setting in."

> V. DE WATTEVILLE

In the left-hand margin is written "Maybe better out.   E.H." **[75/76]**

Presumably Hemingway first intended the passage (from page 129 of *Speak to the Earth*) as a second epigraph to "The Snows," then later questioned it. The passage was not printed with the first *Esquire* version of the story (in the August 1936 issue), nor has it ever subsequently been used. The then editor and now publisher of *Esquire,* Arnold Gingrich, recalls that he felt the two epigraphs were confusing, and he opted for the first one. In any case, Hemingway's marginalium indicates that he was amenable to the omission. The first paragraph of the Texas manuscript then became the four-sentence epigraph that was Hemingway's loose adaptation, in his own words, of a passage from Hans Meyer's *Across East African Glaciers*. This paragraph, printed in italics and describ-

*Robert W. Lewis, Jr., from "Vivienne de Watteville, Hemingway's Companion on Kilimanjaro," *The Texas Quarterly*, IX (Winter 1966), 75–85. Reprinted with the permission of *The Texas Quarterly*.

ing Mount Kilimanjaro and the frozen leopard near its summit, has preceded each published version of the story and has, incidentally, stimulated considerable discussion and speculation.

As Arnold Gingrich has suggested in a letter to Max Westbrook and me, one reason for omission of the Watteville epigraph was that had both epigraphs been retained, an awkward amount of "business" would have divided the title from the story proper. Two paragraphs of three and four sentences would be an unusually long prelude before the story proper, which though called in *Esquire* "A Long Story" was still just a "short story." But even this loose requirement of convention aside, a further more important reason for omitting the Watteville epigraph is the well-known iceberg principle of Hemingway's esthetics. Like the iceberg, seven-eighths of whose bulk was concealed beneath the surface of the water, an author's total meaning should be partly concealed, hinted at, or implied. "If a writer of prose knows enough about what he is writing about he may omit things that he knows and the reader, if the writer is writing truly enough, will have a feeling of these things as strongly as though the writer had stated them." (*Death in the Afternoon*) Hemingway's was the art of omission, not, as Leon Edel has disparagingly put it, the art of evasion; and the Watteville epigraph combined with his own geographical description and a version of Meyer's ecological riddle would have made his intentions too obvious, his meaning too explicit—though perhaps such an assumption by Hemingway would have meant his underestimating the complexity of his story and overestimating the perceptiveness of his readers. The Watteville epigraph and its immediate context in what would have been a readily identifiable book would then have seemed to provide an answer to "what the leopard was seeking at that altitude."

Vivienne de Watteville had been raised in Norway and in her youth had accompanied her zoologist father on East African collecting safaris, on one of which he died after a mauling by a lion. This courageous and self-reliant woman returned to an Africa she had fallen in love with, and from her experiences there came *Out in the Blue* (1927) and *Speak to the Earth* (1935), honest books that might well have appealed to the omnivorously reading Hemingway. [**76/77**]

In *Speak to the Earth* Vivienne de Watteville recounts her wanderings on the high plains near Mount Kilimanjaro and on Mount Kenya. She had a troop of African servants with her, but she was the only European and the only woman in the safari on which she hoped to photograph (as Harry in "The Snows" did) wild animals at close range and also to befriend the potentially dangerous beasts. The presence of Mount Kilimanjaro is important in the first part of the book. Hans Meyer, author of the source for the first or "leopard" epigraph, was a scientist, a geographer, but Watteville was something of a poet, a lover of nature. To her the mountain was a glorious sight from the hot steaming plains below, and it was a "great and splendid" challenge to climb it. In Hemingway's story neither the leopard nor Harry, the leopard's counterpart, was seeking any *thing* on the summit. Like Watteville they perhaps felt the magnetic, poetic, even mystic lure of the awesome peak standing in magnificent relief to the surrounding plains. They perhaps wished to climb it, each in his fashion, simply because it was there, not—for Meyer's reason —because it was unexplored and uncharted. And mountains were the place of challenge where one worked "the fat off his soul the way a fighter went into the mountains to work and train." In any case, Watteville's epigraph would have alluded to the disinterested and idealistic nature of both the totemistic leopard's and Harry's ascents of Kilimanjaro, and it would have emphasized the overhanging importance of time. There would have been no provocative riddle to foreshadow the story, or perhaps the reader would focus on the Watteville epigraph rather than the story itself as the answer to the riddle. Further, there would have been less tension in the concluding pages between the descriptions of Harry's imaginary flight and his actual death. In *Speak to the Earth* reality or the material world (in the forms of the tangible mountain and the historical Watteville as a real though amateurish mountain climber) provides references for Hemingway's concern with a reality beyond history. In a sense, the "real" means of Harry's fictive and unreal ascent are the stories he remembers and that, in a failure of stewardship, he did not write. Hemingway focuses the reader's attention on the concrete things of the physical world, on the local emotions of experience, and yet the result is a strong sense of a large and profound reality. Consider especially the oddity that Kilimanjaro is mentioned only once in the story, and then at the end of the imaginary flight. Yet the title hangs over the entire story, just as Kilimanjaro dominates the real African landscape, and no sensitive reader is ignorant of the mountain's significance by the time of his second reading.

Granting the possibility of such reasons for omitting the Watteville epigraph—as being excessive "business" and violating the iceberg esthetic—it is possible to examine Watteville's two African books for further evidence to indicate Hemingway's intentions, and if such evidence was consistent with intelligent approaches to the story, one could conclude that the Watteville epigraph was not editorially omitted because of irrelevance. The relevancy of it would then lead to a more thoroughgoing and complete critical understanding of the story and, more generally, Hemingway at large. Such are the assumptions of this essay, and the reading of *Speak to the* [**77/78**] *Earth* (and to a lesser extent *Out of the Blue*) unquestionably provided Hemingway more than a source of mere "color" and information. Watteville's books are better than the run-of-the-mill adventure and travel yarns, but she does not have the imagination to vitalize herself or her Africa as Hemingway vitalizes Harry and his Africa. Like many another creative writer, however, Hemingway was able to see the gold in plain narrative. Watteville had a mind and sensitivity, but the context of her epigraph is matter of fact; in the Hemingway story her sentences take on crucial and symbolic meaning. (I am, of course, here making a distinction between the symbolic action of literature and what may very well be equally symbolic action in life, particularly in this instance of Watteville's "irrational" desire to climb mountains.)

Certain important and recurrent ideas in *Speak to the Earth* and *Out in the Blue* are implicit ideas in "The Snows" and, to some degree, in much of Hemingway's work. I emphasize the African short story because first of all the link is strongest and most clearly validated by the Texas manuscript, and secondly "The Snows" provides a good and brief illustration, yet the application of our understanding (in the light of suggestions by Watteville) is to Hemingway as a whole. For instance, both "The Snows" and Watteville are concerned with the nature of death, and clearly that subject is recurrent throughout Hemingway's work.

The strongest parallel between Watteville and "The Snows" is reflected in the omitted epigraph and its immediate context in *Speak to the Earth*. Watteville wanted desperately to climb Kilimanjaro; so apparently did the leopard of the published epigraph; and so subconsciously and metaphorically did Harry—in that he wanted to "work the fat off his soul," even though he never mentions or thinks of the mountain during the course of the story. For all three, the mountain is, if not actually symbolic, a representative lure. While it may not be visible literally, its felt presence dominates the worlds of Watteville, the leopard, and Harry. These figures know its domination, in purity and eternity, of the corrupt, disease-ridden, hate-ridden, sweltering, life-full, death-full plains—the everyday world, life in its usual sense as bounded by birth and death.

Like the archetypal holy mountain, it is the center of this earth of hyena and vulture on the one hand, and noble kudu and lion on the other. (Other Hemingway bestiaries, incidentally, like *The Old Man and the Sea* and *Green Hills of Africa,* similarly divide animals into either the rapacious, foul, cowardly, and villainous or the noble, courageous, and "manly.") But this holy mountain is above and apart from the earth too, and it permits no animal to survive in the glacial thin air on its topmost height, the point most remote from earth and closest to heaven or transcendence. At one point Watteville associates Kilimanjaro with heaven, and Hemingway initially tells us that one name for its topmost peak is the House of God. (Hans Meyer and Robert O. Stephens remind us that the western summit of the twin-peaked Kilimanjaro is also called "Kibo," meaning "the bright," as opposed to the eastern peak, "Mawenzi," "the dark." For mythic and symbolic purposes, it was thoughtful of the Great Geologist to place the higher ice-covered "bright" peak in the west, the direction of death, and the dark, rock-covered [**78/79**] opposite peak of the mythic world in the east.) Watteville longs to climb Kilimanjaro even though she knows that her desire is irrational (just as the leopard's desire was inexplicable), but Kilimanjaro is across the border in Tanganyika, and the Kenyan colonial authorities cannot extend permission to climb it. As death and "ascension" are denied living man, so Watteville cannot cross an imaginary but nonetheless potent geographical frontier. Man longs for this huge tumescent mass of a death mountain, for the eternal snows, for the preserving frost that holds the leopard's body forever inviolate. But in life such transcendence is denied. In the first half of *Speak to the Earth,* Watteville tells of her wanderings on the high plains north of Kilimanjaro, of her sufferings and joys in the midst of hot teeming life, and of her recurrent desire to climb the mountain. Then in the second half of the book she reluctantly leaves the shadow of Kiliman-jaro and settles for Mount Kenya, a very slightly lower mountain that she is permitted to climb and live on the slopes of, and consequently she comes to have a self-ennobling love for this second mountain. In a sense, she abandons a Manichean dualism (symbolized in her life on the plains and her unfulfilled desire for the mountain) for a less ambitious goal and a less troubled soul that places her in unity with life.

Thus the paradox of life as conveyed by Watteville's books and Hemingway's story: one must aspire to unity with nature by a life-long struggle, always toughening the body, mind, and spirit to overcome countless obstacles to this transcendent unity of the one with the all. Self-discipline and love are the chief means to this unity. Yet no amount of courage, control, and love can conquer death, for man is ultimately limited and he cannot count on any paradise beyond life. Nature and luck determine whatever actual success he may have, and thus one must also give up struggling and learn to submit. Essentially, perhaps, this paradox of struggle and submission is Oriental or "primitive" in that it is far from apathy or total passivity but is, rather, an activity of the self that tends to loss of the self *with* or *in* nature rather than a struggling of the self *against* nature. As Harry (in "The Snows") reviews his past life, he remembers it initially as a happy one in which he "lost himself"—a significant and appropriate expression— in his work and his first love. But when he had success in his writing, that is, when his early "struggles" were fruitful, he found himself, he became self-conscious, lionized, susceptible to flattery. His life was filled with activity, but he was no longer doing the honest work that was an overcoming of obstacles, chief among which was selfhood or even selfishness.

Out in the Blue tells of Watteville's first encounter with Africa, and the cost of it was her father's life. Yet she grew strong as a result of this loss and suffering, as Hemingway had said in *A Farewell to Arms* that one could grow strong in the broken places. The "blue" of her title is the nature of sun, hill, mist, sounds, wind, dew, and voices, and "if one did truly belong to those things, they would never give one up, and through all this [trouble], the 'blue' would still be there, waiting."

"Here, in these gentle solitudes, one came to understand that eternity did not necessarily mean the uncounted ages, but might be comprehended and possessed a [**79/80**] hundred times over, in the colors of a sunset, or the dawn, or in the calm outline of the immutable mountains. And to learn that there was no need to be an infinitesimal spark, bound by time and space, but that one might be spread far and wide, a part of the earth, and the sky, and all the elements, was to learn freedom."

Harry of "The Snows" had also had a feeling of freedom when he was first in Africa, and like Watteville, he had returned to recapture the past, to "come out here to start again." But most ironically, he cannot let the "blue" work its medicine. He cannot "work the fat off his soul." He does intermittently see the "pleasant camp" and the "good water," and he can momentarily appreciate Helen's charms and virtues, but his attempt to recondition his soul has failed. He has carelessly got a fatal wound, and "huge, filthy" vultures and whimpering, scavenging hyenas skirt the edge of his "blue," and he has no Edenic Eve, but merely a "rich bitch." If he cannot have Africa, where else can he turn? Most ironically, of course, the other past is fled too, but he pursues it in his artist's imagination to the good times of Paris, to adventures that he knew could have meant something, that he could have written about meaningfully.

Watteville, too, had returned to Africa with some apprehension. For a "realist" the past cannot be recaptured. Any attempt to abstract the virtues of the past, whether of ancient Greece or of one's youth, is extremely hazardous, perhaps "romantic." In the interlude between experience and re-experience the imagination vivifies the dramatic, or the merely colorful, and conveniently ignores the painful, the boring, and the gross. Yet man is the historical animal, and the writer is of that subspecies for whom time not only is of concern but also is the very essence of his story. Existence is built. The feeling man projects and remembers, and in so doing he contrasts the present with the imagined future and the equally imagined past.

Thus the consciousness in modern literature and in Hemingway particularly of time, as indicated by several changes in the final manuscript version of "The Snows." The changes, though slight, suggest Hemingway's attempt to emphasize the contrast between the present and the past (by adding "then" and "now"). Another group of changes adds the phrase "he remembered" or "he thought" in the italicized passages to suggest that those scenes exist in Harry's mind rather than in a general impersonal history.

As noted above, Watteville had a sense of the permanency of the "blue" that would always be waiting: "one came to understand . . . eternity," she writes. Hemingway's most powerful single image of time was to be the Gulf Stream that figures in *To Have and Have Not* (1937), *The Old Man and the Sea* (1952), and, in an interesting geographical shift, most prominently in *Green Hills of Africa*, published a year before "The Snows." Compare these two passages, the first from *Green Hills of Africa,* the second from *Out in the Blue.*

"... when, on the sea, you are alone with it [the indefinable feeling that comes to one when he writes well or works well] and know that this Gulf Stream you are [**80/81**] living with, knowing, learning about, and loving, has moved, as it moves, since before man, and that it has gone by the shoreline of that long, beautiful, unhappy island since before Columbus sighted it and that the things you find out about it, and those that have always lived in it are permanent and of value because that stream will flow, as it has flowed, after the Indians, after the Spaniards, after the British, after the Americans and after all the Cubans and all the systems of governments, the richness, the poverty, the martyrdom, the sacrifice and the venality and the cruelty are all gone as the high-piled scow of garbage, bright-colored, white-flecked, ill-smelling, . . . spills off its load into the blue water . . .; all this well shepherded by the boats of the garbage pickers . . . as interested, as intelligent, and as accurate as historians; they have the viewpoint; the stream, with no visible flow, takes five loads of this [garbage] a day . . . and in ten miles along the coast it is as clear and blue and unimpressed as it was ever before the tug hauled out the scow; and the palm fronds of our victories, the worn light bulbs of our discoveries and the empty condoms of our great loves float with no significance against one single, lasting thing—the stream."

And now Watteville: the Nile River

"flowed by so placidly, neither hurrying nor tarrying, and the little Nile cabbages floated down, eddying in the current, and slipping by and out of sight. Thus might you muse upon it for a few brief hours, or for a thousand years; and it might stand almost for a symbol of time itself, running down through the ages; here still in its beginning, its banks wild and untrodden, its people primitive as the first man, anon flowing through the desert till it flows at last under bridges, and past great civilisations, old and new. About it, and about those natives who sat watching it, there was the same strong patience that would finally conquer all. It is this very patience that is at first so exasperating about Africa and Africans, a kind of apathy and indifference that is callous, and a fatalism that enrages. Yet there, perhaps, lay the solution. Africa is too mighty for anything so brittle as impatience, and one's strength lies not in pitting oneself against it, but in ranging oneself upon the same side."

The similarities in both idea and style provide a strong suggestion of a source for Hemingway's well known image of implacable yet restorative, curing, guiding nature. The image of the Gulf Stream is also an indication of Hemingway's recurrent theme of the dominion of time. Many of his very titles emphasize the concern: *In Our Time, The Sun Also Rises, A Farewell to Arms, Death in the Afternoon,* and *For Whom the Bell Tolls,* not to mention short story titles like "The Short Happy Life of Francis Macomber" or, more importantly, novels and stories in which transitions or changes are crucial such as the group of initiation stories like "Macomber" and "The Killers" and reflective stories like "Soldier's Home" and "Fathers and Sons."

More to the point, of course, is "The Snows," and time figures in that story in at [81/82] least two ways also suggested in Watteville. At one point in *Speak to the Earth,* Watteville contracts malaria (compare Harry's gangrene), and she describes her mind as having "floated away independently" to scenes of her past life. She also had hallucinations of irrational impressions followed by periods of great quiet, refreshment, and happiness—just the state suggested by Harry's imagined flight to death at the end of the story. The shared mental condition of Watteville and Harry is not exceptional, since with extreme fevers such states of mind are not unusual. But the italicized portions of "The Snows" are very important to the story; it would be completely different without them (and considerably less of a story), for the dimension of time has become crucial for Harry. Further, his safari, like Watteville's, was undertaken in an attempt to recapture the past. In Watteville's case, she had literally left her greatly loved father in Africa when he had been killed by a lion. Harry had left his moral and esthetic courage somewhere in the past, and he desired to return to what had been the happiest time of his life, his first safari to Africa when he was writing well and had not sold out to the comforts that Helen and her money and her talented body had brought him. Watteville thinks that perhaps it is foolish to attempt to recover the past; her beloved father is dead; she is not in as good physical condition as on her first trip with him; her spirit is eager, but her flesh is weak. Harry's bitterness and nasty disposition result from similar weaknesses and his suspicion of the futility of his effort. It is too late. He will never redeem himself and his art. Once corrupted, talent is flown.

The losses of talent and love in Hemingway parallel Watteville's losses of health, father, and, momentarily, courage. Hemingway's version is much more artistically conceived, but the function of time is essentially the same with both writers. Time is both tyrannical and but the stream they go a-fishing in, in Thoreau's phrase. Time is part of nature, Watteville's "blue," and nature limits the boundless desires of man, as it had limited to the extreme of death the leopard's will.

Both Watteville and Hemingway recognize an ultimate and irreconcilable gap between man (specifically man's will) and nature. Watteville remarks, "All the love and fearlessness in the world would not win the beasts [man-eating lions] over from acting according to their nature." And later, "Conquering a peak is, I think, only a phrase, and no one ever meant it. For the mountain itself has so much to do with it, and can at any moment turn you back. . . ." Man is merely a puny creature with an overdeveloped mentality; he sees challenges in nature all around him, and at times he is fooled into seeing himself as nature's master. As the omitted epigraph suggests, mere animal hardihood or biological adaptation and timeliness matter more than skill.

Yet while time and the nature of things —"reality"—limit, frustrate, and defeat man, freeze him to death, lion-maul him to death, or inflict a seemingly minor but ultimately fatal thorn scratch—man irrationally struggles. His will *may* remain indomitable, and it is with this quality compounded of endurance, discipline, and [82/83] resistance, whether to nature or to an encroaching *nada,* that Watteville is perhaps most pertinent to Hemingway in general and "The Snows" in particular.

Watteville's own father provided her a remarkable example of endurance in his own death: he was clawed, slashed, ripped by a lion but walked for over two hours rather than be carried or have his daughter sent a message of the accident and be upset. Then he told her, " 'The lion has got me this time,' " and he never complained. (*Out in the Blue*) In a further incidental but interesting parallel, Watteville writes that after her father's death, "All through the night I watched, and the hyenas came so close that, sitting on the floor by B's [her father Bernard's] bed, I could see their ears outlined against the stars. . . ."

Earlier Watteville had mentioned a wounded hyena "snarling and burying its fangs into its fore-paws." In "The Snows" Harry says that death "can have a wide snout like a hyena," and at his death a hyena prowls outside his tent making strange sounds.

Nature too provides object lessons of endurance everywhere in the cycle of changing seasons and the life and death of plants and animals. The lure of Africa for both Harry and Hemingway was similar to its attraction for Watteville, in the same way that wild, abundant nature has been restorative and creative for many American authors as different as Bryant, Cooper, Thoreau, Melville, and Twain. After Watteville's father's death, she reasoned that if this non-human nature of the vital, game-teeming East African highland "could go on just the same, then was that crushing impotence of death overcome. And if I could carry on without outside help, then still it [the procuring of specimens for mounting] would be his [her father's] work." (*Out in the Blue*)

Of course, her safaris in themselves demonstrate her endurance of a physical sort, which is not unimportant to Hemingway, witness the finely ironic stories of endurance like "Fifty Grand" and "The Undefeated." But sheer animal hardihood is not present in human beings, perhaps cannot be present in refined sensibilities, without a corresponding and reinforcing moral endurance, a kind of spiritual belief or faith that makes the body want to endure. In a reflective digression, Watteville wrote, "Love that endures through marriage [as if marriage were like a tough safari!] is something which is quite unmistakable and sent from Heaven. Being poor, enduring hardship, all is bearable where love is." (*Speak*) The quote is redolent of the spirit of Hemingway's early days in Paris as he recalls them in *A Moveable Feast*. "The Snows," interestingly enough, contains scenes that are duplicated in *A Moveable Feast,* . . . but the tone of Harry's reminiscences is not so much nostalgic as bitter. He has not "endured" with his "loves"· who have been too numerous and too shallow. Nor will he live to make those loves endure in stories, as Hemingway finally did. In a *Paris Review* interview published in 1958, Hemingway said, "Survival, with honor, that outmoded and all-important word, is as difficult as ever and as all-important to a writer. Those who do not last are always more beloved since no one has to see them in their [83/84] long, dull, unrelenting, no quarter given and no quarter received, fights that they make to do something as they believe it should be done before they die."

Hemingway's success where Harry failed is a result of more than endurance, however. After all, Harry fails to endure because he dies from an accident; we might as well be generous in believing that had he lived he might have redeemed his dissipated career. Hemingway's career, however, was under the control of a discipline that lapsed, if at all, only momentarily; his comments on writing are generally and remarkably free of a record or sense of the torment that many writers experience in trying to "get going." He was far from being an automatic writer, but at the same time he apparently had a virtually military discipline, a habit of mind regarding writing. Nor is it farfetched to note that the disciplines of sport that so absorbed Hemingway are parallel to those of writing. At least the similarity was often present in Hemingway's own mind when he would think of himself as being in training to beat Turgenev or Maupassant, or defending his own championship in later novels. Harry regards his safari as preparation for a return to serious, honest writing by training like a boxer, working the fat off his soul as he toughens his body. Watteville regarded Africa in a similar way; it was a place to toughen the body, mind, and spirit. In this training camp, one underwent the discipline of hunting in which one had "to learn when to deny yourself that glorious madness, when your heart beats in your ears and you pant with fear and excitement, when you are terrif-

ically frightened, and yet somehow detached and unafraid." (*Out in the Blue*) Is not this feeling of a great emotion that is necessarily under control very much the feeling of the creative writer?

A third quality that Watteville and Hemingway recognized in common is closely akin to endurance and discipline, but it is not passive like endurance nor controlled like discipline. Watteville thought that struggle was also necessary in order for one to be happy; mere passive endurance was not satisfying. As love cannot exist without hate and violence, so happiness cannot exist without a certain tension; one had also to resist, to risk, and to overcome. This is an idea pervasive in Hemingway's work. In "The Snows" Harry's succumbing to the fleshly pleasures of riches and rich women was the very cause of his failure as a writer. Helen's wealth was the armour that shielded him from risk and, paradoxically, killed him because danger was as much the creator's medium as were words.

> Life . . . is glorious only when you live it dangerously, accepting the challenge with glad faith, risking all, giving all. . . . Nothing is securely your own, neither life, love, money nor possessions, unless you are prepared at any moment to give them up. . . . this is the root of all belief. (*Speak to the Earth*)

Watteville's omitted epigraph emphasized the idea of endurance—"one's ability to withstand"—but on the same page that describes the plan of ascent of Kilimanjaro, Watteville wrote that the "insuperable barriers of jungle, . . . the snowy dome itself" could be conquered. (*Speak*) Conquering the unconquerable is the contra-[84/85]diction that Harry faces in the conflict of his will against his nature and the accidents of life. It is the conflict that is similarly resolved in another short story, "The Undefeated." It is the conflict that marks the conclusion of every one of Hemingway's novels: the hero has lost, one way or another, but he has also triumphed. To interpret these similar conclusions as evidence of a Hemingway death wish, as some critics have done, is to miss the point. Like the leopard, the Hemingway hero may lose his life, but he gains his salvation through resistance to the nature of things, to pain, to the common opinion of a weaker mankind, to the easy way out. Certain resistances, like Robert Jordan's of *For Whom the Bell Tolls,* are more noble, less ironic than others, such as Jack Brennan's in "Fifty Grand," but each hero must risk and struggle to overcome. Harry's victory is reduced to an imaginary flight, but we note that it is over a series of obstacles before he can emerge through the rainstorm and the clouds to see the summit of Kilimanjaro. In his mind he creates the barrier that he had avoided in his later life. . . .

PART FIVE

CRITICISM

"Members of the Swedish Academy, Ladies and Gentlemen:

Having no facility for speech-making and no command of oratory nor any domination of rhetoric, I wish to thank the administrators of the generosity of Alfred Nobel for this prize.

No writer who knows the great writers who did not receive the prize can accept it other than with humility. There is no need to list these writers. Everyone here may make his own list according to his knowledge and his conscience.

It would be impossible for me to ask the Ambassador of my country to read a speech in which a writer said all of the things which are in his heart. Things may not be immediately discernible in what a man writes, and in this sometimes he is fortunate; but eventually they are quite clear and by these and the degree of alchemy that he possesses he will endure or be forgotten.

Writing, at its best, is a lonely life. Organizations for writers palliate the writer's loneliness but I doubt if they improve his writing. He grows in public stature as he sheds his loneliness and often his work deteriorates. For he does his work alone and if he is a good enough writer he must face eternity, or the lack of it, each day.

For a true writer each book should be a new beginning where he tries again for something that is beyond attainment. He should always try for something that has never been done or that others have tried and failed. Then sometimes, with great luck, he will succeed.

How simple the writing of literature would be if it were only necessary to write in another way what has been well written. It is because we have had such great writers in the past that a writer is driven far out past where he can go, out to where no one can help him.

I have spoken too long for a writer. A writer should write what he has to say and not speak it. Again I thank you."

Ernest Hemingway, *in absentia*, Stockholm, December 10, 1954; from *Les Prix Nobel en 1954* (Stockholm: Imprimerie Royale P. A. Norstedt & Soner, 1955), pp. 54–55.

Dangerous Game *

CARLOS BAKER. For information about the author, see "The Slopes of Kilimanjaro," reprinted on p. 55.

In the other two stories [i.e., other than *Green Hills of Africa*] which grew out of his African adventure, Hemingway abandoned his experimental attempt to see whether an "absolutely true book" like *The Green Hills of Africa* could compete on terms of equality with a work of the imagination. In "The Short Happy Life of Francis Macomber" and "The Snows of Kilimanjaro" he was still determined to tell "the truth"; but now he was ready to invent the characters, and to imagine the circumstances in which they were to be entangled. The circumstances in these two stories differ markedly. At the same time they share certain inward thematic stresses. Both deal, for example, though in varying ways, with the achievement and loss of moral manhood. Both look further into the now familiar men-without-women theme. The focal point in each is the corrupting power of women and money, two of the forces aggressively men- [186/187] tioned in *The Green Hills of Africa* as impediments to American writing men.

Francis Macomber does not write. He is a wealthy American sportsman hunting the Tanganyika plains with his wife. But he must nevertheless wrestle with problems relating to women, money, and moral manhood. Easily the most unscrupulous of Hemingway's fictional females, Margot Macomber covets her husband's money but values even more her power over him. To Wilson, the Macombers' paid white hunter, who is drawn very reluctantly into the emotional mess of a wrecked marriage, Margot exemplifies most of the American wives he has met in the course of his professional life. Although his perspectives are limited to the international sporting set, the indictment is severe. These women, he reflects, are "the hardest in the world; the hardest, the cruelest, the most predatory, and the most attractive, and their men have softened or gone to pieces nervously as they have hardened." [34] With Margot in mind, this story might well have carried the title which Hemingway attached to one of his despatches from Tanganyika to *Esquire*: "Notes on Dangerous Game." The lion and the buffalo are vanquishable in a way that Margot is not.

Too much money and a woman also underlie the predicament of Harry, the dying author in "The Snows of Kilimanjaro." Having given up to a luxurious way of life by marrying wealth and then growing into complete dependence on it, he has died artistically long before his physical death. What harrows him more than the knowledge of approaching dissolution is the consciousness of all the literary riches, none of them committed to paper, which will go with him underground. Worst of all are the sharply etched memories of his former life—Liberty, Integrity, Opportunity—qualities which were all once joyously owned and now are all irrecoverably lost.

So both stories are moral tragedies tipped with irony. Macomber dies at the very moment he is commencing to live. Harry's death by gangrene symbolizes all spiritual suicides among American writers.

[34] *First 49*, p. 107.

*Carlos Baker, "Dangerous Game," *Hemingway: The Writer as Artist* (Princeton, New Jersey: Princeton University Press, 1963), pp. 186–191. Reprinted with the permission of Princeton University Press.

"We destroy them in many ways," said Hemingway [**187/188**] sardonically in *The Green Hills of Africa*. "First, economically. They make money . . . increase their standard of living and . . . are caught. They have to write to keep up their establishment, their wives, and so on, and they write slop . . . not on purpose, but because it is hurried. . . . Then, once they have betrayed themselves, they justify it and you get more slop." [35] Whether through women or the desire for money, self-betrayal is what kills a man before he has lived out his time. Women and money are nothing but instruments and agents: they exist, sometimes passively, sometimes aggressively, to help the individual writer in his moral self-destruction. If he surrenders, the fault is his own. The emphasis on the value of integrity in these short stories suggests that they may be thought of as two more chapters in the history of Hemingway's artistic obsessions.

The happy life of Francis Macomber begins on the plains of East Africa and lasts about thirty minutes. The tall young man has previously disgraced himself before his wife, his British white hunter, and his gun-bearers, by ignominious flight from a wounded and charging lion. Besides the loss of his own self-respect, such as it was, the extreme mental tortures of the experience include the barbed and vicious scorn of his wife, the lifted eyebrows and unspoken insults of the white hunter Wilson, and the visible disapproval of the native boys in his entourage. After a night of torment, during which he is obliged to watch his wife sleepily returning from the Englishman's tent, the party goes after buffalo. Since the wife knows her husband for a coward, she seems to have him where she wants him, which is under her thumb.

Suddenly, in the midst of the second day's shooting and with the white hunter as an aid, Macomber loses his fear. His wife at once senses and hates this change because it undermines her power. But Wilson silently welcomes Macomber into manhood, and together they enter the tall

[35] *GHOA*, p. 23.

grass after one of the wounded buffalo, leaving the wife behind them in the open car.

Almost immediately the buffalo charges. Fearless and happy in its path stands Macomber, a coward no longer, reveling in his new-found self-trust, firing repeatedly until the buffalo is practically upon him. Then a bullet from his wife's Mannlicher plows [**188/189**] through his skull from back to front and the short happy life is over.

The great technical virtue of this story —and it is one of Hemingway's favorites possibly for this reason—is the development of an emotional intensity to a degree seldom approached in modern literature. The ragged feelings generated by the lion-incident and verbalized in a kind of noon-day nightmare during the conversations in the dining-tent, are just short of unendurable to any who have entered into the spirit of the situation. Yet the tension actually mounts when, during the next day's shooting, we watch the Macombers in their contest for the possession of a soul.

Hemingway silently points up this contest by the varying positions of the central trio in their boxlike open car. On the way to the lion, Macomber sits in front, with Margot and Wilson in the back. After that day's débâcle, Macomber slumps in the back seat beside his frozen wife, Wilson staring straight ahead in the front. When Macomber has proved himself with the three buffalo, it is Margot who retreats into the far corner of the back seat, while the two men happily converse vis-à-vis before her. And finally, as Macomber kneels in the path of the buffalo, it is his wife from her commanding position in the back seat of the car who closes the contest.

Of equal interest is the skill with which Hemingway balances off the two days of hunting against each other. Part of the balance is achieved by the repetition of first effect: the buffalo, like the lion of the preceding day, is wounded, takes cover, and charges without warning. This time, however, the charge moves into a reversed moral situation. Between times, by various devices, the reader has been fully awakened to the degree of physical courage needed in facing wounded and dangerous animals. But where the lion was an instrument for the establishment and build-up of emotional tension, the oncoming horns of the buffalo are the pronged forceps for Macomber's moral birth. Two different worlds fill the two adjacent days.

The yardstick figure, Wilson, a fine characterization, is the man free of woman and of fear. He is the standard of manhood towards which Macomber rises, the cynical referee in the nasty war of man and wife, and the judge who presides, after the mur- [189/190] der, over the further fortunes of Margot Macomber. His dominance over the lady is apparent from the moment she sees him blast the lion from which Macomber ran. But he accepts that dominance only because it is thrust upon him. The kind of dominance he really believes in, and would gladly transfer to the suffering husband, is well summarized in a passage from Shakespeare's *Henry IV* which he quotes as a kind of tribute to Macomber's own loss of fear on the second day: "By my troth, I care not; a man can die but once; we owe God a death . . . and let it go which way it will, he that dies this year is quit for the next. . . ." [36] Having brought out, almost by accident, this attitude he has lived by, Wilson is much embarrassed. "But he had seen men come of age before and it always moved him. It was not a matter of their twenty-first birthday."

Those who object that true manhood is not necessarily proved by one's ability to face a charging beast may be doing Hemingway an injustice. Dramatically speaking, physical courage is often a convenient and economical way of symbolizing moral courage. We are glad, for example, at Hamlet's skill and bravery with the foils. In this African story Hemingway is ob-

viously dealing with both kinds of courage, though, as the situation naturally requires, it is the physical aspect which is stressed.

It would be possible to argue that Francis and Margot Macomber are more nearly caricatures than people. The probability is that the line-drawing in their portraits is the natural consequence of an approach to material chosen for its intrinsic emotional intensity rather than to provide opportunity for depth of characterization. One rightly concludes that they are as fully developed as they need to be for the purposes of the narrative. Further development might well impede the quick march of the short, happy life.

Still it is true that Hemingway's satirical steam, never far below the surface, tends to erupt whenever he deals with leisure-class wastrels. The tendency is visible, for example, in the accounts of Cohn and Campbell in *The Sun Also Rises*. In *Death in the Afternoon*, the author scornfully watches the bored, sport-shod, [190/191] ex-collegians who leave the *corrida* early. The same reaction appears in his sketches of the wealthy yachtsmen in Key West harbor in *To Have and Have Not*, part of which was written at the same time as the Francis Macomber story. It is almost as if, throughout the Depression, Hemingway had resolutely set himself to oppose F. Scott Fitzgerald's temperamental conviction that the rich are glamorous. As Hemingway's scorn rises, the satirical steam-pressure rises with it, and the result is often close to caricature.

If the story of the Macombers is judged, as it probably should be judged, in terms of an experiment in the development of emotional intensity, it is hard to match. As an instance of tragic irony, exemplified in overt action, it has its faults. But dullness is not one of them, and formally speaking the story is very nearly perfect. [37]

---

[36] *First 49*, p. 131. The speech is made by one of the country soldiers, Feeble, in *II Henry IV*, iii, ii, 253–258.

[37] This story was Hemingway's choice for *This Is My Best*, ed. Whit Burnett, New York, 1942. He so wrote Mr. Burnett 5/12/42.

The Hero and the Code *

PHILIP YOUNG (1918–   ) is Research Professor of English at Pennsylvania State University and the author of *Ernest Hemingway* (1952) and *Ernest Hemingway: A Reconsideration* (1966).

[The] . . . distinctions between the hero and his tutor—the man whom the hero emulates, who has the code he would like to operate by, too—clarify and enrich a couple of Hemingway's later, best, and best-known stories, "The Short Happy Life of Francis Macomber," and "The Snows of Kilimanjaro." These long pieces are both clearly ritualistic — one a ceremonial triumph over fear, the other a rite in which a part of the self is destroyed. They present certain difficulties, however, because of new approaches the author took to his material and his protagonists.

Hemingway distinguished between "true" and "made up" stories. Both of these, though they use a great deal of autobiography, are of the latter type. These are personal stories, but they are not literal ones: in Africa in the Thirties Hemingway did not die of an infection, nor was he chased by a lion and murdered by his wife. The protagonists are also "made up" in that in each of the stories the writer adopted a mask that is for once grotesque, incongruous and truly a distortion. Both Macomber and Harry (in "Kilimanjaro") exaggerate some of the hero's weaknesses, failings, shortcomings. Harry is a failure as a man and as a writer; Macomber is a coward. It is very much as if Hemingway was getting rid of things again, but here he took a new and hypercritical attitude toward his protagonists. These men are not wholly unfamiliar as leading players in Hemingway, but they are outside the pattern he built in that they are seen through a glass very darkly or, to put it more cogently, they are seen *in* a glass—as in a Coney Island funhouse —which mirrors into magnified prominence the growing paunch, the receding hairline, the sagging muscles.

"The Short Happy Life" is, among other things, a detailed description of the process of learning the code and its value. Macomber, a frightened man, is seen in the story learning the code from Wilson, his professional [69/70] hunting guide. He is presented as being very ignorant at first, but he painfully learns and he becomes a man in the process. Before that happens, however, it is apparent that Hemingway was using this plot of instruction in courage and honor to comment, as he had not done to this extent before, on many other things. The story is, for example, an analysis of the relationship between the sexes in America, and the relationship is in the nature of declared warfare.

D. H. Lawrence, in an essay on *The Scarlet Letter,* launches an assault on the American male who, he says, has lost his "ithyphallic authority" over the American woman, who therefore dominates and then destroys what is left. "The Short Happy Life" develops and intensifies Lawrence's notion with enormous skill. Francis Macomber, when under the tutelage of the hunter Wilson, learns courage and honor and to embrace the code; he attains his manhood, which is not the same thing as

*Philip Young, from "The Hero and the Code," in *Ernest Hemingway: A Reconsideration* (University Park, Pennsylvania: The Pennsylvania State University Press, 1966), pp. 69–74. Reprinted with the permission of The Pennsylvania State University Press.

losing his virginity or reaching his twenty-first birthday, as the characters point out. When he attains this manhood he regains the ithyphallic authority he had lost and his wife, now panicky herself in her new role, must destroy him literally. Before he became a man she had committed adultery almost in his presence, knowing him helpless to stop her. When he becomes a man, and she can no longer rule him in the Lawrencian sense, she sends a bullet to the base of his skull.

Obviously Macomber is something different from a grown Nick Adams. What he represents instead is an extreme projection of the hero's problem of fear, and the story about him delineates an imagined solution to that problem. Unlike Macomber, Hemingway had never "just shown himself, very publicly, to be a coward." When he wrote the story he had just very publicly and maliciously been *called* one by Gertrude Stein in her *Autobiography of Alice B. Toklas* (1933); he retaliated in *Green Hills of* [**70/71**] *Africa* by calling her a "bitch." But the facts of the matter seem to indicate that she had no more reason for calling him "yellow" than that she knew it was an insult which would hurt, for reasons to be examined later.[*]

However, Macomber is not so extreme a projection that all contact with the hero and with Hemingway is lost. He was given Hemingway's age, his physical fitness and athleticism, and his expertness with big game and fish. Hemingway's own guide, "Pop," in *Green Hills of Africa*, looks very like Wilson, hunting guide of the story. In addition, the extraordinary "immediateness" with which the sensations of fear are felt by Macomber suggests the extent to which the author could feel for him. And fear, after all, was the hero's central problem.

In the course of this story Macomber completely disgraces himself in the presence of his wife and his hunting guide before he learns the code and wins their

[*] This famous quarrel is said to have been patched up in Paris in 1945 but if so, and if Miss Stein could read *A Moveable Feast*, things would assuredly unpatch.

respect. He has already committed the unpardonable sin when the story opens: he ran away from a charging lion, and, as Wilson says, this is just not done—"no white ever bolts." Not only that, but he goes right on committing errors: he asks Wilson not to talk about his cowardice to other people, which for the professional hunter and possessor of the code's book of etiquette is "supposed to be bad form," and after Wilson insults him he spinelessly apologizes. In addition he cannot control his wife, who hounds him without mercy. It had all happened when it came time to track a lion, which he had wounded badly, into the long grass where it lay in wait for those who had shot it. But he had completely failed. First he wanted to send the inadequately armed African "boys" in after the animal; when Wilson refuses to be party to this type of slaughter he [**71/72**] suggests they leave the beast hidden in the grass. He could not have stumbled on a more wretched violation: someone else might meet him unawares and be killed; even if this doesn't happen it is certain that the lion is in considerable pain and it is their responsibility to do for him what cannot be done for human beings. And then when they finally search out the lion Macomber bolts, running wildly away in panic. When the three hunters are reassembled in their car after Wilson has killed the charging, wounded animal, Margot Macomber celebrates the complete loss of her husband's authority by leaning in front of him and kissing Wilson on the mouth. That night Macomber wakes to discover that she is not in her cot in the tent with him. "He lay awake with that knowledge for two hours." This activity does not go against Wilson's code, it is explained; as a matter of fact he "carried a double size cot on safari to accommodate any windfalls he might receive." The standards of the people who hired him were his standards: "They were his standards in all except the shooting."

It is these shooting standards which Macomber eventually learns and which, although they bring his death, make him for a short happy lifetime a man. Quite suddenly when shooting a buffalo he loses his fear. The lessons Wilson has been teaching him are now his own. A wounded buffalo gets away, as the lion did, and he can hardly wait to go in after the beast. In 1942 Hemingway, writing from his own experience an introduction to a collection of war stories, had this to say: "Cowardice . . . is almost always simply a lack of ability to suspend the functioning of the imagination." In "the Macomber affair" he explains it the same way:

It had taken a strange chance of hunting, a sudden precipitation into action without opportunity for worrying beforehand, to bring this about with Macomber. . . . [72/73]

Fear was "gone like an operation. Something else grew in its place. . . . Made him into a man."

Putting the bad things into words may rid one of them, but it is necessary for the earlier-initiated Wilson to make clear to the hero that the same principle applies to so good a thing as the transformation into manhood, which he has just undergone: "You're not supposed to mention it. . . . Doesn't do to talk too much about all this. Talk the whole thing away." Wilson, warming now to Macomber, also confides to him the "thing he had lived by"—a quotation from Shakespeare. The extent to which Hemingway was able to project himself even into this maladroit and cowardly Macomber is further brought out by these lines from Shakespeare. Hemingway revealed this, perhaps without realizing it, in 1942 in the introduction just cited, when he told how in the war, in

1917, *he* learned courage from a British officer (Wilson is very British) who gave him, Hemingway, the identical message Wilson here gives Macomber:

"By my troth, I care not; a man can die but once; we owe God a death and let it go which way it will he that dies this year is quit for the next."

The climax of the story has come, and Macomber's wife, recognizing the hero's new life as a man, cannot tolerate a long denouement. When her husband goes in after the wounded buffalo she—ostensibly and "intentionally" aiming for the beast in order to save Francis—kills him. Aiming at the buffalo, as Hemingway specified, she shot her husband "by mistake on purpose," as wise children put it—or, for adults, in a monumental "Freudian slip." When Wilson accuses her of murder she does not deny it; he prepares to exonerate her with explanatory photographs, and the story ends. Wilson is like the prize-fighter Jack and the gambler Cayetano: he kills—as a profession—animals [**73/74**] who have insufficient chance of protecting themselves; he consorts with rich decadents and adopts their moral standards; he lives a lonely, compromised life. But out of this he builds what he lives by; he has his courage and his honor: he would not "squeal" on his employer; he will not leave the animals he has pitilessly shot to suffer. He bristles with "won't do," "isn't done," "bad form," and "not supposed to." Macomber—not the hero, but like the heroes in this—admires all this code and tries to attain it. He makes the grade, but it costs him his life.

The Shorter Happy Life of Mrs. Macomber *

WARREN BECK is a professor of English at Lawrence University. He has published a critical study of William Faulkner, *Man in Motion* (1961); three novels: *Final Score* (1944), *Pause Under the Sky* (1947), *Into Thin Air* (1951); and four collections of short stories: *The Blue Sash* (1941), *The First Fish* (1947), *The Far Whistle* (1951), and *The Rest is Silence* (1963).

At the climax of Hemingway's famous story Francis Macomber, who had aroused his wife's aversion by cowardice about a lion, now stands up bravely to a charging buffalo and kills it, while almost simultaneously Mrs. Macomber "had shot at the buffalo . . . as it seemed about to gore Macomber and had hit her husband," killing him instantly. Thereupon the English guide Wilson, whose cot Mrs. Macomber had come to the night before, says to the weeping woman, "That was a pretty thing to do. He *would* have left you too." Wilson's assumption that Mrs. Macomber murdered her husband has been rather generally accepted by readers. "Our clue to the full meaning of the act," says one critical discussion in this vein, "is given by the guide." However, one may question not just Wilson's credibility as a witness but his comprehension of Mrs. Macomber and of the Macombers' human situation. And this, in turn, involves larger questions concerning Hemingway's work, as to both its art and its substance.

At the final moment with the buffalo the professionally competent Wilson is off to one side, trying to get in a shot; all through the story he seems off to one side or another in a tangential rather than a comprehensive way of looking at things. The opening pages, with some centering on Wilson's consciousness, emphasize his ambivalent, at times uncertain, and even baffled attitude toward a pair whom he then repeatedly categorizes as familiar types, the wealthy, soft American sportsman and his glitteringly hard wife, whereas the total narrative gives a more penetrating characterization of the Macombers and suggests a more ironic and pitiful denouement than Wilson can realize. While at the end he has "begun to like" Macomber, he never fully or steadily perceives Mrs. Macomber in the largest perspectives the story provides. Might it not be better to read "The Short Happy Life of Francis Macomber" in these dimensions than to take Wilson's word for it?

He had a word for Margot Macomber, of five letters, and apparently he made no substitution for it. He had a four-letter word for Francis, but he dropped that, because Francis had done something Wilson could understand, had lived up to the code of physical courage, thereby coming of age, as Hemingway has Wilson put it. Mrs. Macomber's more complex temperament and moods, however, transcend Wilson's intuition. At one point he had an inkling that there was more in her than conformed to a stereotype, but Wilson, a man of action according to a simplified standard, does not vex himself too long over subtleties; he soon drops back to plainer grounds, as indeed he must, for he has trouble enough approximating consistency within his rather narrowed view.

*Warren Beck, "The Shorter Happy Life of Mrs. Macomber," Modern Fiction Studies, I (November 1955), 28–37. Modern Fiction Studies, copyright © 1955 by Purdue Research Foundation, Lafayette, Indiana.

In the strained conversation with which the story begins, after Macomber's panicky flight from the lion, Wilson is repeatedly confused. When Macomber asks "It doesn't have to go any further, does it?" Wilson thinks "So he's a bloody four-letter man as well as a bloody coward. I rather liked him too until today. But how is one to know about an American?" Determined to withdraw into formality [**28/29**] and take his meals alone hereafter, Wilson is purposely insulting, and while assuring Macomber that a professional hunter never talks about his client, adds "It's supposed to be bad form to ask us not to talk though." Macomber is sorry he hadn't realized that, and admits "There are lots of things I don't know." (This was evident at the very beginning; he had asked not only what he should pay the natives but whether the headman would distribute it equitably.) Wilson, when his first insult fails, tries again, remarking ironically that in Africa no white man ever bolts, to which Macomber says "I bolted like a rabbit," leaving Wilson wondering "Now what in hell were you going to do about a man who talked like that?" Then Macomber suggests he might redeem himself, "fix it up," on buffalo, and Wilson thinks he may have misjudged the man, but cannot hold that thought: "Perhaps he had been wrong. This was certainly the way to take it. You most certainly could not tell a damned thing about an American. He was all for Macomber again. If you could forget the morning. But, of course, you couldn't." The certain thing in this passage, as in others, is that Wilson, between his "perhaps" and "of course," is quite out of his depth.

Does Mrs. Macomber sense this indecisiveness of his and lack of comprehension? Studying him on their return from the lion hunt, she is conscious not only of Wilson's "extremely cold blue eyes with faint white wrinkles that grooved merrily when he smiled," but also of "his very dirty boots," and "she noticed where the baked red of his face stopped in a white line" left by his hat. Whatever she may think of him, he

certainly doesn't know what to think of her. He tries with scant success to take a stand among alternatives, and falls back once more on preconceptions. She has left them in an outburst of sorrowful tears, saying "I wish it hadn't happened. Oh, I wish it hadn't happened," but now she is back, "looking refreshed and cheerful" and asserting that she has "dropped the whole thing." Her glib, brittle, barbed talk leads Wilson to reflect that American women are "the hardest, the cruelest, the most predatory and the most attractive and their men have softened or gone to pieces nervously as they have hardened. Or is it that they pick men they can handle? They can't know that much at the age they marry." Then with these unanswered questions just behind him, he is nevertheless complacently "grateful that he had gone through his education on American women before now." And as Margot, demanding to be taken along on the buffalo hunt, becomes openly vindictive, saying "I wouldn't miss something like today for anything," Wilson weighs her case in her mind as follows: "When she went off to cry, she seemed like a hell of a fine woman. She seemed to understand, to realize, to be hurt for him and for herself and to know how things really stood. She is away for twenty minutes and now she is back, simply enamelled in that American female cruelty. They are the damnedest women. Really the damnedest."

Thus from a glimpse into Mrs. Macomber's deeper nature Wilson returns to the "enamelled" surface, the predatory cruelty which summarizes for him the American female of the safari species, concerning whom he assumes he has learned all there is to know. Then as Margot continues her too sprightly, double-edged talk, he is again uncertain: "So," he thinks, "she *is* giving him a ride, isn't she. Or do you suppose that's her idea of putting up a good show?" But as to what might lie behind the good show, if any, he doesn't inquire; instead he settles for the notion that such women have to be cruel to govern, but all the same, he's "seen enough of their damn terrorism." Admittedly there is more than enough of this to be seen in Margot, but Wilson does not see nearly enough of what else is in her, now and later. These first pages do more than stamp the woman as Wilson finally classifies her; they begin to reveal her variously as Margot-Margaret-Mrs. [29/30] Macomber —and indeed Hemingway's alternation of these names here and throughout the story seems no mere elegant variation but highly implicative, supporting nuances which delineate a volatile but not altogether malevolent personality.

Almost a quarter of the story is given over to this orientation, sketching the three characters in the embarrassing hour after the lion hunt. While the passage shows Francis candid about his cowardice, and hoping to redeem himself, but deeply ashamed and lonely in his shame, and Margot compensating with cruel sarcasm for her genuine disappointment and regret, it centers psychologically upon Wilson. He does his professional best in his hearty laconic way to buck up Macomber, but privately he flounders in an inconclusive attempt to define these two, whom he finally crams into his pigeon holes, none too neatly, but well enough to satisfy his conventional mind. To understand Mrs. Macomber and accord her the degree of compassion she deserves, the reader therefore must put Wilson in his place from the first, as well as later.

After these introductory pages the narrative then drops back, by way of Macomber's troubled night thoughts, to the episode of the lion hunt. The beast had roared nearby all the night before, and Francis is in a funk before they start. Mrs. Macomber tries to cheer him, saying she knows he'll "kill him marvellously." Francis makes one mistake after another, partly from fear but also from naiveté and confusion. He must be told not to shoot from the car, he forgets to throw off the safety on his rifle and loses the best chance for a shot, he wounds the lion but not enough to prevent its getting off into cover, he suggests they send in beaters and

is told a wounded lion will not move on but will charge, he must be told also that they can't just "drop it" and go off, since that would leave the animal suffering as well as dangerous to anyone else who might run onto it. "I see," says Francis, and apparently he does indeed, for then when Wilson offers to go in after the lion alone, saying that's what a guide is hired for, Francis refuses this escape. "I'm just scared, you know," he explains frankly; and twice more (symbol-fanciers may proceed at their own risk) he puts by the temptation of Wilson's repeated offer, each time saying, "I want to go." They go in, the lion charges, and "the next thing he knew" Francis was "running wildly, in panic in the open," leaving Wilson to make a cool, courageous kill of the invincibly brave animal.

Macomber's cowardice leaves him reduced and isolated. His wife does not look at him. She removes her hand when he tries to take it. There is a minimum of talk, and that perfunctory and strained. Macomber, says Hemingway, did not know "how the lion had felt"—did not imagine its sensations which the narrative describes, and did not conceive of its courage as Wilson does when he says "Damned fine lion." Macomber "did not know how Wilson felt about things either," and "did not know how his wife felt except that she was through with him."

At this point the story pauses to characterize the Macombers, especially as to the narrowness of their sophistication, and after a parody passage on them in the manner of a gossip columnist, with a sideswipe at the Martin Johnsons in darkest Africa, Hemingway concludes that the couple "had a sound basis of union," since Margot "was too beautiful for Macomber to divorce her and Macomber had too much money for Margot ever to leave him." Such a sardonic insert may seem, of course, to prepare for the conception of Mrs. Macomber as a woman who would [30/31] shoot her husband for fear that he might leave her, having outgrown her.

However, this sketch of the Macombers from the society-page point of view plus its complement of cynicism is not without an overtone of pathos. Macomber, "very wealthy" and fated to be "much wealthier," has that sad reason for knowing his wife would not leave him. He knows about sports and "most of the other things his world dealt in," but he would have to be "better with women" before Margot would "worry about him getting another new, beautiful wife." Three times in their eleven years together the Macombers had been on the point of separation, but had "made it up." No doubt what entered into those inadequate and inconclusive settlements had been Macomber's "great tolerance which seemed the nicest thing about him if it were not the most sinister." In addition, the story's first passages have told that Macomber "kept himself very fit, was good at court games, had a number of big-game fishing records," and that Mrs. Macomber is "an extremely handsome and well-kept woman" whose looks, five years before, together with her social position, had "commanded five thousand dollars as the price of endorsing, with photographs, a beauty product which she had never used." These then are the assets underwriting the Macombers' "sound basis of union," which is thus revealed as a sorry barter in wealth, beauty, modishness, and mutually demoralizing convenience. But though the exposure of their shallow fashionableness and their somewhat fatalistic view of themselves is gruff, it need not seem incompatible with that veiled, understated compassion which Hemingway often accords the maladjusted, whether among the too sorely beset or the too self-indulgent.

As for the pair's previous approaches to a break-up, apparently Macomber could have brought divorce action more than once on grounds of infidelity. Immediately after the episode with the lion this element enters again. Margot had defiantly kissed "the beautiful, red-faced Mr. Wilson" on the mouth in her husband's presence; that night she leaves the tent she shares with Francis and goes to Wilson's tent. Francis, too disturbed by fear to sleep soundly, is awake when she returns, and to his protest that she had promised there would be none of that, she answers, "That's the way I meant it to be. But the trip was spoiled yesterday." At breakfast the consequent tension among the three is severe, and Macomber, finding that "of all the many men that he had hated, he hated Robert Wilson most," is bitterly irritable.

Again the story begins to touch repeatedly upon Wilson's consciousness; he assumes that Macomber knows of the infidelity and thinks it's the husband's fault for not keeping the wife where she belongs; he reflects that "women *are* a nuisance on safari"; he wants to get the job over with, through buffalo and rhino, and to that end, prudently, "he'd have nothing more to do with the woman." He assumes that Macomber, "poor beggar," has endured plenty of infidelity before, but "must have a way of getting over it," which brings Wilson back, through these alterations of opinion, to the feeling that "it was the poor sod's own bloody fault."

Hemingway explains Wilson further, in that he "carried a double size cot . . . to accomodate any windfalls," since when hunting for "a certain clientele, the international, fast, sporting set . . . their standards were his standards as long as they were hiring him." Except, of course, the shooting. "He had his own standards about the killing," inflexibly held, and he knows "they all respected him for this." (Even as to those standards, however, a variation will emerge; [31/32] Wilson is to violate a game law, apparently without compunction, since his code of personal courage was not involved.) As for his present employers, Wilson thinks that "this Macomber was an odd one though. Damned if he wasn't. Now the wife. Well, the wife. Yes, the wife. Hm, the wife. Well he'd dropped all that." And looking at this woman who had come to his bed the night before but "hadn't talked much," Wilson muses, "What's in her heart, God knows." Thus far then is this a man whose word can be taken concerning Mrs. Macomber when "she shot at the buffalo . . . as it seemed about to gore Macomber"? Perhaps Wilson's absolute and complacent assurance about the things he does understand leads him to estimate too carelessly other matters which may lie beyond his intuitions; or perhaps it is Wilson's naiveté and uncertainty beyond his narrow limits which has accustomed him to muddling along by blunt guesswork. In either case, who is Wilson, that so many readers have strung along with him—this hunter with a first and great commandment and no other, who will welcome an employer's wife to his cot but not if it seems inexpedient, who would illegally order the natives lashed because they may prefer it to having their wages docked, who will illegally chase buffalo in a car as long as the shooting is done on foot to take the chance of the animal's charging, this steely-eyed professional with the muddy boots, this red-faced Mr. Wilson with the white forehead, whose speculations about the Macombers reiterate a yes and then again no.

If beyond his code of bravery Wilson is all adrift, then to take his word for it at the story's end is also to assume the sufficiency of that code, not only for action but for understanding. Philip Young's study, enlarging upon such a tendency in earlier criticism, is inclined to circumscribe Hemingway himself and all his work within such an outlook. Granted that details and instances in Hemingway's fiction do seem to argue not that whoever endures to the end shall be saved but that merely to endure is the best one can do, and that hence the only code is one starkly simplified to an elementary stoicism, in a fatalistic equating of everything to nada. Yet is that the whole Hemingway story? "We all take a beating every day," Wilson remarks consolingly and resignedly, but if Hemingway is thought to be limited to a conception like Wilson's of what may constitute a beating and how it is to be taken, then the less Hemingway he. And if Wilson's criterion of physical courage is adequate to the whole duty of man and man's hope, Hemingway has not found it so in *A Farewell to Arms* or "In Another Country," for instance. It seems desirable and advisable, then, as the buffalo hunt plays itself out toward its awful denouement, for the reader to watch Mrs. Macomber more closely than Wilson had time for, and to estimate her more empathetically than he was able to, bound as he is in a reduced and rigid outlook.

After driving recklessly across a rough plain to intercept three buffalo, Wilson and Macomber dismount and shoot down two, then drive on after the third, dismount again, and shoot it. In the car, frightened by the ride and with a "dreadful headache" from the excitement, "Macomber's wife sat very white faced." She tells her husband, "You were marvellous, darling," and then goes on, "I didn't know you were allowed to shoot them from cars though." Wilson "coldly" says "No one shot them from cars," and when forced to acknowledge that the chase was illegal, he justifies it because the ride itself was dangerous and the animal "could have charged us each time we shot if he liked." Wilson was of course anxious to get the rest of this disagreeable expedition over with, but it may be supposed too that he honestly desired to give Macomber the essential test the man craved and now seemed ready for. [**32/33**]

Margot is not seeing things in such plain terms, however, and her responses are more devious. She asks what would happen if "they heard about" the illegal chase in Nairobi, and Wilson admits he'd lose his license; thereupon Macomber smiles and says, "Now she has something on you," Margot says Francis has "such a pretty way of putting things," and Wilson, as he "looked at them both," thinks "If a four-letter man marries a five-letter woman, what number of letters would their children be?" It is all very unpleasant again, and almost as strained as previous scenes; the chief aspects, though, are Wilson's reduction of the hunter's code from legality to a single rule of risk endured, his irritated retreat to a simplified summing-up of the Macombers in nine letters, and Margot's increasingly disturbed state of mind, which makes her strike out obliquely at both men. A not negligible possibility here is that the challenge of her husband's emerging manhood makes her resentful toward Wilson as the partner of her vengeful infidelity the night before.

This psychological complexity and impasse is broken into by actuality a moment later. A gun-bearer approaches to say that the first buffalo had got up and gone into the bush. Macomber says "Oh," blankly; Margot, "full of anticipation," says "Then it's going to be just like the lion"; and Wilson, whether out of new confidence in Macomber or resentment against Margot or both, tells her "It's not going to be a damned bit like the lion." Macomber, now finding that for the "first time in his life he felt wholly without fear," and having instead "a feeling of definite elation," wants to go in after the wounded buffalo at once. Wilson is amazed at the alternation of opposite characteristics, and his client's inconsistency leaves the guide stranded and almost neutralized in the reflection, "Damned if this isn't a strange one. Yesterday he's scared sick and today he's a ruddy fire eater." Margot meanwhile is definitely disturbed. She asks twice to get into the shade; she is pale, she looks ill.

As they sit in the car under the "single, wide-spreading tree" to wait a little before the men go after the wounded buffalo, a crucial scene ensues, woven of several strands, the subtlest but strongest of which is Margot's implied reaction. Before the lion hunt Margot has said with wifely loyalty that she knows Macomber will "kill him marvellously." After the wild chase and shooting down of the three buffaloes, when Margot says "You were marvellous, darling," the "marvellous" can be read, of course, as more of her sheer sarcasm, but might it not be heard also as a glittery mannerism to mask this "very white faced" woman's deep and increasing

perturbation? The key word recurs—"Wasn't it marvellous, Margot?" Macomber asks, presumably in good faith and genially, but she replies that she hated it, and when he asks why, she is apparently unwilling or even unable to state her whole mind and will only repeat, "I hated it. I loathed it." So Macomber turns to Wilson and begins to discuss with that now receptive companion what has happened to him and how absolutely different he feels, having passed beyond fear. A significant tableau is glimpsed: Margot saying nothing, eyeing her husband strangely, "sitting far back in the seat" while Macomber "was sitting forward talking to Wilson who turned sideways talking over the back of the front seat."

Macomber declares he'd like to try another lion, he's really not afraid of them now, since "after all, what can they do to you?" In this moment Wilson is no longer bewildered. Here is something he understands and honors, and so he brings out the "thing he had lived by," an obvious fact made into a resolute aphorism, Shakespeare's "a man can die but once." Then comes a long passage [**33/34**] in Wilson's thoughts, so staccato as almost to caricature the laconic-hearty Englishman of the "Righto!" kind, cheerily bumping along over his clichés. "The great American boy-men" are "damned strange people," thinks Wilson, but "he liked this Macomber now," though still thinking of him as a "damned strange fellow." This transformation in Macomber "probably meant the end of cuckoldry too. Well, that would be a damned good thing. Damned good thing. . . Beggar had probably been afraid all his life. . . But over now. . . Be a damn fire eater now. . . More of a change than any loss of virginity. Fear gone like an operation. . . Made him into a man. Women knew it too. No bloody fear."

At this juncture Margaret Macomber, "from the far corner of the seat," is looking at "the two of them." Wilson she sees "as she had seen him the day before when she had first realized what his great talent was." The day before means the lion hunt, and Margot's conceiving of Wilson's great physical courage as a talent may suggest that he possesses just this one, a talent held but not improved or extended, which certainly is how the reader has had opportunity to find him all along. Significantly Margot observes that "there was no change in Wilson." There is not, nor is there to be; this man will always rise to the occasion as a hunter, but he will never go beyond that. His stereotyped view of his employers cannot be modified by what he does not notice or has no intimation of.

Meanwhile Margaret also "saw the change in Francis Macomber now," and this leads into half a page of dialogue with further indications of her emerging attitude. As Francis goes on talking about the exhilaration he feels and Wilson says it "doesn't do to talk too much about all this," Margot says they're "both talking rot." Wilson replies, "Sorry. I have been gassing too much," but privately concludes that Margot "is worried about it already" —presumably Wilson's stated and static idea of the predatory American female makes him suppose that what concerns Margot is the possibility of Macomber's getting out of hand, his becoming too much of a man for her to dominate. Macomber, who has not addressed his wife since he asked her if the chase wasn't marvellous and was repeatedly told she hated it, now says, "If you don't know what we're talking about why not keep out of it?" and his wife answers "contemptuously" that he'd "gotten awfully brave, awfully suddenly." "But," Hemingway adds pointedly, "her contempt was not secure. She was very afraid of something."

What this something may be is the crux of the matter, but there is no imperative reason for seeing it as Wilson does, especially since the story omnisciently provides other facts and suggests insights transcending Wilson's. When Macomber responds in good spirit to his wife's contemptuous remark about getting so awfully brave, and laughs, "a very natural hearty laugh," before he says "You know I *have*. I really have," Margot "bitterly" asks, "Isn't it sort of late?" and then Hemingway opens a further perspective, far beyond Wilson's; Margot's bitterness is explained in this conspicuous interpolation: "Because she had done the best she could for many years back and the way they were together now was no one person's fault." And now when Macomber, to Margot's bitterly uttered, ironic and yet perhaps half-tentative question about its being sort of late, answers "Not for me," the woman who could be so ready when a flippant sarcasm sufficed can find nothing to say, but "sat back in the corner of the seat," in that posture not only of withdrawal but of shrinking and retreat. From something perhaps almost too big for her? [**34/35**]

This is the last exchange between the pair. The car is driven closer to where the wounded buffalo took cover, the men get out, and Macomber, "looking back, saw his wife, with the rifle by her side, looking at him. He waved to her and she did not wave back." And then the end. And to support Wilson's suspicion that she murdered her husband there are those sharp details, the rifle handy, and she refusing to answer Macomber's confident and companionable gesture. However, Wilson has been seen plain as an uncertain spectator, given to over-simplification, a man of one admirable talent and only one, and beyond Wilson's cliché of Margot is much weighty evidence of a different kind—that Mrs. Macomber felt deeply her husband's failure with the lion, and passionately wishes it hadn't happened, and weeps over it; that she "had meant it to be" right on this safari; that she "had done the best she could for many years back." In this light must it not be supposed that the "something" she is "very afraid of" touches her even more closely, more personally than a danger that the maturing Macomber will leave her now?

Perhaps what Mrs. Macomber fears is a further challenge to herself as a human being and a wife, the call to try once more, to meet her husband's virtue and friendliness with a reasserted virtue and warmth of her own. Her hesitancy would then seem a quite natural reaction, compounded of an habitual negativism, the cynical pose assumed for protective coloration, plus her real disillusionment after prolonged and repeatedly defeated attempts at something better, and also perhaps a particular reluctance to confess the shabbiness of her revenge for her husband's earlier weakness. It seems conceivable, from data within the story, that Margaret Macomber is at least as good as Lady Brett Ashley, of *The Sun Also Rises,* admittedly a five-letter woman, but also on occasion one capable of deciding "not to be a bitch," being spurred to that assertion by the sight of integrity in a man. Moreover, Brett encounters another man whose standards are almost as simple as Wilson's, the hedonistic Greek count, who will drink no toasts with his wine, lest sentiment intrude upon flavor; and as Hemingway uses him to show that there is more to Brett than the count perceives, appreciative though he is, similarly the short story offers the reader more of Mrs. Macomber than is understood by Wilson, who apparently forgets or at least dismisses his momentary glimpse of what a "hell of a fine woman" she had seemed to be.

That Wilson is scarcely the man to intuit Mrs. Macomber's complex reaction has been indicated by his earlier impercipience of a similar complexity in Francis. Asking about going after buffalo the next day, because he wants the chance to "clear away that lion business," Francis had added that "It's not very pleasant to have your wife see you do something like that." Thereupon Wilson thinks to himself that "it would be even more unpleasant to do it . . . wife or no wife, or to talk about it having done it." Apparently Wilson does not perceive the psychological value of self-examination and confession in the growth of personality, and moreover, while Wilson's sentiments are lofty enough, in the vein of "This above all, to thine own self be true," he does not comprehend what must follow, it being more of his over-simplification to postulate

"wife or no wife." In his commodious cot Wilson had not learned that marriage is not the single life. Macomber, on the other hand, and in spite of the precariousness of his relationship with Margot, knows that as to conduct one never can say "wife or no wife." In his emergence he is more than a man with an eye on a main chance of ingratiating himself with a domineering woman. He is a husband whose con- **[35/36]** cern still, even after all his previous failures, is his marital relationship—a concern not just to retain Margaret in the legal bonds of matrimony and the physical status of cohabitation, but to achieve that mutual honoring without which a spontaneous and sustained intimacy is impossible. Hemingway pictures the lovers in *A Farewell to Arms* thus honoring each other, and while Lieutenant Henry is brave enough to suit Wilson, he is also a man who discovers that in the tests and opportunities of a genuine union one cannot say "wife or no wife."

Both the Macombers, the story indicates, have tried previously to face up to this exacting and promising fact of nature. The reoriented Macomber who has asked his wife whether the buffalo chase wasn't marvellous seems cordially ready for a renewed effort to experience a greater marvel in his relationship with her. But is she ready, the Margot whose bitter "Isn't it sort of late?" has forced Macomber to stand his ground alone in answering "Not for me," the Margot who sits withdrawn in the seat and does not wave back at her husband? Nevertheless, ready or not, Margaret Macomber must face, suddenly, an excruciating moment; and concerning the woman who "had done the best she could for many years," what can be supposed but that she would try again, in a crisis that would bring out what was in the heart of this enamelled but not altogether shallow or selfish human being.

Two further points claim notice. One is the passage describing the shooting. Macomber is indubitably brave; no longer seeing Wilson or depending on him, he is doing it on his own, coolly, "aiming carefully" as he shoots once more "with the buffalo's huge bulk almost on him," so close that "he could see the little wicked eyes," and he sees too that "the head started to lower," his last shot has taken effect. Then in that triumphant moment the bullet his wife has fired kills him instantly. Wilson's assumption at this point, however, must be weighed specifically in relation to what the text says: "Mrs. Macomber . . . had shot at the buffalo . . . as it seemed about to gore Macomber." The danger was indeed acute; the animal fell "not two yards" from him. In that proximity and under such excitement Mrs. Macomber, who has not been shown as an experienced shot or even a participant in the previous hunting, might indeed have killed her husband accidentally. And of chief significance is that the buffalo "seemed about to gore Macomber." This is what she sees, not that Francis, having learned to be brave, probably will leave her, but that in his bravery he is about to be killed. If she wanted him dead, she could have left it to the buffalo, as it "seemed" at that moment. Certainly the passage, with what has gone before, can be read to suggest that she wanted to save him and that she, who had tried so often before, might well have felt he had never been as worthy of her whole effort as he was now.

Furthermore, not only does the story supply throughout insights about Mrs. Macomber which transcend Wilson's view; it is Ernest Hemingway who writes that she "shot at the buffalo." Hemingway is, of course, a highly implicative artist, but he is not notably given to double-talk or passing the buck. Either his statement that she shot at the buffalo must be accepted or else the whistle must be blown and that narrative play discredited as being technically off-side. It is indeed surprising that such a painful doubt about so scrupulous a writer has not moved more of Hemingway's admirers to question whether, after all, we can take Wilson's word for what happened. [**36/37**]

Close examination of that final passage

will show, to Hemingway's credit, the utmost subtlety of method. Wilson's first private statement to the woman "crying in the corner" of the motor car is "toneless," ironic—"That was a pretty thing to do" with the harsh addition, "He *would* have left you too." To that she says "Stop it," and this is all she says, repeatedly, to his continued talk, in which the matter of fact about what needs to be done is mingled with other insinuations. However, it is not only to these that she replies "Stop it," but also to Wilson's sardonic assurances that the death can be proved accidental—an offer which a murderess would scarcely reject. The Mrs. Macomber who "hadn't talked much" to Wilson the night before in his tent now has nothing more to say to this man of one talent, looking at her with "flat blue eyes," incapable of understanding what was in her heart and what is in her heart. At last, however, she varies her answer, saying, "Oh, please stop it. Please, please stop it." What elicits this is not a further accusation of murder, but Wilson's saying "I'd begun to like your husband." It would seem that Mrs. Macomber, while too overwhelmed by grief to contradict the false assumptions of an impercipient, or to care about a morally superfluous testimony of accident, cannot bear this regretful and admiring mention of her husband from a man whose "little" anger is presumably tinged with a shame she must share.

Then Wilson has the last word, that "Please is much better," and stops, in one sense too soon, since he presumes he has taken this woman's full measure and put her in her despicable place. But in Hemingway's stories a last speech is not always Hemingway's last word. In "The Killers" George's "Well, you better not think about it" gives ironic contrast to Hemingway's full intent that we shall think about it. Had Hemingway shared George's attitude, he would scarcely have written "The Killers." Comparably, it seems impossible to believe that Hemingway conceived "The Short Happy Life of Francis Macomber" within the narrow limits of Wilson's view. For it would appear that Mrs. Macomber too had a happy moment of a kind, in which she wished and tried to save her husband, with that access of recognition and penitence and hope in which love can renew itself. If this be the meaning, it is a more profound story, more humane in substance, and a larger and more subtly executed story than Hemingway has been credited with by those who have taken Wilson's word for it.

Finally, if this story (a favorite of Hemingway's) intends this larger meaning, a correct reading is important for more than its own sake. Here then would be evidence in refutation of the charge that Hemingway himself is a traumatic case, bound by insuperable frustration and reduced to a laconic stoicism which, if it were the full measure of the man, would have made impossible both the volume and the most notable heights of his achievement.

Ernest Hemingway: "The Short Happy Life of Francis Macomber" *

R. S. CRANE (1886–1967) was Distinguished Professor of English and Chairman of the Department at the University of Chicago. His essays had enormous impact on critical theory in America. They can be found in *Critics and Criticism: Ancient and Modern* (1952), in *The Languages of Criticism and the Structure of Poetry* (1953), and in the comprehensive two-volume collection *The Idea of the Humanities and Other Essays Critical and Historical* (1967), from which this text is taken.

My Dear M——:*

I am very grateful to you for sending me the three papers on "The Short Happy Life of Francis Macomber." I have read them with much interest, and with only two major reservations.

One of these has to do with your attempt to interpret Macomber as an "Aristotelian" tragic hero. This came as a surprise after your earlier statements about the plot. With these I largely agree. Like you, I think that the action begins with Macomber "in his lowest condition" and proceeds to his achievement, for a brief moment before his death, of a "happiness" greater than he had ever known before; as you put it, he is transformed from an *object* into a *man*. The essential change is thus not one of fortune but of moral character. For such a change the appropriate response of the reader is obviously a pleasurable rather than a painful one, that is, some degree of rejoicing dependent on the depth of "unhappiness" from

which the man has risen, and on the suddenness of the change. That something like this is what we are intended to feel for Macomber is suggested by the reactions of Wilson [**315/316**] in the paragraph beginning, "He was very embarrassed" and in his remark at the end to Margot, "I'd begun to like your husband."

All this you say or imply in the concluding paragraphs of your first section, and here at least you don't treat Macomber's death as a tragic catastrophe, although I think you fail to make sufficiently clear what its relation is to the "emotional satisfaction" of which you correctly say that the "change in Macomber's life is . . . a principal cause." Plainly the answer turns in part on how we construe the act of Margot which brings her husband's "short happy life" to a sudden end; and I am puzzled by W——'s contention, with which you appear to agree, that Hemingway meant to leave us in doubt whether the killing was accident or murder and that this very uncertainty constitutes "the finest artistic touch in the story." I should say, on the contrary, that if "suspension of judgment" about the cause of Macomber's death is the intended final state of mind of the reader, then Hemingway has bungled his job. For the

* Written in 1949 as a letter to a former student who had sent me, for comment, essays on Hemingway's story by himself and two of his colleagues in the Freshman English staff of his university; published in the third edition of *Readings for Liberal Education*, edited by Louis G. Locke, William M. Gibson, and George Arms (New York: Rinehart & Company), © 1957 by the editors; reprinted here with some modifications by permission of the editors and publisher.

*R. S. Crane, "Ernest Hemingway: 'The Short Happy Life of Francis Macomber,'" in *The Idea of the Humanities and Other Essays Critical and Historical*, 2 vols. (Chicago: The University of Chicago Press, 1967), II, 315–326. Originally published in *English "A" Analyst* (Department of English, Northwestern University), No. 16 (November 1, 1949). Reprinted with the permission of *English "A" Analyst*.

climactic emotion in that case becomes a species of wonder, much as in trick stories like "The Lady or the Tiger"; our attention, moreover, is shifted away from Macomber, who up to this point has been the major object of our feelings, and concentrated on Margot, who is suddenly turned into a lady of mystery, with the result that all the reiterated signs of her emotions and intentions during the buffalo hunt become retrospectively ambiguous; and, finally, the doubt about Margot is extended to Wilson, who certainly gives every appearance of being certain about the facts—and what then becomes of our confidence in him as a trustworthy chorus which has been built up through the story? Can we suppose that now, and for the first time, he is wrong in his judgment of Margot? But the whole idea is untenable except on the supposition that Hemingway was no artist or a deliberately irresponsible one.

In spite of the narrator's statement that "Mrs. Macomber . . . had shot at the buffalo" and so on, I think we can no less easily rule out the possibility of accident. To begin with, the theory of accident implies an intention on Margot's part to save Macomber's life, and such an intention doesn't accord either with what we have been led to believe about her character from the beginning or with the clear indications of her growing hatred for her husband in the immediately preceding scene; and, for another thing, it implies that the outcome of her act was determined merely by chance, and there are no previ- [316/ 317] ous instances of this sort of probability in the story. (The last objection can also be brought against E———'s suggestion of "unconscious motivation." Where in the narrative up to this point are the motives of the agents ever presented except as conscious ones deriving from relatively simple states of passion?) But there is also a further and more important objection, which will appear when you ask how our feelings would be affected if we really thought that the killing of Macomber was accidental. Wouldn't the inevitable effect be to arouse some degree of pity for Margot at least at the moment when we see her "crying hysterically" over her husband's body, and hence to make us resent the rough handling of her by Wilson? But I can't think that any reader ever reacted in this way; and we don't so react because, as we are reading the story, we never seriously entertain the notion of accident.

We must suppose, then, either that Hemingway didn't know his business or that Macomber was murdered by his wife. But if he was murdered, why do we continue to feel toward him at the end of the story the "emotional satisfaction" which I agree with you is the effect on us of his final achievement of courage? Or why is it that, although we experience a painful shock when we come abruptly, at the end of the sentence telling us of his victorious stand against the buffalo, to the clause "and he felt . . . ," the shock we then feel is momentary only and the pain never becomes the pity which we normally feel for victims of murder when they are good men whom we know vividly? I think the reason is partly to be found in certain tricks of technique by which, in the first place, our attention is centered so wholly on Macomber and the buffalo during the last stages of the hunt that we don't think of danger from any other source, and by which, in the second place, as soon as Macomber has fallen, our thoughts are turned away from him to Wilson and Margot. But the causes lie also in the plot itself. We tend to feel pity at the murder of anyone whose destruction seems to involve waste or who appears to have unexhausted possibilities of "happiness" or possibilities of greater "happiness" in the future. But Macomber is clearly not so conceived. Within the story he is only (a) the ineffective husband of a "predatory" wife and (b) such a man engaged in an African safari—in short, one who satisfies completely all our expectations and hopes when he finally dominates Margot and acts without fear as a hunter. Once this climax is [317/318] reached he has done the best that is in him, and we have no active desire that he should live on; or rather, as you shrewdly suggest, we take his death as in some sense necessary to our full appreciation of his victory over himself—he is so ordinary a creature that had he survived, the perfection of the moment might well have been spoiled. Again, no matter how nobly a man acts on the eve of his death, we still pity him as long as we think of his courageous act as something done in spite of a natural human aversion to dying. But this is ruled out for Macomber by the very nature of his victory over his previous fear, and here once more, as you point out, Wilson serves as chorus (note his words in the passage beginning " 'You know, I'd like to try another lion,' Macomber said"). Finally, not only is Macomber's death part of his moral triumph, it marks also the complete and deserved defeat of his wife; she has got rid of her husband only to fall under the power of Wilson; and our satisfaction at this, aroused in the concluding dialogue, effectively counteracts our momentary shock at the murder.

But if all this is true, isn't it quite misleading to analogize Macomber to the "Aristotelian" tragic hero? I should think that you would have been more struck by the essential differences between the two than by their superficial likenesses as protagonists who suffer death in serious actions. "Tragedy," as Aristotle defines it in *Poetics* 13 and 14, is a very special plot form, which has been fully achieved, I think, only by a few of the Greeks and by Shakespeare in some of his major works, notably *Hamlet, King Lear,* and *Othello.* Its distinguishing pleasure is a catharsis of fear and pity, the peculiar "tragic" quality of which is determined by the other causes which Aristotle specifies in these two chapters. The formal cause is a change of fortune rather than of character (though this may also be involved) from good to bad, resulting from an unjust deed, productive of great pain and suffering, committed by the protagonist on a friend or friends, as a consequence of which the

protagonist himself is ruined; the material cause is a hero of the intermediate type, not bad but not "preeminently virtuous and just," though within these limits better rather than worse, and also preferably (for then the change will seem all the more impressive) one who enjoys at the beginning great "reputation and prosperity"; and the efficient cause, located in the moral choices of the protagonist, is a course of action motivated not by evil intent [**318/319**] but by *hamartia,* that is, a fundamental error with respect to the circumstances of the situation which is yet compatible with goodness of character, so that though the hero acts voluntarily, the evil results of his acts are non-voluntary and he himself suffers more deeply than any of his victims. When all these conditions are fulfilled in the construction of a plot, the effect for the normally sensitive spectator is tragic fear and pity; and this effect will be enhanced if the change of fortune comes about suddenly and unexpectedly and is accompanied or followed by a change from ignorance to knowledge that reverses the attitudes of the major characters to one another and also, in the best tragedies, to themselves.

But how completely different from this is the plot form of "The Short Happy Life"! The change upon which the effect depends is not a change of fortune from good to bad but of character from bad to good. It comes about as a result of action by the hero (in the buffalo hunt) which involves no injustice, has no destructive effects on anyone who is dear to him, and proceeds not from error concerning the circumstances but from a wholly praiseworthy cause, his conquest of fear. The decision to go on the hunting trip may have been, as you suggest, a mistake; but it is merely one of the given conditions of the plot, not a primary factor in its development or in the determination of our emotions before and at the climax, as is always the case with tragic *hamartia.* Macomber's suffering before the buffalo hunt, moreover, has its source not in any sense of erroneous or misdirected action (as in

Oedipus or Hamlet) but in shame at his own bad conduct in the face of the lion. The only mistake that functions in the plot is that of Margot, for which she pays in the end; but this is not "tragic" either in its motivation or in its results for Macomber; and Margot, in any case, is not the protagonist. (If she had been, a very different plot form would have resulted, but it would not have been "tragic" either.) The only thing, in short, that Hemingway's tale has in common with tragedy, in Aristotle's sense, is that issues of life and death are involved in the change it depicts. But they are involved in such a way that we do not experience fear for Macomber as he proceeds to assert his new-found courage or pity for him when he falls.

Parenthetically, I think that the antecedents and circumstances of the lion hunt are also "conditions"; the action proper begins with the immediate consequences of the hunt in Margot's act of kissing Wil- [319/320] son and in Macomber's shame. Therefore, it seems to me, there is only one formal peripety—Macomber's unexpected coming of age; the murder is a peripety only in a material sense, its formal significance, as I said before, being inseparable from that of Macomber's final act. Because of the nature of the action the only possible kind of discovery is self-discovery, and this occurs when Macomber recognizes that he no longer fears death. There are plenty of "discoveries" to the reader besides the one you mention, but these are not discoveries in a poetic sense, since they proceed not from the events of the plot but from Hemingway's decisions about what he must disclose to the reader and when.

My second reservation about the essays concerns the adequacy of their analytical apparatus. A critic among other things ought to be able to say how successful artistically—as a constructed whole—"The Short Happy Life" really is and to give relevant reasons for his judgment. This necessitates his finding answers to three main questions: How good is Heming-way's plot in producing the kind of pleasure intended? How effectively is it brought before the reader in the words of the story? and How well adjusted to the specific requirements of the plot are the subordinate parts of characterization, thought, and language?

Of these three questions only the first is touched upon in the essays, and it is dealt with for the most part in a fashion that doesn't permit of a critical appraisal of the story. Except for one place in your paper, the three of you are more concerned with the underlying matter of Hemingway's plot than with the plot itself considered as an artistic construction. It is true that you all look for the form of this matter, that is, what holds its successive parts together. But the direction in which you look for it takes you away from the story viewed as a sequential whole with a particularized system of suspense and surprise, and leads to the discovery not of a plot, in the strict sense of the principle that organizes the action and gives to it its peculiar emotional quality, but of some general "pattern" of human conduct in terms of which the things done and thought by Hemingway's characters can be made abstractly intelligible. For E—— the pattern is given by his conception of Macomber as a neurotic egoist who finally frees himself "from the incubus of his heroic self-portrait"; and he has some difficulty in adjusting to this what he calls "the most com- [320/321] plicated dilemma of the story," the question whether the Macomber marriage is or is not "spiritually dead." For W——— the story is essentially an instance of the behavior of "predatory" creatures seeking "advantages" over one another in a "predatory" world. For you the dominant pattern is one which you take to be central in many or most of Hemingway's writings: the problem of how different kinds of men face death. The three of you come out, in other words, in spite of your protests of mutual agreement, with three perceptibly different "plots"! I don't doubt that the story rests on a material substrate of ideas and unconscious associations that can be interpreted, without doing complete violence to the text, in some or perhaps all of these ways. A plot, however, is more than its substrate of ideas or beliefs; it is the form that actually synthesizes the materials and successsive incidents of an individual story and hence, as we infer it progressively from the writer's words, determines the sequence of our emotions with respect to the characters and the changes they undergo.

The difficulty is that the essays tend to approach the story in terms of preestablished formulas applicable to many stories rather than by way of close attention to the successive effects which Hemingway, in this story, is engaged in producing. You are something of an exception, as I have said, and as a result you come nearer to seeing what the form of the story is (in the sense of the working on us of its particularized action) than do your colleagues, who seem to me to be talking about the plot in more or less complete separation from the special sequence of emotions which is at once its artistic end and the principal source of the criteria whereby, at least as a constructed whole, it ought to be judged. I wish, however, that you had elaborated your insight in relation to the peculiar correlation of character and event that produces the effect you recognize and had then gone on to say something about how successful, in the light of its form, you think Hemingway's construction is.

On the first point something might be made of an aspect of the story that struck me when I reread it the other day. Part of the effect depends, I think, on the fact that there has been a long literary tradition of characters like Macomber, cuckolds in subjection to their wives who are also, in moments of physical danger, cowards. Until the middle of the nineteenth century such characters for the most part were comic butts. Then, in various novels and plays, their traits and [321/322] actions were employed to produce "naturalistic" effects of sordidness or the like. In the twentieth century they (and other similar

characters, like alcoholics and ineffectives generally) have often been given the status of protagonists in serious plots, in which a certain impression of nobility is sought by making them unexpectedly act or speak like heroes. I think this is Hemingway's central idea in "The Short Happy Life," as something not greatly different is Eliot's idea in "Prufrock" and Graham Greene's in *The Confidential Agent*. On this view of the story, the function of Wilson in the plot, as distinguished from his technical function as chorus, becomes evident: part of Macomber's triumph is the admiration his action elicits from his latest cuckolder! And so too with Margot. The state of her marriage is not a problem in the sense of being material to the unifying suspense— it is merely one of the preconditions of the action; and Margot's role in the plot is threefold: she is a sign of her husband's initial degradation, the immediate occasion of the hate which frees him from fear, and finally the instrument that makes his heroism complete.

As for the virtues and weaknesses of the plot, I should like to have had your opinion on two points. One is the manner in which Margot's shooting of her husband is related to the previous events. The moral probability is strong enough, but what about the probability that she will have the gun? Is it good enough to support the intended seriousness of the final effect? The other point is more important. I have often thought that the power of the story is considerably attenuated by the fact that the change in Macomber, which ought to have something of the quality of a miracle (it surprises and embarrasses Wilson), is rather too easily foreseeable from the beginning. Macomber has begun as an abject coward and a slave to Margot: what else can he now do except what he does—namely, get over his fear and in so doing emancipate himself from his wife? I grant that there is plenty of suspense during the buffalo hunt, but it turns only on the physical danger, not at all on the complexity of the central action. The plots of the best short stories are not as obvious as this. And there is finally the question of how seriously, in the moral sense, we can take the action as a whole in spite of its fatal ending. Macomber himself, I can't help thinking, is too commonplace a creature to excite in us any strong wishes, on his own account as an individual, that he should rise from the low state in which we first see him. I agree with you that [**322/ 323**] we feel a certain "emotional satisfaction" when he does, but I wonder if this is not to be accounted for by a combination of two things that have little to do with the particularity of his character: our general disposition to take pleasure in any sudden access of virtue in human beings even when, as persons, they are indifferent to us; and our detestation of Margot and consequent desire that whatever would most frustrate and displease her should happen in the story. The effect produced by the change in Macomber is thus of the relatively inferior order which we properly call "sentimental"; it is certainly, for me at least, less "serious" than is (say) the generically similar effect aroused by the emergence of good sense in Jane Austen's Emma.

For an adequate judgment of Hemingway's success, however, it is necessary to go beyond the plot and, holding this constant, to ask about how the story is told. This, you will see, is our old problem of representation as distinct from what is represented, or, in James's words, of "treatment" as distinct from "subject." It concerns all the devices a writer employs, vis-à-vis his audience, for the sake of inducing a proper judgment of the emotional quality, the probability, or the importance of the things going on in his plot when this would not be evident from a simple and direct presentation of them. The sources from which the devices derive are common to rhetoric and poetics, but since the final end to be served is a certain poetic pleasure determined primarily by the construction of the plot, the criteria for judging the success of any representational device must be drawn from a prior consideration of what the plot and its

peculiar "power" are intended to be. You were right therefore to center your first discussion of Hemingway's tale on its action; what I regret is that you did not then proceed to the further question of how well the plot form, as you conceive it, is clarified and sustained by the narrative.

Looked at from this point of view, "The Short Happy Life" is not, it seems to me, one of Hemingway's most expert jobs. Consider the manner in which Macomber's behavior during the lion hunt is made clear to us. We see it first in terms of the effects of his cowardice on himself, his wife, and Wilson (to say nothing of the servants), and then, in a "flashback" that takes off from Macomber's thoughts that night, we are given the incident itself in full and vivid detail. As an expedient for forcing us to attend closely to what has happened before the story proper begins, this inverted order of narration is effective [**323/324**] enough, though a bit shopworn. But think of what the result is for our opinion of the hero. If the story is indeed one in which Macomber passes suddenly (in your phrase) "from *object* to *man*" and if the function of Wilson, in relation to this, is to provide the "norm" by which we are intended to evaluate the change, then clearly nothing should be done in the narrative that will obscure this view of the case. Now I think we do become more or less convinced during the opening scene that Macomber is "less of a man and more of an object than ever before" and that Wilson, if not Margot, is probably right in judging him as severely as he does. But then we learn for ourselves what has actually happened earlier in the day, and I think he would be a rather exceptional reader who could feel quite sure that, if he were put into the same fearsome circumstances as Macomber, and with no more previous experience with African lions, he would not, like Macomber, suddenly find himself "running wildly, in panic in the open, running toward the stream." It may be, as you suggest, that Hemingway wishes us to think of Macomber, in this situation, as "less . . .

even as an *object,* than the lion itself"; and this may be the reason for the otherwise somewhat arbitrary glimpses he gives us into the lion's thoughts. But if so, the device surely misses the mark, with the result that so far from thinking that Wilson's previously indicated contempt has been warranted by the facts, we now tend to feel that he and his professional code are below humanity in a sense in which Macomber's regrettable but wholly natural "cowardice" is not. I repeat that I don't think this is a part of the plot as Hemingway conceived it; about that you seem to me to be right. But certainly to the extent that you are right, Hemingway is wrong! Either he should not have told the story of the lion hunt at all or he should have told it in such a way as to confirm rather than contradict the impression of Macomber's initial moral state which he had been careful to fix in our minds at the start.

It seems to me also that in several parts of his narrative Hemingway has resorted too much to inferior and makeshift devices for keeping the reader aware of what is going on. What we are led to expect from the opening pages is an objective and dramatic rendering of events in the manner, for instance, of "The Killers," and I can see no reason why the whole story could not have been told in this way. The device [**324/325**] is modified, however, in the course of the first scene, by the singling out of Wilson as a kind of observer-chorus whose inferences and judgments about Macomber and Margot are given to us in brief asides. This has some obvious advantages, and entails no great sacrifice of that economy of representation on which Hemingway always prided himself; and if he had been content to do the later scenes in a technique consistent with this beginning, there would be nothing more to say. But then comes the scene of the lion hunt as recollected by Macomber lying on his cot, and here the crudities begin. Observe the flat narrative statements about how Macomber felt as he listened to the night noises; the shift to the lion's perceptions

when the motor car reached the place and the later return to these as the beast is about to spring; the amateurish "He could not know that Wilson was furious because he had not noticed . . ."; and lastly the two paragraphs on the marriage, in which Macomber's reflections are allowed to merge, not imperceptibly, into mere historical report.

And what is done in the final scene of the buffalo hunt is even worse, except that we are spared a look into the buffalo's mind. The scene starts in the manner of the first, with Wilson as chorus in an otherwise dramatic rendering. But this method presently breaks down, and we get many direct statements of thought and feeling not only for Macomber but, in one or two places toward the end, even for Margot, who has hitherto been merely heard and seen (note "but her contempt was not secure. She was very afraid of something" and "Because she had done the best she could for many years back and the way they were together was no one person's fault"). Most of these statements seem to me superfluous in view of what is obviously going on, or, when they serve a purpose, to be clumsy explicit notations of things that could be better shown dramatically. The worst are the reiterated assertions, in the narrator's flat prose, of Macomber's "happiness": "he had no fear, only hatred of Wilson"; "Macomber felt a drunken elation"; "In his life he had never felt so good"; "For the first time in his life he really felt wholly without fear. Instead of fear he had a feeling of definite elation"; and so on. Hemingway at his best would have left all this to the reader's inference, as he does similar things in "The Killers," and he would never have printed a passage like the following: [**325/326**]

Macomber felt a wild unreasonable happiness that he had never known before.

"By God, that was a chase," he said. "I've never felt any such feeling. Wasn't it marvellous, Margot?"

There is in all this little of the concision we appreciate in Hemingway's better work, and the result is a watering down of the effect proper to this crucial part of the story; there is a certain jarring incongruity, too, between the commonplace flavor of Macomber's thoughts as the narrator states them and the relatively heroic quality of his actions. I can explain these lapses only by supposing that, having begun to write like himself in the opening section, Hemingway then suddenly became conscious of the limited intelligence, in matters of art, of his prospective readers in the *Cosmopolitan* magazine!

Macomber and the Critics *

ROBERT B. HOLLAND (1911–   ) is a professor of English and Head of the Department at Mississippi State University. His publications include essays on Ellen Glasgow, Walt Whitman, and "The Agrarian Manifesto."

To an author like Hemingway, to whom the integrity of the word was a religion, the critical fate of "The Short Happy Life of Francis Macomber" must have been, if he knew of it, a sad example of scholarly ineptitude at best and of irresponsible thesis-hunting at worst. It should indeed be a cause of profound wonder to us all that well-educated scholars can write, and reputable journals publish, material whose first premise is based on plain failure to read literally what is, literally, on the page. A brief survey of the critical career of "Macomber" may illustrate how far astray we may go in our judgments of literature, and how greatly and disastrously we may distort and misrepresent the intent, even the plain statement, of the author.

In the climactic scene of the story, which surely must be one of the most frequently explicated scenes in all contemporary literature, Macomber, as he stands alongside the guide, Wilson, firing at the charging buffalo, is killed by a bullet from the gun of his wife, who fires from the back seat of a nearby vehicle. How is this scene of death reported? Here is what Hemingway wrote: ". . . Mrs. Macomber, in the car, had shot at the buffalo with the 6.5 Mannlicher as it seemed about to gore Macomber and had hit her husband about two inches up and a little to one side of the base of his skull." [1]

[1] *The Fifth Column and the First Forty-Nine Stories* (New York, 1939), p. 135.

Here is Edmund Wilson in 1939: "Here the male saves his soul at the last minute, and then is actually shot down by his woman, who does not want him to have a soul." [2] With Wilson, it seems, begins the tide of "Mrs. Macomber as murderess" criticism. Ray B. West, Jr.: Mrs. Macomber, "under a pretense of shooting the animal, sends a bullet into his brain." [3] Philip Young: Mrs. Macomber, "ostensibly aiming for the beast in order to save Francis—kills him." [4] Carlos Baker: ". . . it is his wife from her commanding [171/172] position in the back seat of the car who closes the contest" between herself and her husband. His death is "murder." [5] John Killinger traps Mrs. Macomber twice: It becomes necessary "that she shoot him lest she lose him." "Margot had lost him; so she shot him." [6] Leslie Fiedler: Mrs. Macomber "kills her husband for having alienated the affections of the guide. . . ." [7] Joseph De Falco: She "accidentally" (they are his quote marks) shoots him. The murder "represents the woman's inability to recognize the freedom of the

[2] "Ernest Hemingway," *Atlantic Monthly*, cxxxix (July 1939), 46. In a previous review of *The Fifth Column and the First Forty-Nine Stories* Wilson had not commented on the shooting scene. *Nation*, cxlvii (Dec. 10, 1938), 628–630.
[3] "Ernest Hemingway: The Failure of Sensibility," *Sewanee Review*, liii (Winter 1945), 131.
[4] *Ernest Hemingway* (New York, 1952), pp. 45–46.
[5] *Hemingway* (Princeton, 1956), pp. 189, 189–190.
[6] *Hemingway and the Dead Gods* (Lexington, 1960), pp. 44, 46.
[7] *Love and Death in the American Novel* (New York, 1960), p. 307.

*Robert B. Holland, "Macomber and the Critics," *Studies in Short Fiction*, V (Winter 1967), 171–178. Reprinted with the permission of *Studies in Short Fiction* (Newberry College, Newberry, S.C.)

husband-son figure." [8] André Maurois: ". . . she fires toward the animal and hits Macomber at the base of his skull. He dies instantly. Was it an accident? No; Margot Macomber, accustomed to dominating, felt that once her husband Francis had become a brave man he would no longer be a compliant husband. So she got rid of him —coldly, with no risk to herself." [9] Theodore Bardacke: she "shoots him rather than lose her dominating role." [10] William Bysshe Stein, of the anti-guide school, injects an interesting variation. Assuming that Mrs. Macomber murdered her husband, he makes the murder futile, for Macomber had not really had time to mature and was really still a coward. Mrs. Macomber, however, thinking he had become a brave man, shoots him, and "this, it seems to me, would be the perfect ironical climax to the story: Margot need not have murdered her husband." [11] Finally, a not uncommon extreme: She "degenerates into an hysterical savage who murders her mate in blind, primitive hate." [12]

The critical superstructures these critics have built are often subtle, compelling, and logical. It is tempting to take them into account. But that is not the point. For their fatal flaw is simple: they are built on a false first assumption—namely, that Mrs. Macomber murdered her husband. One is haunted back to Hemingway: ". . . Mrs. Macomber . . . had shot at the buffalo. . . ." We should remember Hemingway's scorn of the loose word, the inexact expression. The battered quote from *A Farewell to Arms* still serves:

There were many words that you could not stand to hear and finally only the names of places had dignity. Certain numbers were the same way and [172/173] certain dates and these with the names of the places were all you could say and have

them mean anything. Abstract words such as glory, honor, courage, or hallow were obscene beside the concrete names of villages, the numbers of roads, the names of rivers, the numbers of regiments and the dates.[13]

In fiction, Hemingway is the counterpart of the poetic Pounds and Doolittles, attempting to restore what they conceived to be the lost integrity of the word. It was Hemingway's virtue to report with exactitude what he saw, to render the thing as it was in all possible clarity. This is not to say that ironies and paradoxes and ambiguities and all sorts of shadowy implications do not exist in the fictional world that Hemingway created, and in the real world upon which he based his creations. It is merely to say that the ironies and paradoxes and ambiguities reside in those worlds and not in Hemingway's reporting.

How then account for the astounding misreading, which continues in spite of a few sensible critiques that one would assume that students of Hemingway had read? As early as 1955, for instance, Warren Beck, in a fine explication, took Hemingway at his word, and in so doing did better by Mrs. Macomber than most other critics. Noting that the wife shot at the buffalo, he builds his case against the integrity of the guide, Wilson, who caps his questionable role by assuming immediately that Mrs. Macomber deliberately shot her husband. In answer to the obvious misreading, Beck is generous enough to the misreaders to assert quietly that Hemingway must have meant what he said, for Hemingway is not an "off-side" writer.[14] Virgil Hutton, in another good explication in 1964, takes a similar point of view, finding the portrait of Wilson an "unrelenting satire," and he speaks of the killing of Francis as Mrs. Macomber's "fatal attempt to save her husband." [15] These represent the wise minority, or at least the minority who read and believed what Hemingway said.

One way to account for the misreading

[8] *The Hero in Hemingway's Short Stories* (Pittsburgh, 1963), pp. 202, 206.

[9] "Ernest Hemingway," in Carlos Baker, ed., *Hemingway and His Critics* (New York, 1961), p. 51.

[10] "Hemingway's Women," in John K. M. McCaffery, ed., *Ernest Hemingway: The Man and His Work* (New York, 1950), p. 349.

[11] "Hemingway's 'The Short Happy Life of Francis Macomber,'" *The Explicator*, xix (April 1961), Item 47.

[12] Arthur E. Waterman, "The Short Happy Life of Francis Macomber," *The Explicator*, xx (September 1961), Item 2.

[13] *A Farewell to Arms* (New York, 1929), p. 191.

[14] "The Shorter Happy Life of Mrs. Macomber," *Modern Fiction Studies*, x (November 1955), 28–37.

[15] "The Short Happy Life of Macomber," *University Review*, xxx (June 1964), 253–263.

of "Macomber" is to assume merely that the critics have read carelessly, that they in fact overlooked what Hemingway said, that they thought he wrote that the wife intentionally killed the husband or that he worded the scene ambiguously. This simple assumption would be the easiest way to account for the flood of misinterpretation that follows [**173/174**] Edmund Wilson's 1939 *Atlantic* piece. But one would not lightly accuse such critics as Wilson, West, Fiedler, Young, and Baker of failing to see the words on the page, although certainly some of the lesser critics have failed to do so. One might assume that some of the latter, rushing to print, scanned the words and heard the Edmund Wilsons and the Bakers, believing what they wanted to believe. It may in fact be that the weight of early evaluation by reputable critics so established the Mrs. Macomber-as-murderess reading that future readers were blinded to what Hemingway wrote.

There remain other reasonable assumptions that might help to explain the matter. The first is that "Macomber," one of two African fictions ordinarily thought of at once, is fair prey for those who are taken with the "Bitch" theory of Hemingway's women. It has become, of course, a critical commonplace that Hemingway's women are on the one hand the good Renatas of *Across the River* and the Catherines of *A Farewell to Arms* and on the other the bitches like Brett of *The Sun Also Rises* or the wife in "Kilimanjaro." And thus The Hemingway Bitch, cold, dominating, materialistic, American, becomes standard. To Leslie Fiedler, for instance, Mrs. Macomber is the "prime example" of the "hopeless and unmitigated" American bitch,[16] beyond whom one cannot go in bitchery. Thus Margot, who has indeed her share of bitchery throughout the story, is at once typed, and must act in character and be a murderess as well, a bitch to the end. For, it would seem, it is not like Hemingway to give her a strain of nobility and compassion. This

would indeed be out-Victorianing the Victorians. Yet nobility and compassion are strong elements in Hemingway's world, as witness Renata, Catherine, The Old Man. Hemingway is as "moral" a writer as the next man. "A writer without a sense of justice and of injustice would be better off editing the year book of a school for exceptional children than writing novels." [17] Nonetheless, the stereotype of the Hemingway Bitch has become a critical commonplace.

A second possibility is that, in spite of the fact that the literary critic should certainly of all men be linguistically responsible and sophisticated, many of us, in a culture of False Speak, of mistrust of the word, of the constant deliberate distortion and misuse of words by the total culture for "respectable" reasons (as witness [**174/175**] much advertising)—many of us cannot recognize, and give credence to, honest words when we see them. Again, in a world trained by Richards to seek ambiguities and levels of meanings wherever one reads, of the new criticism devoted to ambiguities as a virtue of art, the blunt directness of a Hemingway may be old fashioned, and thus to us unthinkable. Irony, indeed, that the author of *A Farewell to Arms,* who rebelled against the elasticity and the generalizing tendency of Victorian diction, should now be read and misinterpreted by a supposedly sophisticated generation that may be really more careless or dishonest, or both, with words than were their forefathers. A plain meaning is thus suspect to the sophisticated modern. If Philip Young and Ray B. West can read plain words—and of course they can—how may we account for their statements that Mrs. Macomber "under a pretense of shooting the animal, sends a bullet into his brain" and "ostensibly aiming for the beast" kills her husband? Surely if Hemingway had meant that there was a pretense of aiming at the animal, if Margot merely "ostensibly" aimed at it, he would

16 Fiedler, p. 307.

17 Quoted by George Plimpton, "An Interview with Ernest Hemingway," in Carlos Baker, ed., *Hemingway and His Critics,* p. 37.

not have written that she "shot at the buffalo." Who was there to deceive? No one was watching her shoot. Was then she attempting to deceive herself? Again, if this were so, would Hemingway have written "she shot at the buffalo"? Hemingway, remember, is the narrator. Is the modern critical mind so self-centered that it finds no depravity in substituting what it wants for what it sees? Or are relativism and skepticism so deeply ingrained in the modern critical mind that it will not believe what it sees? Certainly something of this kind must be the case, else we are driven into the untenable conviction that the author himself did not mean, or know, what he wrote. If this assumption may be established in an honest writer like Hemingway, then criticism is indeed free to substitute its own meanings for those to be found on any page. How free are we to treat literature as if it were propaganda, thus justifying Joseph DeFalco's placing in quotation marks the word "accidentally"? Is nothing sacred to the critic except his own self-expression?

A third possibility is that critics of the present generation are likely to fall prey to *a priori* judgment based on the Freudian psychology, existentialism, myth, or some other frame of reference. Thus we hear that the true theme of Macomber is death; and given the Bitch theory, existentialist death becomes more ironic and thus more "real" if it is the wife who kills the husband, and not he himself, or than if it were the result of a hunting accident. No such [175/176] irony would exist if Macomber were to die simply on the horns of a buffalo, for he had, one might say, asked for it—no tragedy. The density becomes respectable, however, when he dies at the hands of his wife just as he is beginning to live. Again, the mother-son or some similar motif is attractive, involving all the ramifications of domination and sexual conflict. That existentialist and psychological themes are strong elements in contemporary fiction, that of Hemingway included, we may all agree. And it is of course not possible to read the con-

temporary short story from the point of view of nineteenth-century postulates. But thesis-hunting against the plain intent of the author's unambiguous statement—She "had shot at the buffalo"—becomes a sort of intellectual depravity, a critical dishonesty, assuming of course, first, that the critic has read what he is writing about. And if he hasn't, the charge is even more serious.

II

Since the thesis of this essay stands or falls on the validity of my belief that we must take literally the statement, by the "omniscient author," that Mrs. Macomber "shot at the buffalo," any argument from context becomes irrelevant as proof. It is not out of order, however, to attempt to demonstrate that my reading of the crucial statement in no wise goes counter to the context. Although such demonstration is irrelevant as proof if the beginning premise is correct, it should be valuable as supporting evidence of the structural integrity of the narrative.

To begin with the most immediate context, the sentence itself: ". . . Mrs. Macomber, in the car, had shot at the buffalo with the 6.5 Mannlicher as it seemed about to gore Macomber and had hit her husband about two inches up and a little to one side of the base of his skull." It might be inferred that the specificity of "two inches up" is intended to prove that Mrs. Macomber is a good shot, and that, being a good shot, she must have hit what she aimed at. As far as the evidence in the story is concerned, Margot may or may not be a good marksman, for she does not shoot elsewhere in the story, and Hemingway makes no comment about her marksmanship. Leaving this point, then, does the specificity of "two inches up" serve a different, and important, function? I think it does. First, it is a literal fact, as she "shot at the buffalo" is a literal fact. But why does Hemingway present to us this literally irrelevant fact? The reader of Hemingway will surely recognize the typical [**176/177**] Hemingway dodge of taking defense against dramatic emotions by rhetorical matter-of-factness and by ironic heightening of irrelevant literal fact in presenting tragic circumstances. Note "A Natural History of the Dead," as the fragments of bodies are gathered up after battle: "Many of these were detached from a heavy barbed-wire fence which had surrounded the position of the factory and from the still existent portions of which we picked up many of these detached bits which illustrated only too well the tremendous energy of high explosive. Many fragments we found a considerable distance away in the field, they being carried farther by their own weight." The marvelous rhetorical effect of the rare and grammatically "pure" nominative absolute at the end of the passage, and of the prim precision of "illustrated only too well" is to throw about the scene of horror an apparent detached unconcern, indeed to withdraw from the horror into the comforting context of pure structural form, to wrap the reader, in the face of overwhelming tragedy, in the platitude, the triviality, the petty and insignificant.

Again, in *A Farewell to Arms* (p. 4): "At the start of the winter came the permanent rain and with the rain came the cholera. But it was checked and in the end only seven thousand died of it in the army." [18]

Moving to the dialogue between Mrs. Macomber and the guide over the corpse of her husband, we encounter another possible caveat. How are we to take this dialogue? "Of course it's an accident," says the guide. But the guide is being savagely ironic, for he has no doubt, can have no doubt really, that Mrs. Macomber has murdered her husband. "Why didn't you

[18] In any appeal to parallels we must, of course, not overlook the fact that there is a difference between the third person narrative and the first person narrative. *A Farewell to Arms* is a first person narrative, as is *The Sun Also Rises*. This distinction is essential in evaluating the crucial phrase. Hemingway's technique of understatement, however, is recognized as a constant characteristic of style, so that an illustration from his most popular work is not inappropriate.

poison him?" Another twist of the knife. The guide too subscribes to the Bitch theory. (Perhaps he originated it.) The wife is left with her dead husband and with a deadly guide who can find vengeance only by slashing her with his ironic cruelty. After all, Wilson had come to like her husband. He alone can punish her. No law could do it. There is no conceivable legal case against her.

To return to the sentence itself, to the structure immediately following the crucial statement: Margot fires at the buffalo "as it seemed about to gore Macomber. . . ." Seemed to whom? we [**177/178**] might ask. It could seem, as put, only to the narrator or to Mrs. Macomber. Either way, the proximity of "seemed about to gore Macomber" to "shot at the buffalo" certainly may support the supposition that Mrs. Macomber has shot to save her husband, or at least to save a human being. As with California in Jeffers' "Roan Stallion," surely we may accord her a bit of "obscure human fidelity" that leads her, if the terror and the speed of the scene do not, to fire at the beast which seems about to gore a fellow man. We need not even discard the Bitch theory to do this.

One could, I believe, make the same sort of argument for the appropriateness of the crucial phrase to other parts of the context if one wished. From the context, indeed, one can build a reasonable case either way. Margot's peculiar state during the last hunt is quite ambiguous, as well it might be. It is tempting to rework the whole territory. But the critics have done that, on either side of the question: they have thoroughly examined the context. If one chooses to disregard the crucial phrase, one will have no difficulty in finding Margot a murderer by reference to her words and conduct throughout the story. One can find her guiltless by the same examination. My case here rests, as it began, on the plain statement in the text, as Hemingway the narrator wrote it: Mrs. Macomber "shot at the buffalo."

"The Snows of Kilimanjaro": Commentary *

CAROLINE GORDON (1895–   ) has had a distinguished career as a novelist, short story writer, and critic. Her novels include *Penhally* (1931); *Aleck Maury, Sportsman* (1934); *None Shall Look Back* (1937); *The Garden of Adonis* (1937); *Green Centuries* (1941); *The Woman on the Porch* (1944); *The Strange Children* (1951); and *The Malefactors* (1956). Her stories have been collected in *The Forest of the South* (1946) and *Old Red* (1963). In addition she has published two critical studies: *How to Read a Novel* (1957) and *A Good Soldier: A Key to the Novels of Ford Madox Ford* (1963).

ALLEN TATE (1899–   ), one of America's leading poets and critics, has taught for many years at the University of Minnesota. His poetry has been collected in *Poems, 1922–1947* (1948); his criticism, in *Collected Essays* (1959). He has also written biographies of Stonewall Jackson (1928) and Jefferson Davis (1929) and one novel, *The Fathers* (1938).

Edgar Allan Poe, in his review of Hawthorne's *Twice-Told Tales* in *Graham's Magazine* of May, 1842, laid down a fundamental principle for the construction of the "tale" or short fiction:

A skillful literary artist has fashioned a tale. If wise, he has not fashioned his thought to accommodate his incidents; but having conceived, with deliberate care, a certain unique or single *effect* to be wrought out, he then invents such incidents—he then combines such events as may best aid him in establishing this preconceived effect. If his very initial sentence tend not to the outbringing of this effect, then he has failed in the first step. In the whole composition there should be no word written, of which the tendency, direct or indirect, is not to the preestablished design.   **[419/420]**

Ernest Hemingway's *A Farewell to Arms* begins:

In the late summer of that year we lived in a house in a village that looked across the river and the plains to the mountains. In the bed of the river there were pebbles and boulders, dry and white in the sun, and the water was clear and swiftly moving and blue in the channels. Troops went by the house and down the road and the dust they raised powdered the leaves of the trees. The trunks of the trees were dusty and the leaves fell early that year and we saw troops marching along the road and the dust rising and leaves, stirred by the breeze, falling and the soldiers marching and afterward the road bare and white except for the leaves.

The tone . . . of the whole book is set in the first paragraph. The tone, in this case, is a mood, a dramatization of the wistful rebellion of youth, confronted with the hard facts of life, love, and death. This mood, evoked by the very sound of the words in the first sentence: "In the late summer of that year . . ." and persisting throughout the action, swells up at the climax in a crescendo that is so perfectly timed that when one re-reads the book tears spring always to the eyes at the same passage—provided that one is capable of shedding tears over the sorrows of fictional characters.

Another master, Chekhov, might have admired the rendering of the rest of the passage. The action of the sun *shows* the pebbles and boulders that lie in the bed

*Caroline Gordon and Allen Tate, " 'The Snows of Kilimanjaro': Commentary," from *The House of Fiction* (New York: Charles Scribner's Sons, 1950), pp. 419–423. Copyright 1950 Charles Scribner's Sons; reprinted with the permission of Charles Scribner's Sons.

of the river to be *dry* and *white*. The river is clear and moves swiftly; the further specification that it was blue where the water was deepest (in the channels) makes us *see* it flow. We are convinced that the troops passed the house by the fact that enough dust was raised to powder the leaves of the trees and even the trunks. The passage could stand as an amplification of some advice that Chekhov once wrote to his good-for-nothing brother, Alexander:

Descriptions of Nature should be very brief and have an incidental character. Commonplaces like "The setting sun, bathing in the waves of the darkenin̄g sea, flooded with purple and gold . . . The swaḷḷ ws, flying over the surface of the water, chirped merrily"—such commonplaces should be finished with. In descriptions of Nature one has to snatch at small details, grouping them in such a manner that after reading them one can obtain the picture on closing one's eyes.

For instance, you will get a moonlight night if you write that on the dam of the mill a fragment of broken bottle flashed like a small bright star, and there rolled by, like a ball, the black shadow of a dog or a wolf—and so on.

One is reminded of another piece of advice that Chekhov gave:

"If a gun hangs on the wall in the first paragraph of your story it must be discharged at the end"—which is only another way of saying the same thing [420/ 421] that Poe said. The phrase, "The leaves fell early that year," is an admirable preparation for the climax of the action; that is to say, "My love died young." The whole Resolution . . . is, in fact, both prepared for and symbolized in this passage: "We saw troops marching along the road and the dust rising and leaves, stirred by the breeze, falling and afterward the road bare and white except for the leaves." A human heart, ravaged by grief, will ultimately become as bare and as quiet as the white road that the soldiers have passed over.

This kind of writing was rare in the twenties and, indeed, is rare at any time. It calls for a particular kind of response to the natural world, the kind of response that Turgenev, for instance, gave. But we sometimes say that in order to write like Turgenev one would have to be Turgenev. And that, in a measure, was true, up to Hemingway's time. Hemingway has not the range or the depth of the Russian, but possessing a sensory apparatus capable of the same exquisite response to the natural world, he is more deeply grounded in his craft, more athletic. He is, in short, the kind of writer one can learn from as distinguished from the kind of writer, like Turgenev or Tolstoy, who can be safely followed only at a distance. Developing a high degree of technical proficiency, Hemingway fulfilled the promise of early American realistic writers, such as Frank Norris, Ambrose Bierce, Sarah Orne Jewett, and became, like Stephen Crane, a master of naturalism.

There had been masters of naturalism before him, notably in France. Indeed, it might be claimed that the mantle of Flaubert's great disciple, Maupassant, has fallen on Hemingway's shoulders. Some remarks which Henry James once made about Maupassant apply equally well to Hemingway:

"Nothing can exceed the masculine firmness, the quiet force of his style, in which every phrase is a close sequence, every epithet a paying piece, and the ground is completely cleared of the vague, the ready-made and the second-best. Less than any one today does he beat the air; more than any one does he hit out from the shoulder."

"The Snows of Kilimanjaro," one of Hemingway's late and most ambitious stories, exhibits both the virtues and the limitations of his method. He is hitting out from the shoulder as hard—or nearly as hard—as he hits out in his early stories, but his reach isn't long enough. He has chosen an ineffable subject: a man approaching the moment of his death. He uses the snow-covered mountain of Kilimanjaro as the symbol of death, but the symbolism . . . is not a part of the action and therefore does not operate as a controlling image, as in the stories of Joyce, James, and Kafka. The result is a lack of dramatic force. The symbolism seems something the writer has tacked on, rather than an integral part of the story.

As a substitute for the kind of incidents James and Joyce use, incidents which are at once naturalistic and symbolic, Hemingway uses two levels of action: a man who is dying of gangrene alternately talks with those around him and communes with his soul. The incidents are all seen through the eyes [**421/422**] of the chief character. The surface pattern of action, the man's bickerings with his wife, his memories of their past life together, his thoughts about the life they lead together now, his few exchanges with the native servants, are all rendered with precision and fidelity to reality. His reveries about his own life before he met his present wife, his communings, so to speak, with his soul, make an effective contrast to the smooth pattern of their day and also prepare for the Resolution. He not only scents the approach of death, who comes now as a hyena or riding on a bicycle, but he realizes when he first began to die: the day he traded his integrity for security. (The story is, to that extent, a parable of the situation of the artist in the world.) Some of the passages are as lucid and beautiful as any Hemingway has written:

What about the ranch and the silvered gray of the sage brush, the quick, clear water in the irrigation ditches, and the heavy green of the alfalfa? The trail went up into the hills and the cattle in the summer were shy as deer . . .

The African countryside constitutes the Enveloping Action . . . of the story:

He lay then and was quiet for a while and looked across the heat shimmer of the plain to the edge of the bush. There were a few Tommies that showed minute and white against the yellow and, far off, he saw a herd of zebra, white against the green of the bush. This was a pleasant camp under big trees against a hill, with good water, and close by, a nearly dry water hole where sand grouse flighted in the mornings.

On the naturalistic level the Resolution is the death of the hero, and it is well pre-

pared for in the first sentence of the story: "The marvellous thing is that it's painless," he said, and we know that he is talking about dying when he looks out and sees three buzzards squatting on the plain. But the author has made no provision for the climax of his symbolic action. Our attention is not called to the snow-covered peaks of Kilimanjaro until the end of the story; as a result we do not feel that sense of recognition and inevitability which help to make a *katharsis*.

The passage in which the hero and his pilot confront the mountain is well rendered, from the standpoint of naturalism, but something more than naturalism is needed here. "Compie," turning his head and grinning and pointing, is not an impressive Charon and we are not convinced that he and the hero are going to any country that is different from other countries they have known. The passage lacks elevation of tone and the story itself lacks tonal and symbolic unity. . . . Its three planes of action, the man's intercourse with his wife, his communings with his soul, and the background of Enveloping Action, the mysterious Dark Continent, are never integrated. The story does not make the dramatic impact it would have [**422/423**] made had the controlling image operated throughout, tying the several levels of the action together.

Henry James, in "The Art of Fiction," has an explanation for such magnificent failures. He complains that Maupassant omits "one of the items of the problem" when he "simply skipped the whole reflective part of his men and women—that reflective part which governs conduct and produces character." Hemingway's characters reflect, but they do not reflect deeply enough. He, like Maupassant, has limited his field of observation too sharply. Naturalism alone will not sustain the weight of his narrative, and Hemingway, for all his remarkable achievement, remains what James called Maupassant, "a lion in the path."

The Leopard and the Hyena: Symbol and Meaning in "The Snows of Kilimanjaro" *

MARION MONTGOMERY (1925–   ) is an associate professor of English at the University of Georgia. Apart from his numerous critical essays, he has published two books of poetry, *Dry Lightning* (1960) and *Stones from the Rubble* (1965), and three novels, *The Wandering of Desire* (1962), *Darrell* (1964), and *Ye Olde Bluebird* (1967).

In "The Snows of Kilimanjaro" Ernest Hemingway employs specific symbols—a mountain, a hyena, a leopard—to dramatize a favorite theme: heroic perseverance. But the symbols' relationship to the action of the story arouses questions of interpretation which are not easily resolved. It is the purpose of this paper to analyze the story to see just where the symbols, the leopard and hyena particularly, raise problems in the dramatic structure and the meaning of the story and to consider to what extent the problems are solved by the story.

The center of dramatic conflict in "The Snows of Kilimanjaro" is the protagonist's mind, which is constantly agitated by a contrast between the present ignoble situation and the memory of a more heroic past. Harry, a writer, at the point in his life where he should have realized his ideal or should at least find himself still devoted to the ideal, lies dying of gangrene because of his carelessness in not treating a scratch got on a hunt. He knows that he is dying physically, but he knows also that he has died spiritually long before, through his choice of carrion comfort over the lean joys of more dangerous pursuit. Like Eliot's old man in "Gerontion," he remembers his failures sardonically. He adds up the actions of his life,

the motions and facts, that have brought him to a cot in the dry plains of Africa, and he faces despair self-condemned.

If Harry judges himself by his actions, the fact that he does so indicates a positive code against which he measures them. What is that positive code, which he has forsaken? To approach a statement of it, we must make use of two keys which Hemingway provides: one is the leopard described in the headnote to the story; the other is the hyena which functions dramatically in the story. The headnote reads:

Kilimanjaro is a snow covered mountain 19,710 feet high, and is said to be the highest mountain in Africa. Its western summit is called Masai "Ngaje Ngài," the House of God. Close to the western summit there is the dried and frozen carcass of a leopard. No one has explained what the leopard was seeking at that altitude.

This is the only direct reference to the leopard, and therein, perhaps, lies a weakness of the story, a point to be considered later. What is important to note at this point is that a contrast seems to be implied between the leopard of the headnote and the hyena that slinks through the story itself. The hyena's first appearance occurs just at dark when "there was no longer enough light to shoot." Had there been enough light, one may venture to suppose from Harry's attitude that he

*Marion Montgomery, "The Leopard and the Hyena: Symbol and Meaning in 'The Snows of Kilimanjaro,'" *The University of Kansas City Review*, XXVII (Summer 1961), 277–282. Reprinted with the permission of *The University of Kansas City Review* and the author.

would certainly have shot the loathsome creature. From this point on, as [**277/278**] Harry continues to judge and condemn himself, the hyena plays an important role in his thoughts. For instance, when Harry realizes beyond all doubt that he is going to die, we are told that the realization "came with a rush . . . of a sudden evil-smelling emptiness and the odd thing was that the hyena slipped lightly along the edge of it." To extract Harry's code from the story, we must explain the relationship of the leopard frozen on the mountain to the hyena attracted by the smell of Harry's decaying flesh.

Now the quotation just cited might naturally lead one to suppose that the hyena functions in the story as a symbol of death, but its symbolic function is, I think, more complex. Harry has, as a writer, already been considering death's symbols. He has watched the vultures collect, also attracted by the smell of decay. He thinks of death at one point, after remembering his life in Paris, as something that "went on bicycles and moved absolutely silently on the pavements." And late in the story he says to his wife: "Never believe any of that about a scythe and a skull . . . It can be two bicycle policemen as easily, or be a bird. Or it can have a wide snout like a hyena." At this point Harry is already drifting into a dream-like state which will be consummated by his flight to the House of God. He has felt death come and rest its head on the foot of the cot, "and he could smell its breath," this after having just heard the hyena in the darkness. Here Harry is losing control of his thoughts as he drifts into death. His speech and reflections become less clear, less rational, and his association of the hyena with death seems once more quite simple. But death has not been a hyena up to this point; it has been "a sudden evil-smelling emptiness." And the hyena has been to Harry a symbol of a particular kind of life, the life he has followed to that morally "evil-smelling emptiness." We must remember that Harry is a writer, but more importantly we must remember that

he is a hunter. What game is to the animal predator, the book is to Harry. But to Harry the captured game, the finished book, is really of secondary importance. He does regret that he has never written about those things which are clearly important, but even more does he regret having lost sight of their importance. Harry has ceased to be the kind of hunter he holds ideal. To make this point clear, we must note that, while Harry does lament his artistic failure, he judges himself in other terms. In the first part of the story he is angry "that this was the end of it [life]." He is angry, not because of his failure as writer, but because of a moral failure: because he has not been the good hunter.

There are two streams of Harry's consciousness presented in the story, distinguished by typography, in which he considers himself primarily as hunter. The one is in italics, the other in Roman type. The italics embody Harry's reflections concerning the past he approves of; the material in Roman type embodies the past and present he disapproves of. The two play against each other, giving rise to the story's internal and external dramatic tension [**278/279**] sion. For instance, at the end of the first scene, Harry's wife protests against the fate that has caused Harry's discomfort. "What have we done to have that happen to us?" He answers, "I suppose what I did was to forget to put iodine on it when I first scratched it." A whole train of half measures has led to the decaying leg, and Harry's sardonic tone as he relates the neglect reflects a judgment on his failure. But the sardonic tone reflects on more sins than a failure to use iodine. The half measures that have led him to a spiritual rot are gnawing at him, and he remembers himself in a more worthy state in the italicized passage which follows this scene. We do not know at first just what those spiritual half-measures were, because Harry's thought skips that portion of his history for the moment, leaving us to deduce the comparison of the half-measures from the sardonic tone he uses with his wife and the heroic tone of the italicized reflection.[1] (Just so may we deduce Harry's ideal code from the hyena's, the negative code.) Harry recalls a retreat from Thrace and the snow on Bulgarian mountains which brought death to those trapped in their heroic attempt; he recalls the aid given a deserter who won admiration through his courage. He recalls the full-spirited skiing and gambling, and in contrast he recalls Barker who machine-gunned helpless enemy officers. Those were the good days of pursuit for the sake of pursuit which demanded a worthy victim, not the helpless game which scavengers like Barker come by.

Harry breaks his reflections to ask his wife "Where did we stay in Paris?" His mind has turned now, suddenly for the reader, to his own infamous life with his rich wife in a comfortable section of Paris —infamous because it was a life content with an easy pursuit. He is vicious in his repartee with his wife, leading her to ask: "Do you have to kill your horse and your wife and burn your saddle and your armour?" She is a simple woman whose main talent is the bed, and she cannot see that he is scourging himself more than her. She has made possible his comfort and decay through her money, and his desperate, destructive words are his way of "trying to kill to keep . . . alive." When he speaks the cruel truth of his failure, she mistakes his sardonic tone for sarcasm and his words for an attack upon her, and so he slips back into "the familiar lie he made his bread and butter by:" he tells her he loves her. He reflects that "If he lived by a lie, he should try to die by it," an attempt to regain some nobleness of spirit. It is not the woman's fault that he has traded on his talent, accepting the unworthy pursuit of the hollow, decayed

rich, telling his conscience that his end was to write about those spiritually decayed beings. That, then, was the beginning of the half-measures ending in the spiritual rot which left him dead long before the infection of his leg. [279/280] Harry, alone on his cot, recalls how lies became life. "You kept from thinking and it was all marvellous." [2] In other words, Harry began stalking dead game, as Barker did in strafing the helpless enemy officers and as the hyena stalks Harry outside the fire's circle. He recalls next how he was in turn stalked by the woman, as if she caught the scent of his decay. They are alike, he concludes, and in resignation he accepts her again, lying on the cot by the fire while she talks, still unable to reclaim the old ideal that might purge him of the smell of moral decay. It is at this moment in his thought that "it occurred to him that he was going to die," a fact that has already occurred to him and been accepted but which becomes terrifyingly impressive because it is at this point that he senses death as "a sudden evil-smelling emptiness and the odd thing was that the hyena slipped lightly along the edge of it."

Harry remembers next, in contrast to his wife, those women he loved too much, how through the corrosion of quarrelling he and they "killed what they had together." There was unhappiness as a result, but there was no living of a lie. It was a cleaner death he pursued. But now his cruel honesty cannot kill what he and his wife have together any more than the hyena can kill the carrion it stalks. From this point in the story the hyena and the woman are associated, but the equation implied in Harry's thinking is complex— hyena : carrion :: Harry : wife :: death : Harry. In sharp contrast to that animal creature, the Armenian slut, Harry's wife is soft and yielding, the easy death he has sought. "And as he looked and saw her

---

[1] Hemingway has said (in *Death in the Afternoon*, p. 192): "If a writer of prose knows enough about what he is writing about he may omit things that he knows and the reader, if the writer is writing truly enough, will have a feeling of those things as strongly as though the writer had stated them. The dignity of movement of an iceberg is due to only one-eighth of it being above water." There is a great deal of Harry's mind under water so that the reader must fill in transitions for himself sometimes, as in this instance.

[2] Thinking, in Hemingway's stories, seems always to lead to compromising pure action. The relation of thought to lie is an important concern to the protagonists of this story as to those of "The Gambler, the Nun, and the Radio," "A Clean, Well-Lighted Place," and "Soldier's Home," for example.

well-known pleasant smile, he felt death come again." He associates the smell of his physical death and the look of his wife, which remind him of his moral decay.

Harry is, by this time, approaching a moral rejuvenation through self-condemnation. He has come to Africa in the first place to work the fat off body and soul, to give up the easy comforts in an attempt to regain the old hunting form, and it is a wry irony of fate that threatens to destroy him before he can reclaim himself. But in spite of fate, he begins an affirmation. Now rejecting the code of life corresponding to the hyena's in the animal world, he reaffirms that corresponding to the leopard's. He summons memories to strengthen him. There are his grandfather's guns, burned when the family cabin burned. His grandfather, he recalls, refused to let the boy disturb them in their ashes. The image of the burned guns in ashes suggests the leopard of the headnote: there is an unexplained steadiness of devotion in the old man's attitude that is of the same order as that which led the leopard beyond its element. Harry remembers, too, his destitute neighbors in the Place Contrescarpe where he lived before he began living the lie. He recalls those drunkards who killed their poverty with drink and the "sportifs" who "took it out in [**280/281**] exercising" by bicycle racing. Here are the hyenas and leopards of the Paris slum, and Harry, in his reflections, judges the drunkards much as he judges Barker and himself and the hyena. He remembers the halfwit chore boy in Wyoming who remained constant to duty to the point of foolishly shooting a man to protect some hay, and there is in Harry's remembering a note of approval of the boy's action. The full-hearted deed is important to him, not the consequences of appearing ridiculous by defending burnt guns or winning third prize in a bicycle race, or being jailed, perhaps hanged, for shooting a man, or ending up with an Armenian whore instead of a respectable wife.

When his present wife interrupts these reflections of past events to bring Harry more broth, to insist that he do what is good for him, he resists her, more determined than ever, because what she means by *good* is, to Harry, *easy*. Death is Harry's chance of self-recovery. He will not care for death, he reflects, and thus he will overcome it. He is determined he won't spoil this experience as he has so many others. He fears only pain, not the idea, and the pain itself does not bother him now. He drifts into death thinking that he has waited too long and too late, and that his life is therefore wasted. "The party's over and you are with your hostess now." But he is bored with his hostess death. "He looked at her [wife's-death's] face between him and the fire . . . He heard the hyena make a noise." He feels death creep up his leg again and "he could smell its breath." It had no shape. "It simply occupied space," negative being. "You've got a hell of a breath," says Harry, his last words as he feels death crouching on his chest. Then he has the sensation of the cot's being lifted as he is carried into the tent, after which everything becomes "all right." His last thoughts show no fear.

So far the story has held together, but the final two sections are crucial to its success, and it is at this point that the story falls apart. It does so, partly because the device of the fantasy flight to Kilimanjaro seems an artificial contrivance,[3] following as it does the realism of the rest of the story, and partly because the final section, shifting back to the level of conscious reality, also shifts the point of view and seems intended primarily to prevent a possible misunderstanding of the story's outcome, as a sort of footnote to the story.

The next to the last section, Harry's flight to Kilimanjaro, takes us back to the headnote with which the story begins and to the question of the story's basic weak-

[3] This device of the realistic death-dream is very like that used by Ambrose Bierce in his "Occurrence at Owl Creek Bridge," in which story the dream is more purely realistic, springing from the protagonist's dying wish to go home. There is also a suggestion of Bierce's "coup de grâce" in the passage where Harry reflects on the death of his friend Williamson who, with his stomach torn open, begged Harry to shoot him and end his misery.

ness. It is easy enough to accept the plane ride as a possible death dream Harry experiences, for it has been prepared for all along in the story. His wife hopefully argues that the plane will come for him in time to save him, and Harry's rational thought throughout has been patterned by association—the good life with the [281/282] bad, a good woman with bad, and so on. The plane-ride dream, then, is a psychological possibility which one can accept. Further, one is prepared for a psychological use of the mountain, though Kilimanjaro itself does not figure in the story until the dream passage, for Harry's thoughts run to the cool snows of his heroic yesteryears as he lies on the cot on the hot African plain. However, one is not sufficiently prepared for the rather sudden symbolic use of the mountain, for the relationship of the mountain to Harry's moral code is inadequately prepared for in the story itself. One surmises that the leopard's relation to the mountain is in some manner paralleled by Harry's relationship to it, but it is an unclear relationship, whereas Harry's relationship to the hyena and carrion is not.

Further, the use of the mountain as symbol is confused by the last three lines of the headnote as contrasted with the events of the flight and with Harry's self-evaluation. What is the "House of God?" Some positive level of achievement on Harry's part is suggested since he apparently is taken to the summit, some achievement which transcends death on the slopes. Throughout the story the emphasis has been on the ideal of attempt, not on accomplishment; then suddenly one has Harry's final thought on seeing "the square top of Kilimanjaro," the House of

God: "And then he knew that there was where he was going." Has Harry, by his act of renouncing the hyena's way for the leopard's, gained salvation? Is that salvation anything more than the soothing balm of the snows of yesterday recovered through the force of desire? The story's end, one suspects, is not metaphysical so much as it is sentimental. It gives the story a happy ending, useful to lesser attempts of Hollywood, but not justified by Harry's nature. It seems void of any real meaning. The problem is further complicated by the fact that the reader has expected the leopard to become an integral part of the story. When one sees the mountain, first described in the headnote, looming rather suddenly out of the story, he expects to see the leopard also. Then, too, the final line of the headnote keeps bothering the reader. "No one has explained what the leopard was seeking at that altitude." Harry knows the answer to the question in terms of other hunters: his grandfather, the half-wit boy in Wyoming, himself in happier days. And Harry obviously knows the mountain: why does the mountain not appear in his consciousness as would naturally be likely; why is there no thought of the leopard, the natural opposite of the hyena, in the mind of this symbol-conscious writer? As hunter he knows the worthy leopard, even as he knows about that most hated of all animals, the hyena. The answer to these questions seems to be simply that Hemingway does not make efficient use of the leopard and mountain, whereas his use of the hyena is extremely skillful. The headnote and the final two sections protrude from the story, making it an awkward iceberg.

"The Snows of Kilimanjaro": A Revaluation *

OLIVER EVANS (1915–   ) is a professor of English at San Fernando Valley State College. His publications include poetry, *Young Man with a Screwdriver* (1950); history, *New Orleans* (1960); and biography, *The Ballad of Carson McCullers* (1966).

I

When "The Snows of Kilimanjaro" first appeared in *Esquire* (August 1936), it attracted immediate attention. It was promptly reprinted (in *Best American Short Stories of 1937*) by Edward J. O'Brien, who, praising it in his preface, remarked: "Nothing is irrelevant. The artist's energy is rigidly controlled for his purpose." Since then it has been anthologized many times, and now it is probably safe to say that, with the possible exception of "The Killers," none of Hemingway's stories has enjoyed greater popularity than this one. Hemingway's own opinion was that it was "about as good as any" [1] of his shorter works.

In the last ten or fifteen years, however, "The Snows" has come in for considerable disparagement, mainly from the so-called New Critics and their followers. In 1945 Ray B. West, Jr., wrote in *The Sewanee Review:* "While I consider this story one of Hemingway's best . . . it is spoiled for me by the conventionality of its leading symbol: the White-capped mountain as the 'House of God.' " [2] In 1950 Allen Tate and Caroline Gordon, referring to it in *The House of Fiction* as a "magnificent

failure," complained that it lacked "dramatic force" and objected that the symbolism was not properly integrated with the action.[3] And in 1956 William Van O'Connor characterized it as a "rather puzzling story" and expressed dissatisfaction with the ending.[4]

Even critics who have praised the story without reservation have differed widely in their interpretation of it, so that one might well wonder if the symbols through which it communicates its meaning are indeed as conventional as Mr. West has found them. The fact is that no other story of Hemingway's has caused quite so much critical controversy, and the main reason for this is disagreement on the meaning of the symbols. [601/602]

II

. . . The level of present action in the story is negligible; most of the action occurs in the past, at various levels, but "The Snows" is not, primarily, a story of action at all: its interest lies in the *situation,* and in the conflict between idealism and materialism that takes place within the protagonist. To charge that the story lacks "dramatic force" is to conceive of drama solely in terms of external action, and this

---

[1] See Carlos Baker, *Hemingway, the Writer as Artist* (Princeton, 1956), p. 191.
[2] LIII, No. 1 (January–March), 131.

[3] Allen Tate and Caroline Gordon, *The House of Fiction.* (New York, 1950), pp. 421–423.
[4] William Van O'Connor, "Two Views of Kilimanjaro," *The History of Ideas News Letter,* II, No. 4, 76–80.

Oliver Evans, from " 'The Snows of Kilimanjaro': A Revaluation," PMLA, LXXVI (December 1961), 602–607. Reprinted with the permission of the Modern Language Association.

does not do justice to Hemingway's intention.

III

As for the symbols, there is, first of all, Africa itself, the Dark Continent, which stands in the story for the mysterious nature out of which man comes and into which he returns at last. Since the natural and the good are, in Hemingway's system of values, usually identified, this symbol has a moral significance; to Harry, Africa means the hope of moral regeneration: "Africa was where he had been happiest in the good time of his life, so he had come out here to start again. . . . He had thought he could get back into training that way. That in some way he could work the fat off his soul the way a fighter went into the mountains to work and train in order to burn it out of his body."

It will be seen that Harry here associates Africa with the creative phase of his life, when he was leading a "natural" existence before the corruption of money set in. Since he was happy there, he thinks of it nostalgically as a kind of spiritual home, to which he returns now in the hope of recovering something of his lost integrity. The therapeutic value of nature is, of course, an obsessive theme with Hemingway: it occurs in many of the stories in his first book, *In Our Time* (1925), and in the novel which he published the following year (*The Sun Also Rises*), where Jake revives himself, after his dissipations in Paris, by going on a fishing trip with Bill to a remote spot in Spain. Spain, indeed, had for Hemingway in the 'twenties something of the symbolic value that he later attached to Africa: W. M. Frohock, speaking of the Basque peasants in *The Sun Also Rises*, comments, "We get the feeling that to Hemingway, unspoiled people of this sort are always good," [5] and notes the admiration which Hemingway expresses, in *Green Hills of Africa*, for certain African tribes.

[5] W. M. Frohock, *The Novel of Violence in America, 1920–1950* (Dallas, 1950), p. 171.

The main symbol, of course, is the snow- [602/603] covered mountain top. To say (as do Tate and Gordon) that it represents death is to misread the meaning of the story, for while it is true that the mountain stands for a kind of perfection that is attainable only in death, through union with nature (the peak, as has been mentioned, is called by the Masai the "House of God"), it operates in the story not as a symbol of death but of life-in-death. The snow with which it is covered is, of course, a traditional symbol of purity: this is the reason it figures so importantly in Harry's recollections of his early life, when he was still happy in the possession of his integrity. It is associated in the story with life, not with death—or with death only in the sense that it is the means of achieving eternal life.[6]

As the mountain symbolizes life-in-death, the plain on which the man is dying symbolizes death-in-life, and the essential contrast in the story is between the two. The plain is hot and full of glare (we are told this several times), and it is associated with the joylessness of his recent existence, an existence which is in fact a form of death-in-life. Mountain tops and hilltops are traditionally symbolic of the ideal (one *strives* toward them), and low-lying plains, by contrast, symbolize earthly and material values; it is by these that Harry has lived, and on his deathbed his mind dwells wistfully on thoughts of snow and high places. The situation is coherent also on the realistic level, since a feverish man might be expected, in his delirium, to think of coolness. Cold and hot; high and low—these are the two extremes that Hemingway chooses to dramatize Harry's

[6] Alfred G. Engstrom ("Dante, Flaubert, and 'The Snows of Kilimanjaro'," *MLN*, LXV, March 1950, 203), suggests that Hemingway may have got the idea of his symbolic peak from a passage in Flaubert's *Correspondence* in which the striving for artistic perfection is likened to the ascent of a snow-covered mountain. However, as Douglas Hall Orrok points out (*MLN*, LXVI, Nov. 1951, 441), there is as much—or as little—reason for believing that the source was a passage from Victor Hugo's *William Shakespeare*. Like Tate and Gordon, Engstrom believes the peak stands for death: "The Holy Hill for Dante is that of Righteousness. For Flaubert, it is Art in its perfection. But for Hemingway, in 'The Snows of Kilimanjaro,' it is death."

situation, and they are admirably illustrated in the symbols of mountain and plain.

I tend to agree with Charles Walcutt that "the conflict in the story is between a fundamental moral idealism and the corrupting influence of aimless materialism." [7] Harry's idealism reveals itself in his sense of frustration and despair, and it contrasts oddly with the mechanistic views which he expresses from time to time. Thus, when Helen asks, speaking of his illness, "What have we done to have that happen to us?" he answers, "I suppose what I did was to forget to put iodine on it when I first scratched it." His wife replies, "I don't mean that," whereupon he says: "If we would have hired a good mechanic instead of a half baked Kikiyu driver, he would have changed the oil and never burned out that bearing in the truck." Helen says again, "I don't mean that," and Harry continues: "If you hadn't left your own people, your goddamned Old Westbury, Saratoga, Palm Beach people to take me on. . . ." Here he refuses to acknowledge a plan, an intention in the scheme of things, and clings stubbornly to the view that all is accident. Again, several pages later, he reflects that "now this life she had built again was coming to a term because he had not used iodine two weeks ago when a thorn had scratched his knee as they moved forward trying to photograph a herd of waterbuck standing, their heads up, peering while their nostrils searched the air, their ears spread wide to hear the first noise that would send them rushing into the bush." This is the habit of thinking, in terms of mechanical cause and effect, into which he has fallen since his association with Helen, and it is only occasionally that his old idealism asserts itself. It must be remembered too that Harry is a sick man, the external illness being but a symbolic manifestation of the sickness of the soul from which he has long been suffering: these are the thoughts

of a man without faith, a man who is morally ill.

The gangrene symbol has been chosen as carefully as the others: for rotting flesh, read rotting soul. The story begins with Harry's remark, "The marvelous thing is that it's painless. That's how you know when it starts." The death-in-life which Harry has been living was an easy, comfortable one, and the moral disintegration, like the physical, occurred stealthily and by degrees: "But he would never do it, because each day of not writing, of comfort, of being that which he despised, dulled his ability and softened his will to work so that, finally, he did no work at all."

Contrasted with the symbol of the man rotting away in the heat of the plain is the symbol, in the epigraph, of the leopard which, having attained the summit—and died in the effort—leaves his body preserved immaculately and eternally in its snows. The contrast may be merely ironical, in which case the epigraph appears rather gratuitous, justifying the objection of Tate and Gordon that the symbolism "seems something the writer has tacked on rather than an integral part of the story" (p. 421). It is probable, however, that Hemingway intended to identify the man in some way with the leopard. What has happened to the leopard is a pretty obvious example of life-in-death, and what has happened to the man is, as has been noted, a form of death-in-life. The man has two dimensions, spiritual and material, and the leopard symbolizes the former: thus, Harry too achieves life-in-death, through union with what is ideal and eternal, but only (like the leopard) at the cost of his earthly existence. [8] It should also be noted that the leopard, being a *spotted* animal, is peculiarly appropriate as a symbol of Harry's moral identity: what is maculate, both in the beast and in

---

[7] C. C. Walcutt, *The Explicator*, VII (April 1949), Item 43.

[8] Douglas Hall Orrok notes (p. 444) that "the African belief in the external soul, which supposes a blood kinship between the leopard and the man, would explain the death of the leopard as the Döppelganger of the man Harry near the west peak of Kilimanjaro."

the man, has become immaculate in eternity.[9]

Of all Hemingway's symbols, the leopard in this story has provoked the most controversy. Ten years ago, Alfred G. Engstrom asked rhetorically, "As for the other symbol in the epigraph, can there be any doubt as to its meaning?," and went on to declare: "The leopard is Dante's—the symbol of worldly pleasure and lechery—one of three beasts, in the first Canto of the Inferno, that stood between the medieval poet and his own Delectable Mountain" (p. 205). It did not require much ingenuity for Douglas Hall Orrok, the following year, to refute this interpretation, but the one with which he attempted to replace it called for a great deal: he suggested that the leopard symbol was taken from Revelation xiii. 1, in which there is mention of a beast "like a leopard" which is blasphemy, and that Harry, by neglecting his talent, has been guilty of literary blasphemy. "The Snows of Kilimanjaro," he wrote, "is a fable of literary integrity. The artist who blasphemes against the Gods of Parnassus is sacrificed in the ascent of the mystic peak" (p. 445). This theory does at least establish an identity between the man and the beast, but it breaks down when we apply it to the contrasting set of circumstances under which Harry and the leopard meet their death, nor does it fit into the total symbolic framework of the story. Charles Walcutt, in 1949, was the first critic to suggest that the leopard was a "symbol of Harry's moral nature," but he was unable to integrate the symbol into the story satisfactorily because his conception of the mountain did not include the associations of life-in-death; he thought of the peak merely as "a symbol of Truth, meaning— or an incarnation of the ideal." [10] Agreeing with this view, E. W. Tedlock, Jr., pointed out the "leopard and mountain represent those things which do not decay" [11] in

contrast to the man who is dying on the plain; he did not, however, explore the implications of this contrast. In 1952, Philip Young, whose book on Hemingway has the kind of biographical emphasis that enables him to view "The Snows" as "a fictionalized purge, in this case of a whole set of guilty feelings . . . an exercise in personal and aesthetic hygiene," [12] identified the leopard with the kind of literary work that Harry (i.e., Hemingway) would like to leave behind him: "He dreams of immortality for some of what he has done; he thinks, that is, of writing prose that will be so pure that it can never spoil, that will be permanent" (p. 48). Besides limiting the meaning of the story rather narrowly, this interpretation does not sufficiently account for what happens in it: Harry's integrity as a man as well as a writer is involved in "The Snows," and his situation has universal moral interest and application. Curiously enough, Young also accepted Engstrom's theory that the leopard symbolizes the worldly pleasure that stood between Dante and the Holy Hill, as well as the notion (also from Engstrom) that one of Flaubert's letters was the source of the mountain symbol: how these can be reconciled to the idea that the beast represents Harry's unaccomplished literary ambitions is by no means easy to see. In the most recent (1956) analysis of the story, Carlos Baker, agreeing with Walcutt and Tedlock, fitted their interpretation of the leopard into his theory that the mountain as Home, and plain as Not-home, underlies most of Hemingway's early work. Baker succeeded brilliantly in correlating the story with the Hemingway *Weltanschauung*, but he did it insufficient justice in its own right.

The vultures and the hyena, of course, are symbols of death, and they are associated with the death-in-life of the second phase of Harry's career, after he has made the fatal sacrifice; they are contrasted in the story with the leopard, which is asso-

[9] For this idea I am indebted to Robert A. Pratt, of the University of Illinois.
[10] Op. cit., loc. cit.
[11] *The Explicator,* VIII (October 1949), Item 7.

[12] Philip Y. Young, *Ernest Hemingway* (New York, 1952), pp. 46–48.

ciated with the earlier, purer phase [**604/ 605**] of his life, the period of idealism, and also (as we have seen) with the eternal life which is achieved only in death: life-in-death. Few creatures could be more unlike, on the realistic level, than the skulking, cowardly hyena, which feeds chiefly on carrion, and the bold and graceful leopard which attacks living prey.

What has apparently escaped all the critics is that Harry's wife, Helen, is herself a symbol—and by no means the least important one in the story. Beyond noting that her influence is generally inimical (Edmund Wilson was the first to do this), no one has shown how skillfully and how consistently Hemingway employs her throughout as a symbol of death, or rather of death-in-life. Take for example the following passage: "Drinking together . . . he could feel the return of acquiescence in this life of pleasant surrender. She *was* very good to him. He had been cruel and unjust in the afternoon. She was a fine woman, marvelous really. And just then it occurred to him that he was going to die."

This is his first premonition of death, and note that it occurs immediately after his reflection that his wife is a "fine woman." Helen *is,* of course, a "fine woman" in the sense that she is "very good to him," but it is exactly this which is fatal for Harry—the comfort and security which she represents results in a "pleasant surrender" on his part, and lead to death-in-life. A few pages later we read: "She looked at him with her well-known, well-loved face from *Spur* and *Town and Country* . . . and as he looked and saw her well known pleasant smile, he felt death come again."

This is his second premonition, and again it occurs while he is with the woman, watching her "pleasant smile." Shortly before he enters his final delirium, we find the following: "He looked at her face between him and the fire. She was leaning back in the chair and the firelight shone on her pleasantly lined face and he could see that she was sleepy. He heard the hyena make a noise just outside the range of the fire."

The contiguity of this description of the woman with Harry's intuitions of his approaching death, and with the hyena, make it probable that Hemingway is using Helen quite consciously as a symbol of death-in-life. Finally there is the passage:

. . . if it was no worse than this as it went on there was nothing to worry about. Except that he would rather be in better company.

He thought a little about the company he would like to have.

No, he thought, when everything you do, you do too long, and do too late, you can't expect to find the people still there. The people are all gone. The party's over and you are with your hostess now.

His "hostess," on the realistic level, is Helen; on the symbolic, it is death. It is, after all, only right that Helen should have this function in the story, since Harry's moral infection, the gangrene of his spirit, dates from his association with her. Of the various death symbols, Helen is the most important: the vultures and the hyena are waiting in the hope that he will die; Helen is waiting in the hope that he will live—but live a death-in-life. In this context, Harry's reflection, that "She shot very well, this good, this rich bitch, this kindly caretaker and destroyer of his talent," takes on a strong ironical significance.

In describing the early relationship of Harry and his wife, Hemingway writes: "The steps by which she had acquired him and the way in which she had finally fallen in love with him were all part of a regular progression in which she had built herself a new life and he had traded away what remained of his old life." The inference is that what has been bad for Harry has been good for Helen: she has thrived at his expense. But she does not thrive on his *vitality;* she thrives, as would the hyena, on *what is dead* in him: "The people he knew now were all much more comfortable when he did not work at all." This conception of women, that they can live comfortably with their men only when the latter are dead morally, may be found also in that other, simpler story about Africa that Hemingway wrote about the same time, "The Short, Happy Life of Francis Macomber," where Margot, when her husband belatedly asserts his identity, shoots him. According to Edmund Wilson, "the emotion which principally comes through in 'Francis Macomber' and 'The Snows of Kilimanjaro'—as it figures also in *The Fifth Column*—is a growing antagonism to women." [13] Indeed, the women characters of Hemingway's early and middle period frequently have a menacing quality: they interfere with the pursuit of masculine ideals, whether aesthetic or athletic. In as early a book as *The Sun Also Rises* we find the innkeeper, Montoya, a dedicated *aficionado* of the bull-ring, fearful of Brett's influence over the toreador Romero; and when Pop, in the autobiographical **[605/606]** *Green Hills of Africa,* asks the author, "What are the things, the actual, concrete things that harm a writer?," Hemingway replies: "Politics, women, drink, money, ambition."

IV

If the New Critics, preoccupied with surface technique, have failed to evaluate "The Snows" properly, other critics, preoccupied with biographical considerations, have succeeded scarcely better. It is true that, as in almost all of Hemingway —especially the early Hemingway—the biographical element looms large. Philip Young, the champion of this school, states that in 1936 Hemingway, who had been "chasing about Europe and Africa with the very rich and drinking too much" (p. 48), felt depressed about his own work; he asserts that the model for Helen was Hemingway's second wife, Pauline Pfeif-

fer, a wealthy fashion writer for *Vogue;* he points out that much of the material in the flashbacks came straight from Hemingway's own experience (the fishing and skiing episodes, the descriptions of Paris neighborhoods, and the incidents in the Turkish-Greek War and on the Austro-Italian line in World War I); and he notes that the "Julian" of the story was F. Scott Fitzgerald, that in the first printing of "The Snows" (in *Esquire*) he is called Scott Fitzgerald instead of Julian, and that Hemingway himself once made the reply, "Yes, they have more money," to Fitzgerald's observation, "The rich are very different from you and me," attributed in the story to Julian (pp. 46–47). And Carlos Baker tells us that in January 1934 (only two years before "The Snows" was written), Hemingway was taken seriously ill of amoebic dysentery in Tanganyika while on safari and was flown past Kilimanjaro to Nairobi for treatment: "During the flight east, and no doubt also during the period of treatment in Nairobi . . . Hemingway had time to reflect on a topic which would naturally occur to him in such a situation: the death of a writer before his work is done" (p. 192).

Now all of this may be true—some of it certainly is—but Hemingway intended "The Snows" to be more than a slightly fictionalized diary, and the perceptive reader will find that he succeeded in that intention. *In Our Time, A Farewell to Arms,* and *The Sun Also Rises* are also to a large extent personalized fiction, but the critic is dangerously myopic who sees in them only, or chiefly, the biographical element. It also limits the story, though much less narrowly, to regard it merely as a parable of the artist. Engstrom makes this mistake, as do also Orrok, Tate and Gordon, and, to a certain extent, Baker, who states that the central theme is the same as James's in "The Lesson of the Master." [14]

---

[13] In *The Wound and the Bow* (Cambridge, Mass., 1949), p. 237. Perhaps the first specimen of what Wilson calls "American bitches of the most soul-destroying type" is Frances, in *The Sun Also Rises:* her dialogue with Robert Cohn anticipates that of Margot with her husband.

[14] "Don't become in your old age what I have in mine," Henry St. George, the novelist in James's story, says—"the depressing, the deplorable illustration of the worship of false gods . . . the idols of the market;

I have suggested that the theme of "The Snows" involves a contrast between life-in-death, of which the leopard and mountain are symbols, and death-in-life, with which is associated a group of symbols that includes Harry's wife, Helen, and the physical illness from which he is suffering. To appreciate fully the moral meaning of the story, it is necessary to understand the conditions under which Harry first contracted his spiritual sickness. Hemingway tells us that when Harry met Helen he had already exhausted his capacity for love: "It was not her fault," he has his protagonist reflect, "that when he went to her he was already over," and again: "He had never quarreled much with this woman, while with the women that he loved he had quarreled so much they had finally, always, with the corrosion of the quarreling, killed what they had together. He had loved too much, demanded too much, and he wore it all out." It is this inability to love which is his real sickness, and it is aggravated by the deception which he practices—and practices successfully—upon his wife: "But when he no longer was in love, when he was only lying, as to this woman, now . . . it was strange that when he did not love her at all and was lying, that he should be able to give her more for her money than when he had really loved." The definition of love that he frames now, in his sickness ("Love is a dunghill. And I'm the cock that gets on it to crow") contrasts powerfully with the wistful, almost sentimental manner in which, in the flashbacks, he recalls his early love affairs.

Life without love is death-in-life: this is the real moral of the story, as it is the moral of "The Ancient Mariner"; Hemingway's protagonist, however, is less lucky than Coleridge's, for it is only in death, or life-in-death, that he will recover his integrity and achieve identification with

that which is infinite and perfect. It is significant that Harry's disintegration as a writer began at the moment he felt himself incapable of [**606/607**] love: when he stopped loving, he stopped creating. This is the reason, too, for the boredom he now feels about almost everything, even death: "For this, that now̄ was coming, he had very little curiosity . . . I'm getting as bored with dying as with everything else, he thought." When he lost his ability to love, he lost his curiosity about life as well as his capacity for it.

It is very important to realize that the story ends on a note of triumph. Harry does gain the mountain top, not merely *in his delirium,* as William Van O'Connor thought, but *in death.* It is because O'Connor did not, apparently, understand this that he found the story "puzzling." Had Harry's delirium been merely that, and had it not been followed by his death, "The Snows" would indeed have been puzzling, but Hemingway is careful to depict the delirium in such a way that its climax is synchronous with Harry's death: "And then he knew that there was where he was going." Death is the price that he must pay, but life-in-death, Hemingway is telling us, is preferable to death-in-life at any cost. "Only in fantasy does he escape from the nature that pulls him down," O'Connor objected, but Harry's escape from the plain to the peak is real and absolute: it is there, in the "House of God," that he is reunited to that which is ideal and permanent, to that which never rots.

"The Snows of Kilimanjaro" is Hemingway's most religious story. For man, the only alternative to love is death, as W. H. Auden has often insisted;[15] and this is the lesson which Hemingway's parable dramatizes. It is a larger lesson than that which Henry St. George, in James's story, gives to his disciple, and it is essentially a religious one. Hemingway's religion, like that of the American Transcendentalists with whom he has more in common than

money and luxury . . . everything that drives one to the short and easy way." Baker also sees in "The Snows" another Jamesian theme, the confrontation (as in "The Jolly Corner") of an ego by an alter ego.

15 See, *e.g.,* "1st September, 1939" in *Collected Shorter Poems, 1930–44* (London, n.d.).

has usually been supposed,[16] is to a large extent a religion of nature, containing elements of pantheism and Platonism. From the point of view of the latter doctrine, "The Snows" is the story of a man who, having lost contact with divinity when the spark of human love (an emanation of divine love) is extinguished within him, is returned to the Original Source of all love. From the time of his first novel, *The Sun Also Rises,* one of Hemingway's most consistent convictions has been that to the extent man is in tune with nature he fulfills the divine plan and his own proper destiny: this is the reason for his insistence on the therapeutic value of nature, and I think it explains also, at least partially, his obsessive interest in those activities which he regards as "natural," such as hunting and fishing. This is, of course, a romantic attitude, and indeed the number of critics is increasing who would agree with Malcolm Cowley that Hemingway is only superficially a realist.[17]

There are other romantic themes in "The Snows," such as that of the *femme fatale,* which, as Mario Praz has shown in *The Romantic Agony* (where he traces it to Greek mythology), is one of the most characteristic preoccupations in the literature of Western Europe.[18] Hemingway has less in common with Dreiser than with Hawthorne and Melville—the men, as Cowley puts it, "who dealt in images that were symbols of an inner world" [19]—which is merely another way of saying that he writes, as nearly all important romantic authors have written, out of an obsession. To the extent that this "inner world" resembles the outer one, and its symbols are intelligible, the romantic writer succeeds. Hemingway, of course, has been unusually successful.

[16] Twenty years ago, F. O. Matthiessen (cited by Baker, p. 178), pointed out certain correspondences between Thoreau and Hemingway. For a study of Hemingway's affinity with Emerson, see C. Hugh Holman's essay, "Hemingway and Emerson," in *Modern Fiction Studies,* I (1955), No. 3, 12–16.

[17] See Cowley's Introduction, *Ernest Hemingway* (New York, 1944). The opinion of Tate and Gordon (p. 421) that "the mantle of Flaubert's great disciple, Maupassant, has fallen on Hemingway's shoulders" has meaning only where technique is concerned: the sensibilities of Maupassant and Hemingway are poles apart.

[18] Other romantic attitudes in Hemingway are his primitivism, which is similar to Thoreau's, and his intuitionism, his distrust of verbalization, which is strongly reminiscent of D. H. Lawrence's and which pervades the early stories as well as *The Sun Also Rises,* where Jake tells Brett, who wants to discuss her affair with Romero: "Don't talk about it or you'll lose it." It is significant, too, that words are to blame, in "The Snows," for the death of Harry's early love affairs; it is the "corrosion of the quarreling" that has killed them. For related aspects of Hemingway's romanticism, see the article previously referred to, by C. Hugh Holman; Tom Burnam, "Primitivism and Masculinity in the Work of Hemingway," *Modern Fiction Studies,* I, No. 3, 20–24; and Lois Barnes, "The Helpless Hero of Ernest Hemingway," *Science and Society,* XVII (1953), No. 1, 1–25.

[19] Op. cit., loc. cit.

"The Snows of Kilimanjaro": Harry's Second Chance *

GLORIA R. DUSSINGER (1932–   ) is a graduate student at Lehigh University. Among her forthcoming publications are essays on Conrad, Faulkner, and Hemingway.

The similarity of Harry's memories in "The Snows of Kilimanjaro" to those of Hemingway in *A Moveable Feast* reveals the autobiographical intensity of this short story. When Hemingway speaks through his protagonist, *"He had seen the world change. . . . He had been in it and he had watched it and it was his duty to write of it . . . ,"* [1] he makes clear that Harry's story is his professional manifesto. In his narration of the experiences of a dying man, Hemingway proves by example the one thing needful to the writer's pursuit of his hallowed calling. Hemingway embodies in "The Snows of Kilimanjaro" his idea of the writer's vocation, the artistic form giving it a validity that public, non-fictional statements lack.

If "The Snows of Kilimanjaro" expresses Hemingway's artistic credo, why has the story been so variously interpreted and even rejected by Hemingway critics? An obvious answer lies in the symbolism; Hemingway, with uncharacteristic directness, included the symbols of the mountain and the leopard in an epigraph, where they cannot be ignored. Most of the criticism of this story founders on the two symbols: commentators have made numerous attempts to locate literary and natural sources for them, to discover their meaning, and to evaluate their success. [2] [54/55]

When passing an aesthetic judgment on the symbols in "The Snows of Kilimanjaro," students of Hemingway follow one of three courses. The first is to grant the leopard and the mountain their full idealistic value, but to deny Harry a place among them. [3] Only by reading the story

[1] *The Short Stories of Ernest Hemingway*, Modern Standard Authors edition (New York, 1938), p. 66. Subsequent quotations from this edition appear in parentheses in the text.

[2] Alfred G. Engstrom, "Dante, Flaubert, and 'The Snows of Kilimanjaro,'" *MLN*, LXV (1950), 203–205,

likens Kilimanjaro to Flaubert's mountain of art. The resemblance is applicable if Flaubert is understood as an analogue, not a source. I cannot accept, however, his equating the leopard with Dante's symbol of lechery: the leopard must balance the hyena (leopard aspiring and preserved, hyena slothful and corrupted), or the story falls apart. Douglas H. Orrok, "Hemingway, Hugo, and Revelation," *MLN*, LXVI (1951), 441–445, draws allusion to many mountains and leopards, none of which illuminates the story. William Bache, "*Nostromo* and 'The Snows of Kilimanjaro,'" *MLN*, LXXII (1957), 32–34, presents an extremely strained argument for *Nostromo* as the story's source.

Carlos Baker, *Hemingway: The Writer as Artist* (Princeton, 1963), p. 193, seeks a naturalistic justification for the symbols: the snowy mountains of the epigraph, the death-dream, and the flashbacks represent, physically, a feverish man's desire for coolness; spiritually, they represent the good life. Barney Childs, "Hemingway and the Leopard of Kilimanjaro," *American Notes & Queries*, II (September 1963), 3, reports on a natural source for the leopard symbol: a British mountain climber discovered the frozen remains of a leopard on Kilimanjaro.

Of the critics who interpret the meaning of symbols in this short story, Montgomery and Evans are the most thorough. Marion Montgomery, "The Leopard and the Hyena: Symbol and Meaning in 'The Snows of Kilimanjaro,'" *University of Kansas City Review*, XXVII (1961), 277–282, contrasts the hunting habits of the leopard and the hyena and then turns hunting code into aesthetic code. This contrast does harm to the leopard symbol since it is not the usual but the extraordinary behavior of the leopard that earns him a place in the epigraph. Oliver Evans, "'The Snows of Kilimanjaro': A Revaluation," *PMLA* LXXVI (1961), 601–607, equates the mountain with life-in-death and the plain with death-in-life. He gives the story its broadest interpretation, raising it from a tale of artistic integrity to a religious work on love as the vitalizing force of existence.

[3] William Van O'Connor, "Two Views of Kilimanjaro" in *The Grotesque: An American Genre and Other Essays* (Carbondale, 1962), p. 122, states, "Only in fantasy does he [Harry] escape from the nature that has pulled him down." In the opinion of R. W. Stallman, "A New Reading of 'The Snows of Kilimanjaro,'" in *The Houses*

*Gloria R. Dussinger, " 'The Snows of Kilimanjaro': Harry's Second Chance," Studies in Short Fiction, V (Fall 1967), 54–59. Reprinted with the permission of Studies in Short Fiction (Newberry College, Newberry, S. C.)

ironically, by regarding the symbols of permanence and purity as a mockery of Harry's unwholesomeness, can one maintain this critical position. It ignores the formal characteristics of irony, the implied meaning of snow and mountains in Harry's honest past, and the self-evident validity of Harry's final vision. Although Hemingway has made Harry's ascension to the House of God true by *seeing* Kilimanjaro through the eyes of his protagonist, these critics refuse to believe.

A second critical group, accepting the metaphysical meaning of the symbols and also accepting the apotheosis of Harry, cannot reconcile the two. Feeling that Hemingway has insufficiently proven Harry's worthiness, these critics call "The Snows of Kilimanjaro" a magnificent failure. Gordon and Tate accuse Hemingway of tacking on the symbol of the mountain for which they fail to find a counterpart in the action. Montgomery insists that Hemingway has not related Harry's moral code to the mountain, nor integrated the leopard into Harry's death-dream. Consequently the end of the story appears to Montgomery sentimental and inorganic.[4]

The third approach to "The Snows of Kilimanjaro" subscribes unreservedly to both the transcendental import of the symbols and the transfiguration of the protagonist.[5] Critics who follow this [55/56] approach see the significance of the snowy mountains of Harry's reminiscences and the truth of his recognition of Kilimanjaro as his goal. To justify Harry's spiritual elevation, they point out that, in spite of self-betrayal, Harry retains enough honesty to judge himself rightly in his last hours. He strives to write then all that he had evaded earlier, assured that quality more than makes up for quantity.[6] Moreover, Harry matches the leopard in surmounting the naturalism of his contemporaries.[7] The riddle of the epigraph is analogous to the surprising fact that Harry, despite the destruction of his talent, despite the changing of the world, has never lost his curiosity.[8] The willingness to go on experiencing, even when experience must serve as its own end—this is Harry's affirmation.

If the obvious meaning of the symbols in the epigraph and the equally obvious linking of them with Harry's past and Harry's death were all that Hemingway offered in support of his writer-hero, critics would be justified in questioning the organic soundness of the symbols. Were such the case, it would be plain that Harry has not earned the redemption Heming-

---

That James Built and Other Literary Studies (East Lansing, 1961), p. 198, "He's no leopard transcending reality; Harry's merely the common bestial man devoid of transcendent virtues." Michael F. Moloney, "Ernest Hemingway: The Missing Third Dimension," in *Hemingway and His Critics*, Carlos Baker, ed. (New York, 1961), p. 182, also rejects Harry's triumph. He finds a tragic pathos in Harry's recognition that the opportunity for repentance is lost.

4 Caroline Gordon and Allen Tate, *The House of Fiction* (New York, 1950), p. 421; and Montgomery, p. 282. Ray B. West, Jr., "Ernest Hemingway: The Failure of Sensibility," *Sewanee Review*, LIII (1945), 131, complains that the conventionality of the leading symbol—the white-capped mountain as the House of God—spoils the story for him despite its technical complexity. This critic should be reminded that organic function, not conventionality, should be the criterion for judging a symbol.

5 E. W. Tedlock, Jr., "Hemingway's 'The Snows of Kilimanjaro,'" *The Explicator*, VIII (1949), Item 7, declares, "But Harry's inner struggle ends in victory. In his final delirium he achieves the summit of the mountain." Evans, p. 607, believes that because Harry's vision is synchronous with death, "the story ends on a note of triumph." Joseph DeFalco, *The Hero in Heming-*

way's Short Stories (Pittsburgh, 1963), p. 210, also shares this view: "Death may be a form of transcendence if the subject has undergone an ordeal of suffering and if he has achieved insight and illumination."

6 Harry is confident about quality: "it seemed as though it telescoped so that you might put it all into one paragraph if you could get it right" (p. 68). Tony Tanner, *The Reign of Wonder* (Cambridge, 1965), p. 233, comments on the urge of the Hemingway hero to elevate the experimental moment over the movement of history: "And they would agree that if your senses are properly attuned and at work 'it is possible to live as full a life in seventy hours as in seventy years.'"

7 Charles C. Walcutt, "Hemingway's 'The Snows of Kilimanjaro,'" *The Explicator*, VII (1949), Item 43: "It is just as naturalistically illogical that Harry should continue to believe in man and search for meanings and values as that a purely predatory leopard should climb up into the frozen desert. . . ."

8 When a scrupulously careful artist like Hemingway twice employs the same phrase within a short story, the critic had best be alerted to its significance. In his first weary statement about death, Harry says, "For this that now was coming, he had very little curiosity" (p. 54). His senses have become jaded by years of comfortable living—"by drinking so much that he blunted the edge of his perceptions" (p. 60). However, during the course of the story, his memories increasingly freshen his senses, enabling him to face his final experience, the one he vows not to spoil (p. 67), with acuity. He announces, in almost his last words, "You know the only thing I've never lost is curiosity" (p. 74).

way awards him.[9] But Hemingway, with superb artistry, has developed Harry's value through the narrative structure and then firmly established that value by subjecting it to a test. Harry's death-dream is a brilliantly contrived technique for measuring the intrinsic worth of the protagonist. In his flight toward death, Harry's behavior achieves Hemingway's personal standard; therefore, that section of the story simultaneously vindicates the hero and voices the author's creed: to be true to the senses is the writer's ultimate duty.

An analysis of the narrative will make clear Hemingway's design. From the beginning of the story, Harry knows that he is dying but [**56/57**] knows it with an intellectual detachment. His relationship with the woman is that of the friendly enemy—a quarrelsome, superficial connection. Within the first series of reminiscences, Harry's thoughts turn to snow scenes, mountains, betrayal, good skiing, and the birth of God (four Christmases are mentioned, pp. 56–57). This juncture of disparate topics mirrors the chaotic world of the war generation. The topics are somewhat general; Hemingway indicates that they do not touch the inner Harry by causing Harry to break them off, returning the story to the present. The memory of the German inn triggers Harry to ask Helen about a Paris hotel. His willingness to exchange the past for idle chatter with the woman proves his lack of commitment to it. Moreover, the past has not yet cauterized Harry's festered spirit: he slips easily into the familiar lie (p. 58) that symbolizes his lost integrity.

Between the first and second sets of flashbacks, Harry makes plain to the reader the determinism that permits him so easily to deceive himself: "We must all be cut out for what we do, he thought. However you make your living is where your talent lies" (p. 61). On two previous

occasions Harry had revealed a deterministic philosophy: by reasoning, "Maybe you could never write them, and that was why you put them off and delayed the starting" (p. 54) and by his strictly naturalistic answers to Helen's metaphysical question: "What have we done to have that happen to us?" (p. 55). Soothed by determinism, which makes no demands upon the moral responsibility of the individual, Harry slips again into the lie (p. 64).

The second set of recollections uncovers the real Harry; it deals with his loves and with his wartime trauma, "the things that he could never think of" (p. 66). In the section following these memories, one can note several changes in the protagonist: he passionately desires to write (p. 67), he no longer falls back on deterministic reasoning, he associates the woman with death and therefore cannot maintain the lie (p. 67 and p. 74), and he feels death with his senses (p. 67 and p. 74). The narrative reflects the nearer approach of death by dwelling increasingly on the past and shortening the present passages to interludes.

A third group of reminiscences contains a brief reference to the castration theme [10] but centers on Harry's vocation and its begin- [**57/58**] ning in Paris. Hemingway shows the renewed sensitivity of Harry to physical phenomena in the Place Contrescarpe section: Harry cannot dictate these memories because they are not actions but raw, unclassified sensations— sights, sounds, smells. The accuracy of the sense impressions signifies the rebirth of Harry's artistic integrity, for the Hemingway hero holds to the truth of the sensations, honesty perceived and recorded.[11] Additional proof of Harry's forsaking the

---

[9] Earl Rovit, *Ernest Hemingway* (New York, 1963), p. 37, makes a virtue of necessity by calling "The Snows of Kilimanjaro" a *tour de force* in which Hemingway compels his audience to accept a morally rotten protagonist as a superior man. Rovit senses the unfitness of Harry as hero which the usual reading of the story cannot evade. My reading, I hope, will show Harry's true stature.

[10] Tom Burnam, "Primitivism and Masculinity in the Work of Hemingway," *Modern Fiction Studies*, i (1955), 23, finds the gangrenous leg a castration symbol; he blames the writer's loss of talent on the loss of his dominant position in marriage. The inclusion of the castration theme in the third flashback has psychological validity. Retreating into the self, Harry naturally touches upon the pivotal experience in the growth of the psyche —the establishing of sexual identity. The emasculation of his grandfather was an awesome and irrevocable event in the life of the child Harry. His fear of a similar catastrophe sapped some of Harry's self-confidence, making him seek security at the expense of integrity.

[11] Tanner, p. 229.

lie can be found in the fourth flashback. Here Harry names himself the betrayer, an admission he had skirted in the first series, pointing at Nansen and Barker instead.

Harry in his restored honesty straightens out his false relation to the woman. He acknowledges that he will never write about her (p. 72), and thus cuts himself off forever from his conscience-salving rationalization (p. 59). By portraying the gradual retreat of Harry into the truth of his past, away from the woman and the falsehood of the present, Hemingway reveals his understanding of the psychology of a dying man. Harry is left with his naked self, the irreducible *I am* that defies chaos: "He could beat anything, he thought, because no thing could hurt him if he did not care" (p. 72). Realizing now that the power to mold reality lies within the self, Harry has transcended the scientific materialism to which he was prey at the beginning of the story. His final memory takes the form of a death-wish, for Harry guesses that his state of self-illumination is threatened by time: "It's a bore. . . . Anything you do too bloody long." (p. 73) [12]

Had "The Snows of Kilimanjaro" ended here, the reader would remain unimpressed by Harry's conversion. True, he had established honest relations with his fellow man (represented by Helen) and with himself, both of which were founded on the clarity of his senses. But what dying man, if he had the time, would not do as much? The test of Harry's integrity, the ordeal which proves his sincerity, is a second chance. Up to the paragraph beginning "It was morning" (p. 75), this has

been the story of a man convinced [58/59] that he must die. From that paragraph forward to "the square top of Kilimanjaro" (p. 76), it is the story of a man confident of living.[13] By structuring the story in this way, Hemingway gives his writer-protagonist what Dencombe pleaded for in James's short story "The Middle Years," and, in so doing, makes manifest the value of Harry.

Scrutiny of Harry's response to his second chance will settle the question of his merit. Toward others the redeemed Harry shows a sympathetic understanding that contrasts with his previous egocentricity: he twice offers breakfast to Compton rather than trying to hurry him; he calls the woman by her name, acknowledging her separate identity. What Harry does *not* do is lie. He does not tell himself that the rich are worth writing about after all; he does not try to avoid writing by reasoning naturalistically that he lacks talent; he does not tell Helen he loves her in order to insure his job after the hospital stay; he doesn't sell his spiritual vitality for physical comfort. What Harry *does* do is record faithfully and in precise detail the sensory impressions of his journey. The passage narrating the flight contains colors, textures, motions, temperatures conveyed in the incisive Hemingway prose style.[14] It is the restoration of the seeing eye, which perceives the final flight with as much sensory accuracy as the flashbacks, that announces Harry's victory.

---

[12] Hemingway's horror of doing anything too long is dramatized starkly in "An Alpine Idyll." A philosophic base for this characteristically modern trait can be found in the notion that order and meaning must be imposed on chaotic phenomena by the active self. This making of the world out of nothing must be neverending. When a temporary construct is retained too long, it takes on the appearance of permanency. The subject tends to forget that the order he observes is his own; he may begin to think it is constituted in the universe by some external power. If he bows before an order, he loses his selfhood, for selfhood is the process of controlling nothingness.

[13] I did not include the final sentence: "And then he knew that there was where he was going" (p. 76) because in this sentence Harry recognizes death as his destination. Earlier Harry had felt death as an "evil-smelling emptiness" (p. 64), the "emptiness" being equivalent to Hemingway's omnipresent nada but the "evil-smelling" suggesting a negative moral value. After his conversion, Harry no longer attaches this sentimental badness to death; he greets death in its totally amoral whiteness.

[14] Could it be that the uncharacteristic "telling" of Harry's musings: "He had destroyed his talent by not using it . . ." (p. 60), is a stylistic device employed by Hemingway to indicate how far Harry has strayed from true art? If the clear description of the recollections is contrasted with the sloppiness of Harry's statements in the narrative present—"rich bitch," "rotten poetry," etc. —the reader can *see* that Harry has dulled his ability to write. Harry's return to honest reporting in his death-flight becomes the objective correlative of his salvation.

Suggested Topics for Controlled Research

Finding facts is obviously an important aspect of literary research. Only research could reveal the existence of an unpublished epigraph on the typescript of "The Snows of Kilimanjaro"; and only research could reveal that Hemingway composed the following epigraph to the collection of stories *Winner Take Nothing:*

"Unlike all other forms of lutte [contest] or combat the conditions are that the winner shall take nothing; neither his ease, nor his pleasure, nor any notions of glory; nor, if he win far enough, shall there be any reward within himself."

Epigraphs, as the discussions in this anthology of both the published and unpublished epigraphs of "The Snows of Kilimanjaro" dramatize, are important mirrors of Hemingway's themes. The epigraph from *Winner Take Nothing*, for example, reflects one of the most prevalent metaphors in Hemingway's fiction—the contest.

Facts such as these are interesting, but they are not necessarily significant in themselves. We must, as if making fire from sticks, rub facts together before new ideas, insights, or truths will be kindled. The traditional way of creating such friction is through comparative analysis. If we analyze the epigraph from *Winner Take Nothing*, and compare its implied comment on the contest of life with the themes and actions of the African stories, we will, if nothing else, raise certain important questions: What do Macomber and Harry win? What do they lose? What are the rules of the contest? What constitutes victory or defeat? It is clear that we would have to do more research before we could come up with answers. It is just as clear, however, that even through this tentative comparison, we have already raised some good "thought" questions— and it is out of such questions that research topics grow and develop.

No more meaningful contest existed for Hemingway than the bullfight. There must be complete honesty, he repeats in *Death in the Afternoon:* the matador must demonstrate true courage as he directs and leads the bull through the three-act ritual to a point when, at greatest risk to his own life, and thus with the greatest awareness of its true value, he faces the bull, taking the bull's life while recognizing the truth of his own. If the matador reveals cowardice, or if he fakes danger through tricks of cape or body action, then the audience is cheated of its wish to identify with his "moment of truth," his grace and courage in the face of the dark forces of life symbolized by the bull.

How can bullfighting be compared to the theories, techniques, and themes of Hemingway's fiction? A careful analysis of Hemingway's literary theories will provide some answers, questions—and topics about his conception of "truth" in fiction. To explore the results and effects of his theories, however, we must compare them to his experiences and the objectification of these experiences in his stories. Though recognizing that Hemingway's accounts of his experiences are already one step away from the actual events themselves, the accounts do, nevertheless, give us a basis for comparison and allow us to observe the process of selection and transformation which produced the stories.

Again, though "The Short Happy Life of Francis Macomber" and "The Snows of Kilimanjaro" were initially inspired by the same African experiences, their technical development is obviously very different. Notice, for example, that while "The Short Happy Life of Francis Macomber" focuses on the present and external actions of Macomber's final moments of life, "The Snows of Kilimanjaro" focuses on the internal actions of Harry's memories and ultimate fantasy in death.

The exploration of these differences in theme and technique is not only a prerequisite for a clear understanding of the stories; it will also lead to worthwhile topics for discussion and research. From this initial consideration we might then move to a profitable evaluation of both stories in light of the suggested sources and influences collected under the headings "Experience" and "Context."

Keeping in mind that Hemingway took certain artistic license in *Green Hills of Africa,* we might, for example, study the development of the stories from the "Tanganyika Letters" and *Green Hills of Africa.* Some relevant questions: How close are Macomber's physical and emotional experiences to Hemingway's? How close are Harry's? What artistic alterations of the original experiences are there in the stories? Were these changes made to create suspense, atmosphere, irony, etc.? Or were they made to develop themes and ideas beyond the effective capacity of the original experience?

We soon observe in reading the materials reprinted under "Context" that scholars do not entirely agree about Hemingway's literary debts. Was there really a leopard on Kilimanjaro? Carlos Baker suggests that Hemingway learned of it in a conversation. Would this necessarily rule out literary influences? Why does Hans Meyer not mention a "Leopard's Point" as H. W. Tilman does? Are there any clues in descriptive and stylistic parallels? Would Hemingway's emphasis on the "truth" of experience have any bearing on the general question? On the other hand, what is the thematic and the stylistic significance of the epigraph taken from Vivienne de Watteville's *Speak to the Earth?* Are Robert Lewis's speculations on the reasons for both its inclusion and final omission valid? Can we apply similar reasoning to the deletion of the name "Henry Walden" (see frontispiece) from the same typescript? Carlos Baker points out that, though Hemingway says, in *Green Hills of Africa,* that he has "not yet been able to read it [*Walden*]," there are striking parallels between Thoreau's discussion of "Where I Lived and What I Lived for" in *Walden* and the central theme of "The Snows of Kilimanjaro." Why does Hemingway give Harry this surname? Does the theory of the "iceberg" apply in his final decision to omit it?

Like the author, the critic has an experience—in his case the literary experience of reading a story. Is what he perceives and feels an accurate or true response to the story? Or is it a distorted reaction caused by preconceived ideas and prejudices about the author and his characters? Obviously, since all art plays on the emotions, the critic, like the author, can only strive for objectivity through introspection and discipline. Thus an honest evaluation of an honest story is a process of self-discovery for the critic as well as for the author. Even then, whether professional or apprentice, each critic possesses a unique composite of acquired experience, and therefore a unique way of seeing life, actual or literary. In the reprinted "Criticism" many different "truths" are perceived—all valid responses by sensitive and intelligent critics who agree and yet disagree, each seeing and communicating literary experience in slightly different terms.

Carlos Baker, for example, calls "The Short Happy Life of Francis Macomber" a satire on the corrupting power of women and money, in which Hemingway sacrifices depth of characterization for the intensity of an elaborately structured action. Philip Young calls the story a "ceremonial triumph over fear," a process of initiation in which Macomber learns the "code" of manhood from Wilson and then is murdered by Margot in a "monumental 'Freudian slip.'" Warren Beck, on the other hand, believes that Margot tried to save her husband, and that Wilson's observations are untrustworthy. Wilson must be trusted as an observer, says R. S. Crane, who notes a growing hatred in Margot and argues that the resolution of the story is an artistic failure. The "ambiguity" is in the minds of the critics, says Robert B.

Holland, who argues that we have no reason not to believe the narrator when he says that Mrs. Macomber "shot at the buffalo." What is the "truth"? Only through a careful study of the argument and evidence for these and other ideas in the essays can we reach a meaningful decision.

The obvious points of contention in interpreting "The Snows of Kilimanjaro" arise, of course, over how to evaluate the symbolic meaning (if there is any) of the mountain, the leopard, and the hyena. But it is also probable that those critics writing before 1966 were unaware of either the second epigraph or the "Walden" surname, since both were first mentioned in print by Robert W. Lewis, Jr., and his colleague Max Westbrook, in their monograph on the typescript. Would earlier critics, knowing these facts, have in any way altered their interpretations? This question might lead to some important insights and interesting topics. For more facts—and questions—however, we must eventually depend on our own reading of the texts and sources.

Suggested Topics for Library Research

This anthology focuses on the genetic development and esthetic dimensions of Hemingway's African stories. In many cases the reprinted materials are representative rather than definitive. Library research, however, offers unlimited opportunities for deeper and wider exploration than is possible in controlled research. Yet in doing so, it also places a greater burden on the researcher: Where to begin? How to proceed? We have moved in the anthology from theory to experience, to context, to criticism. A tentative step toward expanding these areas in your library research might be to study the footnotes to the reprinted materials, since footnotes are, traditionally, implicit suggestions for further study: they give sources, of course, but they often list relevant criticism, offer parenthetical discussion, and in some cases, even offer ideas for consideration which the critic wants to share with his readers but chooses not to develop in his essay.

But this is only a beginning. Our focus is still, in one sense, "controlled" by the arguments and perceptions of the scholars who make such references. The only objective source of relevant materials and criticism is a bibliography; and Hemingway scholars are fortunate in having Audre Hanneman's *Ernest Hemingway: A Comprehensive Bibliography* (Princeton, 1967), which not only lists all primary and secondary sources, but annotates many citations as well. Should this work be temporarily unavailable, you may, as an alternative, consult three separate bibliographies that, in combination, offer approximately the same coverage. Two of the bibliographies are compiled by Carlos Baker: 1) "A Working Checklist of Hemingway's Prose, Poetry, and Journalism—with Notes" is printed in the appendices of *Hemingway: The Writer as Artist;* 2)

"A Checklist of Hemingway Criticism" is printed in the appendices of *Hemingway and His Critics: An International Anthology* (New York, 1961); the third bibliography is compiled by Warren S. Walker: *Twentieth Century Short Story Explication,* 2nd ed. (Hamden, Conn., 1967). Whether you use the Hanneman bibliography or these three together, you must pick up where they leave off by turning next to the annual *PMLA Bibliography,* to the quarterly checklists of *American Literature,* and, ultimately, to the more tedious process of checking the most recent critical journals whose articles have not yet been listed in *American Literature.*

The major sources of ideas remain, of course, the book-length studies. The commentaries by Carlos Baker and Philip Young on "The Short Happy Life of Francis Macomber" are followed in their books, for example, by equally perceptive analyses of "The Snows of Kilimanjaro." But there are other often valuable books on Hemingway's fiction: Earl Rovit studies the technique and psychological implications of Hemingway's fiction in *Ernest Hemingway* (New York, 1963); Sheridan Baker emphasizes biography and experience in *Ernest Hemingway: An Introduction and Interpretation* (New York, 1967); and, as the titles indicate, Robert W. Lewis, Jr. studies *Hemingway on Love* (Austin, 1965); Joseph Defalco, *The Hero in Hemingway's Short Stories* (Pittsburgh, 1963); John Atkins, *The Art of Ernest Hemingway: His Work and Personality* (London, 1952); and John Killinger, *Hemingway and the Dead Gods: A Study in Existentialism* (Lexington, 1960). A glance at these titles suggests a wide range of critical emphases. Indeed a careful survey of the opinions in these books might lead to some illuminating topics on the nature of the critical process and its effect on the interpretation and the reputation of not only the African stories, but Hemingway's fiction in general.

It is interesting to consider the response of the general reader at the time the stories were first published. The country was still suffering from an economic depression. Would the general reader be sympathetic with the fictional problems of characters on safari in Africa when millions were hunting jobs in America? R. S. Crane suggests, in his essay on "The Short Happy Life of Francis Macomber," that Hemingway tried too hard to please the readers of *Cosmopolitan.* Is this a valid criticism? To explore some of the topics that these questions raise, you might study those of the magazine's articles, photographs, advertisements, and fiction that provided a cultural as well as a literary context for the publication of each story.

Do the African stories mark any changes in theme or technique? To answer this question you must compare them with other stories by Hemingway. The best source for a comparative study of this kind is *The Short Stories of Ernest Hemingway,* collected in May, 1938. Since Hemingway published only seven stories after this date, the problem of locating them is relatively simple: The first three are a series of stories in *Esquire,* using a bar in Madrid as a setting: "The Denunciation," X (November 1938); "The Butterfly and the Tank," X (December 1938); and "Night Before Battle," XI (February 1939). The fourth story, unreprinted, involves a Spanish Civil War veteran who is traced to Havana and killed: "Nobody Ever Dies!" *Cosmopolitan,* CVI (March 1939). The fifth is again about the Spanish Civil War: "Under the Ridge," *Cosmopolitan,* CVII (October 1939). And the last two were published under the general title "Two Tales of Darkness" in *Atlantic,* CC (November 1957), and individually under the titles "A Man of the World" and "Get a Seeing-Eyed Dog."

The two notable exceptions (stories published before 1938, but *not* reprinted in *The Short Stories*) provide, however, a striking parallel to "The Snows of Kilimanjaro," since they also portray a character named Harry. The first story, "One Trip Across," was published in *Cosmopolitan,* XCVI (April 1934), shortly after Hemingway's return from Africa; the second, "The Tradesman's Return," was published in *Esquire,* V (February 1936), at about the same time that Hemingway began the final draft of "The Snows of Kilimanjaro." With revision, particularly of "The Tradesman's Return," these stories became parts one and two of the three-part novel *To Have and Have Not* (1937), in which the protagonist, Harry, is given the surname "Morgan," an allusion, critics agree, to Henry Morgan, the famous buccaneer. Equally striking is the introduction, in part three of the novel, of a subplot involving a spiritually corrupted writer, Richard Gordon, and his wife, Helen.

Only our time and interest will limit the possibilities for thematic and stylistic comparison that a consideration of the total body of Hemingway's stories provides. The topic of bullfighting, already suggested as a topic for controlled research, might, for example, be expanded to include a study of the ways in which Hemingway uses this ritualistic contest as a theme, an action, or a background in such stories as "The Capital of the World," "The Undefeated," and "Banal Story"; and to what extent these stories, in turn, may be compared to "The Short Happy Life of Francis Macomber" and its "bullfighting" protagonist. Boxers, like bullfighters, often suggest the values of what Philip Young calls the "code hero." But not always; and an equally illuminating study might be made of the contrasting themes in "The Killers," "Fifty Grand," and "The Battler."

On the other hand, the theme of "initiation," an integral part of the "code" motif, informs most of the Nick Adams stories, as well as many of Hemingway's themes on the "failure of love." Indeed, themes of "initiation" and "failed love" are so prevalent in Hemingway's collected stories that a list would closely approximate the table of contents, and either theme might be developed in relation to the African stories. (Typically, Hemingway combines most of these themes in his novels. In *The Sun Also Rises,* for example, a bullfighter, Pedro Romero, and an amateur boxer, Robert Cohn, dramatize opposing standards of behavior for the sexually impotent Jake Barnes.)

Fishing, though not so prevalent an action as the contest or hunt in Hemingway's stories, often carries a greater burden of meaning—or possibly, as some critics suggest, it is only more obvious in such stories as "Big Two-Hearted River" and "Now I Lay Me" (not to mention *The Old Man and the Sea* and *The Sun Also Rises*). What is this extra burden of meaning? Oliver Evans suggests, *contra* Gordon and Tate, that Hemingway's "sensibility" is not naturalistic, but romantic and primitivistic, more like Thoreau's than Maupassant's (footnotes 16–18). To explore such a thesis, we might compare the two fishing stories with the African stories and, after reaching some conclusions as to their non-literal properties, with a few representative stories by Maupassant, such as "The Story of a Farm Girl," "A Piece of String," or "The Necklace." Before attempting such a study, however, we must arrive at a clear understanding of such terms as "sensibility," "naturalism," "romanticism," and "primitivism," which critics generally take for granted in developing a study of fiction.*

We often look for clues to an author's sensibility in what he prefers to read. In *Green Hills of Africa,* for example, Hemingway singles out three American writers for praise: Henry James, Stephen Crane, and Mark Twain. Was he influenced by these writers? Though critics have tried to answer this question with respect to each of the three, research still remains to be done. What does Hemingway mean, for example, when he says, in the same passage, that "All modern American literature comes from one book by Mark Twain called *Huckleberry Finn.*"? Many have wondered and written on the subject—Philip Young devotes a chapter to a comparison of Hemingway and Twain, for example—but there is still room for exploration, as there is in the often suggested parallels between Hemingway's "The Snows of Kilimanjaro" and James's stories involving writer protagonists: "The Lesson of the Master," "The Jolly Corner," and "The Middle Years"; and between "The Short Happy Life of Francis Macomber" and Stephen Crane's fiction, especially "The Blue Hotel" and *The Red Badge of Courage* (1895).

Hemingway often draws attention to the writers of previous generations (as in "Monologue to the Maestro," for example); less often to his American contemporaries, such as William Faulkner, F. Scott Fitzgerald, Ring Lardner, Sherwood Anderson, and Gertrude Stein. An illuminating comparison might be made, nevertheless, between "The Short Happy Life of Francis Macomber" and Faulkner's famous hunting story "The Bear," published in *Saturday Evening Post,* CCXIV (May 9, 1942), and widely reprinted. And though Hemingway saw little or nothing of Faulkner personally during their lifetimes, he had a long, if rather uneasy, friendship with F. Scott Fitzgerald, from 1925 to Fitzgerald's death, in 1940. Ostensibly, Hemingway's inspiration for the writer "Julian," whom Harry remembers in "The Snows of Kilimanjaro," was Fitzgerald's own published confession of an artistic "crack-up" in a series of three essays beginning in the February issue of *Esquire* and ending in April, 1936. They have since been reprinted, along with other essays, letters, and miscellany, in *The Crack-Up* (New York, 1945), edited by Edmund Wilson. A comparison of the ideas and attitudes in Fitzgerald's "crack-up" essays with those implicit in "The Snows of Kilimanjaro" might lead

---

* Some useful sources of definitions for such literary terms are: M. H. Abrams, *A Glossary of Literary Terms* (New York, 1957); Alex Preminger et al., eds., *Encyclopedia of Poetry and Poetics* (Princeton, 1965); Joseph T. Shipley, ed., *Dictionary of World Literature,* rev. ed. (New York, 1953).

to some valuable insights about the pit-
falls of the literary artist—and, by extension, to a study of the friendship and
literary careers of both authors. Some
relevant sources are Hemingway's account
in *A Moveable Feast* (1964) of their first
meeting and adventures in Paris; Morley
Callaghan's memories of meeting them
both, a few years later, in *That Summer
in Paris* (New York, 1963); Carlos Baker's
discussion of the relationship in his biography *Ernest Hemingway: A Life Story*
(New York, 1969); and the following Fitzgerald biographies and studies: Arthur
Mizener's *The Far Side of Paradise* (New
York, 1959); Andrew Turnbull's *Scott
Fitzgerald* (New York, 1962); Henry Dan
Piper's *F. Scott Fitzgerald, A Critical Portrait* (New York, 1965); and William Gold-
hurst's *Fitzgerald and His Contemporaries*
(Cleveland, 1963).

Though the same biographical approach
might be taken in a consideration of Hemingway's relationship to Anderson and
Stein, both of whom he knew quite well
at a crucial moment in the development
of his style, his debt to Lardner was in-
curred at an earlier date, while he was still
writing humor for his high school newspaper. Probably the best analysis of the
initial influence of these three writers on
Hemingway is Charles A. Fenton's *The
Apprenticeship of Ernest Hemingway*
(New York, 1954). Other valuable studies
of influence on Hemingway's style and the
characteristics of its form are Austin M.
Wright's *The Short Story in the Twenties*
(Chicago, 1961); Frederick I. Carpenter's
"Hemingway Achieves the Fifth Dimen-
sion," *PMLA,* LXIX (September 1954);
John Graham's "Ernest Hemingway: The
Meaning of Style," *Modern Fiction
Studies,* VI (Winter 1960–1961); Robert
C. Hart's "Hemingway on Writing," *Col-
lege English,* XVIII (March 1957); and
Harry Levin's "Observations on the Style
of Ernest Hemingway," *Kenyon Review,*
XIII (Autumn 1951).

Coming full circle, what parallels can
be drawn between the themes of Hemingway's stories, and the major interests

which his life reflected; between the characters who inhabit his stories, and the
actual persons he knew; between the
events which occur in his stories, and his
own experiences? Easily the best source of
Hemingway's own opinions on any single
aspect of this composite question is his
interview with George Plimpton, first
published in the *Paris Review,* XVIII
(Spring 1958), and reprinted in *Writers at
Work: Second Series* (New York, 1963).
Then, following a rough chronology of
Hemingway's life, we might consult Mar-
celline Hemingway Sanford's *At the Hemingways* (Boston, 1962); Constance Cappel
Montgomery's *Hemingway in Michigan*
(New York, 1966); Leicester Hemingway's
My Brother, Ernest Hemingway (Cleveland, 1962); the journalism which mir-
rored Hemingway's life and inspired much
of his early fiction: Gene Z. Hanrahan,
ed., *Hemingway: The Wild Years* (New
York, 1962), William White, ed., *By-Line:
Ernest Hemingway* (New York, 1967), and,
once again, the finest study of these early
years, Charles Fenton's *The Apprenticeship of Ernest Hemingway.* Major sources
for Hemingway's years in Paris are Harold
Loeb's *The Way It Was* (New York, 1959);
Morley Callaghan's *That Summer in
Paris;* and, of course, Hemingway's own
volume, *A Moveable Feast.* The thirties
and after are touched on by Leicester
Hemingway's *My Brother, Ernest Hemingway,* and by Jed Kiley's anecdotal volume, *Hemingway: An Old Friend Remembers* (New York, 1965); the fifties and after
by A. E. Hotchner's *Papa Hemingway*
(New York, 1966); and, again, the whole
spectrum by Carlos Baker in his biography
Ernest Hemingway: A Life Story.

One final question: are movies better
than ever? What violence is done to "The
Short Happy Life of Francis Macomber,"
for example, when Robert Wilson falls in
love with Margot, loses his hunting license,
and promises to marry her after the trial
in Nairobi? What violence is done to
"The Snows of Kilimanjaro" when Helen
nurses Harry back to health and renewed
love? (In disgust Hemingway nicknamed

the movie "The Snows of Zanuck"!) "The Short Happy Life of Francis Macomber" was produced under the title "The Macomber Affair" in February, 1947; "The Snows of Kilimanjaro" retained its title when it was produced in September, 1952. A careful study of the movie reviews, which are listed in *A Reader's Guide to Periodical Literature,* will dramatize once and for all what Hemingway meant by "truth."

Guide to Research

THE IDEA OF RESEARCH

Research is the organized, disciplined search for truth; the aim of all research is to discover the truth about something. That thing may be a historical object like the Stonehenge monuments or a historical event like the Hungarian Revolt or the Battle of Waterloo. It may be a work of literature like Shakespeare's *Julius Cæsar* or Miller's *Death of a Salesman*. It may be a recurring event like the motions of the planets or the circulation of the blood. It may be an experimentally repeatable phenomenon like behavior of rats in a maze or perception apparently unaccounted for by the five senses. Or it may be a political problem like the decision to use the atomic bomb in World War II. Archeology, history, political science, literary criticism and scholarship, astronomy, physiology, and psychology—these are some of the many divisions of research. Indeed, all the sciences—physical, biological, and social—and all other scholarly disciplines share this organized, disciplined search for truth.

The search for truth has often been confused with such aims as confirming prejudice, instilling patriotism, and praising friends and blaming enemies. The attempt to prove the preconceived conclusion *that* one college is superior to another, for example, is not research (though the attempt to discover *whether* one college is so superior is). Research is hostile to prejudice.

General Methods of Research. The best general method of research is first-hand observation. But this method is not always possible and, when it is possible, not always practical.

The best method to begin discovering the truth about something is to observe that thing and the circumstances surrounding it. To discover the truth about *Julius Cæsar* or *Death of a Salesman*, get the play and read it, or go to the theatre and watch a performance. To discover the truth about the planets, observe them through your telescope. To discover the truth about the intelligence of rats, build a maze and run some rats through it.

This first-hand observation is not always possible, however. To discover the truth about the Battle of Waterloo, you can't observe the battle. The best that you or anyone else can do is to observe other persons' observations, the recorded observations of eye-witnesses: diaries, letters, and memoirs, for instance, of soldiers and generals who were in the battle. With more recent historical events—for example, the Hungarian Revolt—you are better off. You can watch films and listen to tape recordings. You may be able to interview people who were there. But these observations are still second-hand; and, on the whole, history can be observed only at second-hand. The sole exception is history that you have been part of. You may have fought in the Hungarian Revolt—though, if you did, you may be prejudiced.

Even when first-hand observation is possible, it is not always practical. You may have a copy of or tickets to *Julius Cæsar* or *Death of a Salesman* but not know enough about the principles of dramatic criticism to interpret the play unaided. You may have a telescope but not know how to use it or, if you do, not know what to make of what you observe through it. You may have some rats but not know how to build a maze or, if you do, not know enough about animal psychology to run your rats through it properly. The best that *you* can do under these circumstances is to supplement whatever first-hand observations you can make with observations of the first-hand observations of other people better-trained or better-equipped than you. Read *Julius Cæsar* or *Death of a Salesman* and also critics' interpretations of the play. Observe the planets, if you can, and read treatises on astronomy. Do what you can with your rats, and read reports of experiments with rats. After all, no one can master the special methods and come by the special equipment of all scholarly disciplines. Indeed, few people can do this with more than one discipline, and then not before they're thirty. But all people who want a liberal education should try to discover as much of the truth about as many scholarly disciplines as their abilities and their circumstances permit. Indeed, the achievement of this is what is meant by "a liberal education."

Primary and Secondary Sources. As the foregoing account of the general methods of research suggests, there is, ultimately, only one source of the truth about something—the thing, the event, or the phenomenon itself: the Stonehenge monuments, the Hungarian Revolt, or the Battle of Waterloo; the text of *Julius Cæsar* or *Death of a Salesman;* Robert Oppenheimer's testimony on the use of the atomic bomb against Japan; the motions of the planets or the circulation of blood; extrasensory perceptions or rats running in a maze. Such a source is a *primary* source. And, in historical research, where the thing itself (the Hungarian Revolt or the Battle of Waterloo) cannot be observed at first hand, a report of an eyewitness or a film or a tape recording is also counted as a *primary* source. But any other second-hand source (an interpretation of *Julius Cæsar* or *Death of a Salesman,* a treatise on astronomy, a report of an experiment with rats) is a *secondary* source.

A primary source is, of course, better. But, if a primary source is unavailable to you (if it is a book, perhaps your school library does not have it) or if you are not trained or equipped to use it (you don't know how to run rats through a maze or you have no telescope), then a secondary source must do. In any case, except for the most mature scientists and scholars, a good

secondary source is useful and often indispensable.

It is worth noticing that being primary or being secondary is not an intrinsic characteristic of the source itself. It is, rather, a relationship that either exists or does not exist between a given source and a given topic of research. Consequently, a given source may be primary in relation to one given topic but secondary in relation to another. Two examples may serve to make this important point clear. Edward Gibbon's *The Decline and Fall of the Roman Empire* (1776-1788) is a secondary source in relation to the topic of the Roman Empire but a primary source in relation to that of eighteenth-century English prose style or that of eighteenth-century historiography. Samuel Taylor Coleridge's *Lectures on Shakespeare* (1811-1812) is a secondary source in relation to the topic of Shakespeare's plays but a primary source in relation to that of nineteenth-century principles of dramatic criticism or that of Shakespeare's reputation.

It is worth noticing also that a given source may be primary or secondary in relationship to more than one topic. James Joyce's novel *A Portrait of the Artist as a Young Man* is a primary source in relation not only to the topic of the structure of *A Portrait of the Artist as a Young Man* (and dozens of other topics on the novel itself) but also to the topic of use of the stream-of-consciousness technique in twentieth-century fiction.

THE RESEARCH PAPER

A research paper is a paper giving the results of research, the methods by which they were reached, and the sources, primary or secondary, which were used. A research paper attempts to tell the truth about a topic, and also tells how and where this truth was discovered. As we have seen, the sources of a research paper may be either written sources (literary texts and historical documents, for example) or sources of other kinds (experiments, for example). Since a research paper written in school is almost always based upon written (printed) sources, we shall here discuss only that kind. A research paper based upon written sources may be either a library-research paper or a controlled-research paper. A library-research paper is a research paper for which your search for sources is limited to those sources contained in the libraries available to you; a controlled-research paper, to those sources contained in one anthology —to those contained in this volume, for example. Here we shall emphasize the latter kind.

Finding Your Topic. The first step in writing a research paper based upon written sources, whether a library-research or a controlled-research paper, is finding a topic. We say "finding a topic" rather than "choosing a topic" because the process is more like finding a job than choosing a sandwich from a menu. Unless your instructor assigns you a topic, which he may do, you must look for one; and the one you find may not be just what you want but the best one that you can find. But, if you look long and carefully, you may find a topic that so well suits your interests, your capacities, and the time and the space at your disposal that your paper will almost surely be a success.

Finding a topic is the most important single step in writing a research paper, and the things that you should have in mind when looking for a topic are (1) your interests, (2) your capacities, and (3) the time and the space at your disposal. If you are interested in a topic, if you know something about the special methods of research that the topic requires, and if your topic is narrow enough to require no more time than you have for research and no greater development than you can give it in a paper of the length assigned you, then the paper that results will probably be satisfactory. For example, the topic of figures of speech in *Julius Cæsar* may interest you greatly. But, if it does, you must ask yourself whether you know enough about figures of speech to do research on them

and, if you do, whether this topic is narrow enough. Even the topic of metaphors in the play would be too broad for most papers; metaphors in Brutus' soliloquies might be about right. In any case, before you take a topic for a paper, you should do some reading on that topic; otherwise, you won't know whether it is interesting, within your ability to handle, and within the scope of your assigned paper.

Once you think that you've found a topic, take great care in phrasing it. The best phrasing is a question or a series of closely related questions. Better than "The character of Brutus" is "To what extent is Brutus motivated by self-interest and to what extent by the public interest?" The latter is not only more narrow and more precise; it provides you with a criterion of relevance in selecting your sources. At the end of this volume, you will find a list of suggested topics, intended to call your attention to topics that might not occur to you. But these topics are suggestive rather than definitive or precise.

Finding Your Sources. Finding sources for a library-research paper and finding ones for a controlled-research paper, though different in several respects, are alike in certain others. Finding sources in the library requires knowledge of how to use the card catalogue, periodical indexes, special bibliographies, reserve shelves, and encyclopedias. Finding sources in this volume or a similar one does not. But, in either case, you must have a clear idea of what you are looking for; and you must be prepared to put up with a high ratio of looking to finding. In other words, you must have not only criteria of relevance but also a willingness to do a good deal of skimming and a good deal more of careful reading, some of it fruitless.

The basic criterion of relevance you provide by careful phrasing of your topic, a problem discussed in the preceding section. The other criteria you provide by making a preliminary or tentative outline —perhaps in the form of subtopics, perhaps in the form of questions. Such an outline is not to be used for your paper. The outline for your paper will probably be quite different and, in any event, cannot be made until after you find your sources and take your notes. This preliminary outline guides your research and, as we shall see, provides you with the subtopic headings necessary for your note-cards (see "Taking Your Notes," page xiii).

Making Your Working Bibliography. Once you have found a promising source ("promising" because, though it seems to be relevant, it may turn out not to be) you want to make some record of it so that, once you have completed your search for sources, you can turn back to it, read it, and, if it turns out to be relevant, take notes on it. This record of promising sources is your *working* bibliography. It is so called for two reasons: first, because you work with it as you proceed with your research and the writing of your paper, adding promising sources to it and discarding irrelevant ones; and, second, because this designation distinguishes it from your final bibliography, which appears at the very end of your research paper and contains only sources actually used in the paper. For a controlled-research paper, your working bibliography may be nothing more elaborate than a series of check marks in the table of contents of your research anthology or a list of page numbers. For a library-research paper, however, you need something quite different.

A working bibliography for a library-research paper is a collection of three-by-five cards each representing a promising source and each containing full information about that source. Once you have completed your research, written your paper, and discarded all promising but (as they turned out) irrelevant sources, this bibliography is identical with your final bibliography. Having a separate card for each source enables you to add and to discard sources easily and to sort and arrange them easily in any order you please. Eventually, when this bibliography becomes identical with your final bibliography, you will arrange sources alphabetically by au-

thors' last names. Having full information about each source on its card enables you to turn back to it easily—to locate it in the library without first looking it up again. You find this information in the card catalogue, periodical indexes, or other bibliographical aids; or, when browsing through the shelves or the stacks of the library and coming upon a promising source, you find it in or on the source itself—for example, on the spine and the title page of a book.

If the source is a *book,* you should put the following information on the three-by-five working-bibliography card:
(1) the library call number,
(2) the author's (or authors') full name (or names), last name first for the first author,
(3) the title of the book,
(4) the name of the city of publication,
(5) the name of the publisher (*not* the printer), and
(6) the year of publication (often found on the other side of the title page).
See the example of such a card on the opposite page (note the punctuation carefully).

If the source is a *periodical article,* you should put the following information on the three-by-five working-bibliography card:
(1) the author's (or authors') full name (or names),
(2) the title of the article,
(3) the name of the periodical,
(4) the volume number,
(5) the week, the month, or the season of publication, together with the year, and
(6) the page numbers covered by the article.
See the example of such a card on the opposite page (note the punctuation carefully).

These two forms take care of the two standard cases. For special cases—such things as books with editors or translators as well as authors, books published in several editions or in several volumes, and daily newspapers—see any good handbook of composition.

860.3
J23
Jones, John A., and William C.
Brown. A History of
Serbia. New York: The
Rowland Press, Inc., 1934.

WORKING-BIBLIOGRAPHY CARD FOR A BOOK

Smith, Harold B. "Fishing
in Serbian Waters." Journal
of Balkan Sports, VII
(May 1936), 26-32.

WORKING-BIBLIOGRAPHY CARD FOR A PERIODICAL ARTICLE

Taking Your Notes. Once you have found sources, entered them in your working bibliography, read them, and found them relevant, taking notes requires your exactly following a standard procedure if your notes are going to be useful to you when you come to write your paper. An extra five minutes given to taking a note correctly can save you a half hour in writing your paper. Here is the standard procedure:

(1) Take all notes on four-by-six cards. Never use notebooks, loose sheets of paper, or backs of old envelopes.

(2) Limit each note **to information** on a single subtopic of your preliminary outline *and* from a single source. It follows from this that you may have many cards on the same subtopic and many cards from the same source but that you may never have one card on more than one subtopic or from more than one source.

(3) On each card, in addition to the note itself, put

(a) the appropriate subtopic heading in the upper left-hand corner,

(b) the name of the source (usually the author's last name will do) in the upper right-hand corner, and

(c) the page number (or numbers) of that part (or those parts) of the source that you have used in taking your note. If you have used more than one page, indicate your page numbers in such a way that, when you come to write your paper, you can tell what page each part of the note comes from, for you may not use the whole note. (If you follow these first three rules, you will be able, when you come to outline and to organize your paper, to sort your notes in any way you please—by subtopic, for example—and to arrange them in any order you please. Such flexibility is impossible if you take your notes in a notebook. If you follow the third rule, you will also be able to document your paper— write footnotes, for example—without again referring to the sources themselves.)

(4) In taking the note itself, paraphrase or quote your source or do both; but do only one at a time, and use quotation very sparingly.

Paraphrase and quotation require special care. Anything between paraphrase and quotation is not acceptable to good writers: you either paraphrase or quote, but do nothing in between. To paraphrase a source (or part of a source) is to reproduce it in words and word orders substantially different from the original. When you paraphrase well, you keep the sense of the original but change the language,

retaining some key words, of course, but otherwise using your own words and your own sentence patterns. To quote a source (or part of a source) is to reproduce it exactly. When you quote well, you keep both the sense and the language of the original, retaining its punctuation, its capitalization, its type face (roman or italic), and its spelling (indeed, even its misspelling).

Omissions and additions require special care. If, when quoting, you wish to omit some of the original, you may do so only if the omission does not change the sense of the original (never leave out a "not," for example!) *and* if it is indicated by ellipses (three spaced periods: ". . ."). If you wish to add something to the original, you may do so only if the addition does not change the sense of the original (never add a "not"!) *and* it is indicated by square brackets. The most usual additions are explanations ("They [i.e., the people of Paris] were alarmed") and disclaimers of errors in the original, indicated by the Latin *"sic,"* meaning "thus" ("Colombis [sic] discovered America in 1592 [sic]"). You must, of course, carry these ellipses and square brackets from your note-cards to your paper. And, if you type your paper, brackets may be a problem, for most typewriter keyboards do not include them. If your keyboard does not, you may do one of two things—either use the slash ("/") and underlining ("__" and "—") in such a way as to produce a bracket ("⌐" and "⌐") or draw brackets in with a pen. In any event, don't substitute parentheses for brackets.

In your paper, quotations no longer than three or four lines are to be enclosed within a set of quotation marks and run into your text; longer ones are to be set off from the text, without quotation marks, by indention from the left-hand margin and, especially in typewritten copy, by single-spacing. But never use either of these devices unless the language is exactly that of the original.

Your usual treatment of a source should be paraphrase; use quotation only if the

Fly - fishing   Smith
   Smith says that fly-fishing is a
method of fishing used chiefly by
wealthy Serbians and foreign tourists,
that the flies used are generally imported
from Scotland, and that "Serbian trout
are so snobbish that they won't glance [27/28]
at a domestic fly."
   [Query: How reliable is the information
in this rather facetious article?]

NOTE-CARD

language of the original is striking (strikingly good or strikingly bad), if it is the very topic of your research (as in a paper on Shakespeare's style), or if it is so complex (as it might be in a legal document) that you don't want to risk paraphrasing it.

Let us look at the sample note-card above. The topic of research is methods of fishing in Serbia; the subtopic that the note deals with is fly-fishing in Serbia; the source is Harold B. Smith's article "Fishing in Serbian Waters," from the *Journal of Balkan Sports* (see the second of the two working-bibliography cards on page xiii).

Note the subtopic heading ("Fly-fishing") in the upper left-hand corner; the name of the source, abbreviated to the author's last name ("Smith"), in the upper right-hand corner; the page numbers ("[27/28]"), indicating that everything, both paraphrase and quotation, up through the word "glance" is from page 27 and that everything after that word is from page 28; the sparing and appropriate use of quotation; and the bracketed query, to remind the note-taker that he must use this source with caution.

Writing Your Paper. Many of the problems of writing a research paper based upon written sources—organization, the outline, the thesis paragraph, topic sentences, transitions, and the like—are problems of expository writing generally. Here we shall discuss only those problems peculiar to such a paper. Two of these problems —paraphrase and quotation—we discussed in the preceding section. Two·others remain: reaching conclusions and avoiding the scissors-and-paste organization.

When you come to make the outline for your paper and to write your paper, you will have before you three things: (1) your *preliminary* outline, containing ordered subtopics of your topic; (2) your working bibliography; and (3) your note-cards. These are the *immediate* results of your research; they are not the *final* results. They are only the raw material out of which you must fashion your paper. At best, they are an intermediate stage between finding your topic and making your final outline. The preliminary outline will not do for the final outline. The working bibliography will almost certainly require further pruning. And the note-cards will require sorting, evaluation, organization, pruning, and exercise of logic and common sense. All this needs to be done, preferably before you make your final outline and begin to write your paper, though almost inevitably some of it will remain to bedevil you while you are writing it. To put the matter in another way, you are, with these things before you, a Sherlock Holmes who has gathered all his clues but who has reached no conclusions from them, who has not come to the end of his search for truth. You must discard irrelevant clues, ones that have no bearing on the questions that you want answered. You must arbitrate the claims of conflicting or contradictory clues. You must decide which one of several probable conclusions is the most probable.

Once you have reached your conclusions, you must organize your paper and set forth this organization in your final outline. Organization and the outline are, of course, problems common to all expository writing. But a problem peculiar to the research paper is avoiding the scissors-and-paste organization—avoiding a paper that looks as though you had cut paraphrases and quotations out of your note-cards, pasted them in columns on paper, and connected them only with such phrases as "Jones says" and "On the other hand, Brown says." Such an organization is the result of a failure to reach conclusions (with the consequence that there is nothing but "Jones says" to put in between paraphrases and quotations); or it is a failure to see the necessity of giving the conclusions reached *and* the reasoning by

which they were reached (with the consequence that, though there is something to put between paraphrases and quotations, nothing is put there, and the reader is left to write the paper for himself).

Documenting Your Paper. To document your paper is to give the source of each paraphrase and quotation that it contains, so that your reader can, if he wishes to, check each of your sources and judge for himself what use you have made of it. To give the source is usually to give (1) either the information that you have about that source in your working bibliography (except that the name of the publisher of a book is usually not given) or the information that accompanies each source in a research anthology *and* (2) the information about page numbers that you have in your notes. This information you may give either formally or informally, as your instructor decides.

Formal documentation is given in footnotes. For a full discussion of footnotes, see any good handbook (one cheap and widely accepted one is *The MLA Style Sheet*). The form of footnotes is similar to, but not identical with, the form of bibliographical entries. With these three sample footnotes, compare the two sample working-bibliography cards on page xiii:

[1] John A. Jones and William C. Brown, *A History of Serbia* (New York, 1934), p. 211.
[2] Harold B. Smith, "Fishing in Serbian Waters," *Journal of Balkan Sports*, VII (May 1936), 27.
[3] Smith, pp. 27-28.

Informal documentation is given in the text of the paper, usually parenthetically, as in this example:

Fly-fishing in Serbia is chiefly a sport of wealthy Serbians and foreign tourists (Harold B. Smith, "Fishing in Serbian Waters," *Journal of Balkan Sports*, VII [May 1936], 27), though in some mountain districts it is popular among the peasants (John A. Jones and William C. Brown, *A History of Serbia* [New York, 1934], p. 211). The flies used are generally imported from Scotland; indeed, Smith facetiously adds, "Serbian trout are so snobbish that they won't glance at a domestic fly" (pp. 27-28).

As this example suggests, however, informal documentation can be an annoying distraction. It probably works out best in papers that use only a few sources. In such papers, there are few occasions for long first-references to sources: for example, "(Harold B. Smith, "Fishing in Serbian Waters," *Journal of Balkan Sports,* VII [May, 1936], 27)." But there are many occasions for short succeeding-references: for example, "(Smith, pp. 27-28)" or "(pp. 27-28)." Occasionally, informal documentation may be profitably combined with formal, as in a paper about Shakespeare's *Julius Cæsar.* In such a paper, references to the play might well be given informally —for example, "(III.ii.2-7)"—but references to critics formally.

How many footnotes (or parenthetical documentations) do you need in your paper? The answer is, of course, that you need as many footnotes as you have paraphrases or quotations of sources, unless you group several paraphrases or quotations *from the same page or consecutive pages of a given source* in such a way that one footnote will do for all. One way to do this grouping—almost the only way— is to introduce the group with such a sentence as "Smith's views on fly-fishing are quite different from Brown's" and to conclude it with the raised numeral referring to the footnote. Your reader will understand that everything between the introductory sentence and the numeral comes from the page or the successive pages of the source indicated in the footnote.

Making Your Final Bibliography. Your paper concludes with your final bibliography, which is simply a list of all the sources—and only those sources—that you actually paraphrase or quote in your paper. In other words, every source that you give in a footnote (or a parenthetical documentation) you include in your final bibliography; and you include no other sources (inclusion of others results in what is unfavorably known as "a padded bibliography"). The form for entries in your final bibliography is identical with that for ones in your working bibliography, given above. You should list these sources alphabetically by authors' last names or, if a source is anonymous, by the first word of its title, but not by "a," "an," or "the." For example:

BIBLIOGRAPHY

Jones, John A., and William C. Brown. *A History of Serbia.* New York: The Rowland Press, Inc., 1934.

"Serbian Pastimes." *Sports Gazette,* XCI (October 26, 1952), 18-19, 38, 40-42.

Smith, Harold B. "Fishing in Serbian Waters," *Journal of Balkan Sports,* VII (May 1936), 26-32.

MARTIN STEINMANN, JR.